Singing Our Unsung Heroes:
(Re)Membering Manu Dibango, Celebrating Cameroon Music

Edited by

Walter Gam Nkwi

Langaa Research & Publishing CIG
Mankon, Bamenda

Publisher:
Langaa RPCIG
Langaa Research & Publishing Common Initiative Group
P.O. Box 902 Mankon
Bamenda
North West Region
Cameroon
Langaagrp@gmail.com
www.langaa-rpcig.net

Distributed in and outside N. America by African Books Collective
orders@africanbookscollective.com
www.africanbookscollective.com

ISBN-10: 9956-551-09-0

ISBN-13: 978-9956-551-09-5

© Walter Gam Nkwi 2021

All rights reserved.
No part of this book may be reproduced or transmitted in any form or by any means, mechanical or electronic, including photocopying and recording, or be stored in any information storage or retrieval system, without written permission from the publisher

About the Authors

Chapter 2
Henry Kam Kah is Associate Professor and Acting Head of the Department of History at the University of Buea in the South West Region of Cameroon. His research interest is in the area of gender, conflict, and culture. He has several published scholarly papers to his credit, a book and co-edited book with Professor Bea Lundt of Flensburg University Germany. Dr. Kah has presented papers at several international symposia, workshops, seminars, and conferences. He is a member of several learned societies including the American Political Science Association (APSA), the Council for the Development of Social Science Research in Africa (CODESRIA), the West African Research Association (WARA), the Pan African Anthropologists Association (PAAA), the African Politics Contact Group (APCG) and the Association of Friends of the Archives and Antiquities Cameroon (AFAAC). Dr Kah is also associate research fellow of the Institute of African Studies, University of Ibadan, Ibadan Nigeria since 2008 and was DAAD Guest Professor at the Department of History at the Heinrich Heine University Dusseldorf between October 2015 and March 2016. He is currently involved in a team research on grassroots voices with regards to the Anglophone crisis in Cameroon. Email: henry.kah@ubuea.cm; ndangso@yahoo.com

Chapter 3
Peter Wuteh Vakunta hails from Cameroon Grassfields. He holds a Ph.D. in French Literature and Francophone Studies. Vakunta is author of several books in French, English, Pidgin English and Camfranglais. He has taught at a number of Universities in Africa and the United States. At present, he is Professor of French Language and Cultural Studies at the Unites States Defense Language Institute located in Fayetteville, North Carolina. During his leisure time, Vakunta loves to play soccer and the Xylophone. He has published many books amongst which are the following: *Tragedy of the Commons; Ntarikon: Poetry For the Downtrodden;Grassfields Stories from Cameroon; Straddling the Mungo: A Book of Poems in English and French*

(English and French Edition); *A Nation at Risk: A Personal Narrative of the Cameroonian Crisis; Cam Tok and Other Poems from the Cradle; From Pidgin to Camfranglais: The Making of a New Language in Cameroon*; Carton Rouge à Paul Biya, Président de la République du Cameroun: Lapiro's Songs of Protest (Vol. 1). His other works are available on https://www.amazon.com/s?k=vakunta&i=stripbooks&ref=nb_sb_noss_1. His email:vakunta@gmail.com

Chapter 4

Primus M. Tazanu teaches at the Department of Sociology and Anthropology, University of Buea, Cameroon and is affiliated, as senior guest research, to the Centre of African Studies, University of Copenhagen, Denmark. Primus holds a PhD in Social Anthropology from the University of Freiburg, Germany. His research focuses on social practices and the production of meanings through media technologies: new/social media/smartphones and sociality, media, and Pentecostalism as well as media and racism. Primus is interested on the ways in which the liveness of media influences sociality and users' sensory experiences, expectations and distanciations that arise in mediated communication, smartphones/social media and connectivity, smartphones/social media and electronic identities, media, and self-presentation. His research on Pentecostalism revolves around the mediatization of Christian beliefs and practices in Cameroon. As concerns racism online, Primus looks at racist discourse and representations, philosophical anthropology, questions of freedom, decoloniality and social justice. Dr Tazanu has been a postdoctoral fellow at the University of the Witwatersrand in South Africa as well as a guest lecturer at the universities of Basel (Switzerland) and Freiburg. Aside from his book *Being Available and Reachable: New Media and Cameroonian Transnational Society* (2012), Primus has published in many peer-reviewed journals including *New Media and Society, Africa, Mobile Media and Communication, Journal of African Media Studies, Journal of Religion in Africa, Journal of Asian and African Studies and the International Journal of Critical Diversity Studies*. Dr Tazanu is an Editorial board member of Spears Books, an African Committee member on Social Science One and a Senior Researcher at Langaa Research and Publishing Common Initiative Group. His email: tazanu@gmail.com

Chapters 1, 5 & 8
Walter Gam Nkwi holds a PhD in Social History/Social Anthropology from the Leiden University. Before embarking on his PhD studies, he read African and Cameroonian history at undergraduate and post graduate levels at the University of Buea. He is teaching Social and Labour History at the Department of History, University of Buea, Cameroon. Dr. Nkwi has a passion for the history of communication technology, migration, social, indigenous conflict management, pre-cultural history, and global labour historical issues of Africa. He was a Visiting Research Fellow at the International Institute of Social History (IISH), Amsterdam from 1st September 2012 to 31st January 2013. In January 2015, Dr. Nkwi was made the Faculty Officer of Engineering and Technology at the University of Buea. Dr. Nkwi belongs to several intellectual associations. He has published books, book chapters and peer review journals. He is the author of *Voicing the Voiceless; African Modernities and Mobilities: An Ethnographic History of Kom, Cameroon, c.1800-2008*; With Francis B. Nyamnjoh and Piet Konings *University Crisis and Student Protests in Africa: The 2005-2006 University Students Strike in Cameroon*; *Kfaang and its Technologies: Towards a Social History of Mobility in Kom, Cameroon, 1928-1998*. His recent publications include: . "*Afoysiina-a-kfaang* (food of newness): Cultigens in Global migration flows in Kom, Cameroon since the 1650s "*Leidschrift, jaargang 35, nummer3*, (November 2020): 35-53; "Roman Catholicism and the Conundrum of Polygamy in Njinikom (Cameroon)" pp.193-122 In Henry Kam Kah and Bea Lundt (eds) *Polygamous Ways of Life Past and Present in Africa and Europe-Polygame Lebensweisen in Vergangenheit und Gegenwart in Afrika und Europa*. Berlin: LitVerlag, 2020; "*Wain nii yi dzwin*: Children as Social Security in Kom, Cameroon" pp.327-347. In Samuel Ntewusu and Nina Paarmaan (eds) *Jenseits van Geschichte, Gender und Kultur in Afrika und Europa* (Berlin: Lit Verlag, 2020). Dr Nkwi is an Editorial board member of Spears Books, an African Committee member on Social Science One and a Senior Researcher at Langaa Research and Publishing Common Initiative Group. His email: nkwi.walters@gmail.com

Chapter 6

Hassan Mbiydzenyuy Yosimbom holds an MA in Comparative Literature (2000) from the University of Buea, Cameroon and a PhD in African Literature (2016) from the University of Yaoundé 1, Cameroon. He was a 2019 ARUA-Mellon Fellow (University of Ghana, Legon) and during his tenure, he researched on "Mobility and Sociality in Africa's Emerging Urban." He is the 2020 recipient of the Centre for African Studies, University of Cape Town's, Postdoctoral Fellowship on "Entanglements, Mobility and Improvisation: Culture and Arts in Contemporary African Urbanism and its Hinterlands." His research interests include identity dynamics, mobility, postcolonial studies, and cosmopolitanism. Additionally, he is interested in understanding the links between postcolonial and postmodern theories, and how their interplay shapes and nurtures multiple-layered identity formations and performances in postcolonial societies, especially Cameroon. He is also keen on researching Latin American epistemological foundations such as transmodernity, coloniality, decoloniality, and pluriversality and how they could be used to de-/re-construct postcolonial African societies. His major publications include: "Imperial Localism, Cosmopolitan Localism and the Cameroon Anglophone Decolonial Option" (*Scrutiny 2: Issues in English Studies in Southern Africa* 2016), "Francis Nyamnjoh's *The Disillusioned African*: A Philosophy of Liberation" (*The Repressed Expressed: Novel Perspectives on Black and Diasporic Literature* 2017), "Mapping Heterotopias of Apocryphal History" (*Lit: Literature Interpretation Theory* 2018), "Unmasking Francophone Cameroons' Epistemicide" (*Living (In)Dependence: Critical Perspectives on Global Interdependence* 2018), and "Shadow Lines: Confrontations, Configurations and Transpositions" (*Rethinking Language and Literature in a Changing World* 2019). His email: yoshassmbiy@yahoo.com

Chapter 7

Godwin Gham Nyinchiah is a PhD student in history. He graduated from the University of Buea, Cameroon with Masters in African History. He is currently a Research Fellow at the same University, Department of History and African Civilization where he is currently writing his PhD Thesis on 'The Resilience of British Southern Cameroons Statists Identity, 1940-2017'. His research interest is wide and includes amongst other themes: democracy, politics, minority issues, gender, history education. He is much more interested in the development of African history generally. Mr. Nyinchiah has published on a range of different areas among which are; 'The varied Nature of History textbooks in Cameroonian schools', *Yesterday and Today*; 'Multiparty Politics, Violence and Coping Strategies among Victims in Bamenda, Cameroon, 1990-1992', *Afro Asian Journal of Social Sciences*, "*Suffer Don Finish*", counting the cost of multiparty upheavals in Bamenda, Cameroon in the 1990s, *International Journal of Research and Innovation in Social Science*; 'A Comparative Analysis of Representation of Historical Facts in History Text Books In Cameroon Schools', *International Journal of Arts, Humanities & Social Science*. His email.gnyingchia@gmail.com

Table of Contents

Acknowledgments xi

Chapter 1
Introduction:
The Eternal Relevance of Music
in Society 1
Walter Gam Nkwi

Chapter 2
The Pan-African and Global Appeal of
Manu Dibango's Music 29
Henry Kam Kah

Chapter 3
Arrest the Music! The Rebel Art and
Politics of Lapiro and Valsero:
A Pedagogical Perspective 49
Peter Vakunta

Chapter 4
Lapiro, the Political artist:
Chronicler of Cameroonians' Precarity 79
Primus M. Tazanu

Chapter 5
Understanding Female Mobility in
Post-colonial Cameroon History
through Francois Misse Ngoh's U go Cry 109
Walter Gam Nkwi

Chapter 6
Singing, Dancing, Listening and Interpreting
the Mimboland Unsayable and Unwritable:
The Power of Music and the Music of
Power in Francis B. Nyamnjoh's Oeuvre........................... 137
Hassan Mbiydzenyuy Yosimbom

Chapter 7
Longue Longue: History, Identity and
Music and the 2016 Anglophone
Crisis in Cameroon... 177
Godwin Gham Nyinchiah

Chapter 8
Epilogue: Which way Forward? 213
Walter Gam Nkwi

References 219

Acknowledgments

I want to thank Professor Francis Nyamnjoh from two perspectives. Firstly, for his having sown the seed that has germinated into this book during a telephone conversation I had with him in April 2020 about Manu Dibango's passing on; and secondly, for his having granted me the permission to quote generously from his eulogy in honour of Manu Dibango in the introduction to this book.

I also wish to thank the entire team of contributors to this volume for the commitment and passion with which they timeously submitted their individual chapters. My special thanks go to Dr. Hassan Mbiydzenyuy Yosimbom who proof-read the introduction and made very relevant comments and suggestions. With Dr. Primus Tazanu they joined me in icing the cake, especially in the epilogue. Their suggestions and comments were valuable. My sincere thanks as well, go to the anonymous reviewers whose comments and suggestions have enriched and strengthened this book immensely.

Lastly, I wish to thank the authors whose works have been cited in this collection, because their works were veritable buildings blocks of our project. Furthermore, my thanks equally go to the workers of the National Archives in Buea whose diligence and professionalism have, despite the challenges, contributed in no small way in moulding us as researchers and scholars of Cameroon. However, for those errors of fact or interpretation which might have eluded all efforts at keeping them out, the different authors and I alone are responsible.

Chapter 1

Introduction:
The Eternal Relevance of Music in Society

Walter Gam Nkwi

Unsung Musical Heroes that Effortlessly Inspire

This book collates thematic reflections on Cameroon music exalting Manu Dibango, one of the first-generation Cameroonian musicians who bowed to Covid-19 on 24 March 2020. Granted his enormous contribution to Cameroonian, African and world music, one would have expected that an encyclopaedia of recognition be written to his honour after his demise. However, that has not yet been done. Like many other musicians in Cameroon, neither much seems to have been written about him nor his music in the academic domain. The inspiration for this book was drawn from the conviction that one of the best ways of honouring and valorising him would be by taking the cue from his music and then collecting essays generally on music in Cameroon.

While drawing from the biography of Manu Dibango the collection expands into different directions to show how important/relevant music has been in postcolonial Cameroon and more specifically in the Cameroon's second Republic under Paul Biya (1982 till date). As the musicians strike the strings of the guitar, while people listen tirelessly to the rhythms or dance, under these strings lie a wealth of coded history, anthropology, sociology, and poetry. All these need to be decoded. The timelessness of music cannot be over emphasised. For instance, during a Press Conference held in Yaounde on 11 November 2020, captioned *Kassav Returns To Cameroon Musical Arena: Musical Concert Announced At Press Conference*, it was announced that on Friday, November 13, 2020, Jocelyne Béroard, Jacob Desvarieux, Jean-Philippe Marthély, Jean-Claude Naimro, Claude Vamur and Georges Décimus were expected to be on stage at the Boucaro lounge in Yaounde. This information was announced to media men and women during a press conference organised by the French Caribbean band called Kassav at the Yaounde Djeuga Palace Hotel. Forty years or so ago, the Kassav Band made inroads into Cameroon and thrilled public spaces. It has remained relevant till today, evidenced by the band's return to stage in the country.

The group that was formed in 1979 in Guadeloupe has thrilled music lovers with songs from over 20 albums and 12 solo albums by band members. During the press conference, the Kassav group members told media practitioners the modalities of the would-be musical event. It was also an occasion to shed light on their musical career from when it started in 1979 and how they had managed to stay together as a team all along to the heights they had reached then. The musicians highlighted the love for music, commitment and hard work which had taken them to numerous countries where they had shared their passion with their fans.

They also talked about role models like Ndedi Eyango and many more who had been great motivations to them in the music industry. On the sidelines of the press conference, the Kassav crew spent time with curious fans. Jocelyne Béroard told journalists that besides music she is also a philanthropist who offers help to the less privileged. They also noted that entry to the concert would be limited because of #Covid-19 barrier measures imposed by the government and the World Health Organisation (WHO) would have to be respected.

The exchanges between the Kassav Group members and the

media men and women with the promise of a heart-stopping concert reminded the audience that music and society are inextricably linked or intimately related. In its modest forms it reflects and creates social conditions which amongst other things include the factors that either facilitate or impede social change. Technological innovations have facilitated interaction between musicians and their audience. For example, developments of recording techniques in the latter half of the 20th century has revolutionized the extent to which most people have access to music. All kinds of music are available to most people, 24 hours a day, at the touch of a switch. One could even observe that people the world overtake it for granted that music is easily available nowadays. In this book, we demonstrate that under the belly of the readily available music lies a wealth of information that needs to be decoded. This is one of the gaps which the essays in this volume attempts to fill.

Music is a very powerful medium and in some societies there have been attempts to control its use. It is powerful at the level of the social group because it facilitates communication which goes beyond words, enables meanings to be shared, and promotes the development and maintenance of individual, group, cultural and national identities. It is powerful at the individual level because it can induce multiple responses – physiological, movement, mood, emotional, cognitive, and behavioural. Few other stimuli have effects on such a wide range of human functions. The brain's multiple processing of music can make it difficult to predict the particular effects of any piece of music on any individual.

The power of music to act therapeutically has long been recognized. Therapy can involve listening to or actively making music. Increasingly it may involve both. Music can be effective in conjunction with other interventions in promoting relaxation, alleviating anxiety and pain in medicine and dentistry, and promoting well-being through the production of particular endorphins. Its therapeutic uses have been explored extensively with particular groups of patients: the elderly, those with brain damages, and those with persistent pains. It has also been used to promote appropriate behaviour in vulnerable groups and enhance the quality of life of those who cannot be helped medically (Novotney, 2013).

Music can play an important part in human development in the early years, stimulating foetuses and infants in such a way as to promote their wellbeing. Early interactions between mother and child have an essentially musical quality which assists in the development of communication skills. Listening to music or being involved in making it does not seem to directly affect intelligence, although active involvement in music making may enhance self-esteem and promote the development of a range of social and transferable skills. Listening to quiet, relaxing background music can improve performance on a range of academic tasks, while exciting music may interfere. Memorisation can be particularly affected. Adults are able to mediate the effects of interference through the adoption of coping strategies (Novotney, 2013).

The increased availability of music seems to be encouraging people to use music to manipulate their own moods, reduce stress, alleviate boredom while undertaking tedious or repetitive tasks, and create environments appropriate for particular kinds of social occasion. In short, music is being used by individuals to enhance the quality of their lives. In parallel with this, there is a large industry concerned with the effects of music on workers, consumers and on politics and politicians especially in repressive regimes. Music can influence the people and help them show their disproval and frustrations to governments in many ways. Such a demand for music is likely to continue to increase. To support our appetite for music, the music industries in the developed world constitute a major element of the economies of many countries. They are in danger of losing their skilled work force in the future because of the extent to which music is progressively being taken for granted.

Much of the research into the effects of music on intellectual and personal development, concentration, anxiety, pain reduction, and behaviour in a range of settings has tended to ignore the possible effects of cognition at the individual level (Schellenberg, 2013). This is an important omission. Such research suggests that our thinking about music has a powerful impact on our responses to it. If we wish to understand how music affects our lives we have to take account of the experiences of the individual. The evidence suggests that many people have already discovered that music is good for them (Schellenberg, 2013). Now we need to develop an understanding of exactly why and in what circumstances. This will require a multi-disciplinary approach to take account of the many factors which may be important.

In a world characterized by incompleteness, no one discipline is competent or complete enough to dig deep into any research domain. Nyamnjoh's (2015) assertion of incompleteness in "Incompleteness: Frontier Africa and the Currency of Conviviality" is very relevant for this collection as the chapters draw from different backgrounds, disciplines, and methodologies. That notwithstanding, the essays also affirm that music may include the society or culture to which the individual belongs, sub-group membership, individual characteristics including gender, age, prior experiences of music, current mood, whether the music is self or other selected and the extent to which music is considered important in the individual's life. To explore these issues a wide range of methodologies that explore the individual's subjective experiences of music will be adopted, taking into account those responses the actors may be unaware of.

There is also a need for more systematic investigation of the ways that music can impact on groups of people in social settings. Research by anthropologists as well as ethnomusicologists suggests that music has been a characteristic of the human condition for a millennia or so (Blacking,1976; Brown,1999; Mithen, 2005; Dissanayake, 2012; Higham *et al.*, 2012; Cross, 2016). The potential for musical behaviour is a characteristic of all human beings, with the environment shaping the experiences of individuals who act and react in groups (North and Hargreaves, 2008; Welch and McPherson, 2018). Listening to music, singing, playing (informally, formally), creating (exploring, composing, improvising), whether individually and/or collectively, are common activities for the vast majority of people the world over. Music represents an enjoyable activity in and of itself, but its influence goes beyond simple amusement and transcends almost all the strata of the society. To date, research has tended to focus on commercial and work environments and even more on music in Africa but not much on Cameroon.

The Advancements in Science, Technology and Ever-Increasing Availability of Music in Our Everyday Lives

Never before in the history of humanity have so many different kinds of music been so easily available to so many people. The development of the electronic media in the latter part of the 20th Century has revolutionized access to and use of music in our everyday lives. We can turn on the radio, play a CD or tape, or listen to music on video or TV with very little effort. Newer technological blogs like Youtubes, twitters, Facebook, and recording gadgets have led to the explosion and dissemination of music consumption around the world and Africa/ Cameroon has not failed to be part of the bazaar. Prior to these developments, music was only accessible for most people if they recorded it themselves or attended particular religious or social events. The effects of these changes have been dramatic. It is now possible for us to use music to manipulate personal moods, for arousal and feelings, and to create environments which may manipulate the ways in which other people feel and behave. Individuals can and do use music as an aid to relaxation, to overcome powerful emotions, to generate the right mood for going to a party, to stimulate concentration, in short, to promote their wellbeing. It has become a tool to be used to enhance Africans/Cameroonian self-presentation and promote their development.

Probably, the most significant development in music in the last century was the development of the technology which enabled the recording of sound. This has made music easily accessible to everyone. As a result of this, music has become a major industry worldwide. People do not only listen to music, they actively take part in making it. In 1993 alone, in the USA, 62 million people said that they sang or played a musical instrument (Gilliland, 1969; Anderson, 2012). Similarly, in the UK millions of people sing or play instruments for the love of it. In 1999, 49% of children took instrumental music lessons (Alleyne, 2000; Bennet, 2007). The decision to learn an instrument was generally theirs, although teachers were influential in the process, more so than parents. Approximately half of the children who played had a friend or family member who also played an instrument. Estimates of adults playing an instrument have varied between 24-30%. The instruments most likely to be played by children are the recorder, electronic keyboard, or piano. The piano is the main instrument for adults. These trends and/or developments in (musical) science are making music increasingly available in our everyday lives thereby affirming its importance are a veritable fleshpot for research.

The Place of Music in Cameroon Scholarship

This book focuses on music in Cameroon. There seems to be no better way of illustrating the omnipresence of music in the past and in the present and above all the immortal relevance of music than by beginning with an anecdote, a conversation between a young man and Nyamsi Theodore Auger alias Kotto Bass who died in 1996 and whose popular hits such as "Yes Bamenda," "Ponce Pilate," and "Ok Mado" still thrill music lovers twenty-four years after his demise. In the conversation, the young man assumes that he is talking with Kotto Bass and creates his own questions purportedly coming from Kotto Bass. In the conversation, Kotto Bass and the young man interchangeably act as interviewer and interviewee as occasion demands.

The young man starts by asking Kotto Bass whether Paul Biya was there (in heaven) but suddenly remembers that Biya should be in the other room which is purportedly hell. After a humorous discussion with the "ghost of Kotto Bass," he touches on Makossa. Kotto Bass seeks to know how makossa has been going on in Cameroon since his demise. The young man laments that there is no more Makossa. He says that Makossa died a long time ago. On the other hand, comes Richard Bona's "Allo Foukou" criticising the government of Paul Biya for overstaying in power. According to him the regime is characterised by corruption and pillage. He further maintains that 38 years of power has been characterised by dictatorship and under this "we can't speak, can't shout. The only thing we can do is to call Foukou. Thirty-eight years of reign equals 38 years of suffering and when it comes time for evaluation, they give us hatred. We could have discussed rather than burning down villages" (Bona, 2019).

The above anecdote illustrates the place of politics in music in present-day Cameroon. Music has become a potential weapon in the hands of musicians to criticise the regime. Nyamnjoh and Fokwang, (2003) were one of the first scholars who put music in historical perspective with the changing political regimes and rhetoric in Cameroon. The authors argue that the contents of political songs in Cameroon have changed with the fortunes or misfortunes of politics and politicians in high office. Furthermore, Nyamnjoh and Fokwang (2005) examine the nexus between musicians and political power in Cameroon in order to understand the dynamics of agency and identity politics among musicians. They also argue that politicians in Cameroon and indeed the rest of Africa have tended to appropriate musicians and their music in order to maintain themselves in power. This book takes inspiration from these authors not only to write about Manu Dibango but to chronicle music and musicians – both dead and alive – in Cameroon –from diverse perspectives.

Elsewhere, Nkwi (2006) argues that music had a relationship with history in 18th and 19th century Kom, Northwest Cameroon. Kah (2015) uses *"country don spoil"* by Ndi Tansa alias Awilo, to show that music can be used to satirize socio-political decay and conflict in Cameroon history focusing on 20th and 21st centuries. This book aims at further affirming such a perspective. For instance, in the song "Ayo Africa" by Longkana Agno Simon, aka Longuè Longuè, major historical themes such as colonialism, racism, neo-colonialism, and exploitation are asserted. Apart from Manu Dibango's and Francis Bebey's biographies, how much of the biographies of Cameroonian musicians do Cameroonians know? How does their music reflect major themes in Cameroonian society? This book takes its cue from the near lack of any profound research done on music and musicians in Cameroon. The scant literature on Manu Dibango, that is, a glaring absence of text about him after his demise, suggests that there is a gap to be filled by scholars of music in Cameroon. This book hopes to achieve this objective by asserting that between the strings of the guitar or within the gourds of a balafon lies a wealth of the history of the society that has not yet been documented.

Over the past decades, visual as well as non-visual sources have evolved as powerful means of gaining access to alternative histories. As has been argued elsewhere (Nkwi, 2006), it is increasingly being acknowledged that non-visual and visual records, whether art or documentary, offer new routes to the past and present, especially where the life experiences and the expression of people in most societies have been marginalised in the dominant written narratives. The significance of such an approach cannot be left in doubt. Thus, this book further affirms that music provides an alternative source through which we could fully understand various African societies. Music *per se* comprises the culture and daily lives of most people which is not written in the western sense of the word but is preserved through oral traditions or by way of mouth (Leach, 1950). These groups of people are primarily rural and are better able to preserve some of the older cultures of the national unit of which they form a part than the population of the cities with its more sophisticated, more international civilization, which is subjected to faster changes and fluctuations of fashion. Music could be understood as folk culture and therefore used for African community spirit, symbolizing solidarity, and unity (Tala 1987/1988: 102).

However, aside focusing on history and politics, this collection takes into consideration sociology and anthropology, thematizing the masses and society and probing into how people interact with their societies and/or environments. Such a consideration ties in with Nyamnjoh's (2003) argument that Onguene Essono (1996) discusses critical Bikutsi songs composed by popular and village musicians disillusioned by a regime that has promised without fulfilling. The songs, Nyamnjoh argues, reject the god-like status which President Biya has assumed and the torture that the insensitivities of his regime have imposed even on his own supporters from the same ethnic origin.

The Place of Music in African Scholarship

In Africa, music has historically been appropriated by social actors with a variety of interests. Veit Erlmann (1997:170), shows how South African music has served contradictory Western perceptions of Africa as 'civilized' and 'uncivilized'; and through Johannes Brusila, how the category of 'world music' permits the West to construct and essentialize the 'rest' as musical others, and how African musicians have sought to negotiate an identity for themselves within the imposed dichotomy of 'traditional' and 'modern' music. While Western music is differentiated into various nuanced categories, 'world music' collapses the music forms of various localities, regions and cultural spheres into a homogenous bloc configured to suit every consumer's exotic fantasy (Feld, 2000:151).

In colonial times, missionaries greeted African musical practices with ambivalence and a tendency to police their expressive lyrics and dance forms. Veit Arlt (2002) recounts how emerging popular highlife music in colonial Ghana was perceived by missionaries as 'obscene' and diabolical, a threat to the Christian values they sought to instil. Throughout the colonial era, African songs and dance steps were perceived with suspicion and absurdity. This was factored by the notion that orality was not a source for historical reconstruction, that its authenticity could not be tested, verified, and trusted. It was for this reason that scholars and Africanist championed the oral source as a foundation of history. They included Thomas Hodgkin, Basil Davidson, Terence Ranger, Philip Curtin, Steven Feierman, Leonard Thompson, Jan Vansina, Kenneth Onwuka Dike and B.A. Ogot.

It was Melville Herskovits, a renowned Anthropologist who first advocated the role of oral transmission, when he pointed to the surviving aspects of African culture among the New World Africans in the Diaspora in what he called 'cultural tenacity' (Freud,1998:8). Certain aspects of culture that existed in African societies were still prevalent among the Africans in the Americas. Music especially became central in historical reconstruction in Africa (Nkwi, 2010:39). This genre of the reconstruction of African history was first tested in the Great Kingdoms of Mali, Songhai, Ghana, Egypt and later Nigeria, and Zimbabwe. Music was used to narrate the paths of migration and settlement.

Africans have continuously shaped and are being shaped and informed by their music in various but amazing ways. For instance, David Coplan, a specialist in the ethnographic history and performance culture of the Basotho of southern Africa is one of those scholars who relate how Lesotho migrant labourers in South African mines have used their songs "to domesticate intractable contradictions between the symbolically reconstituted past and the uncertain constitution of the present; life at home and at the mines; …family solidarity and long-term separation; …autonomous self-image and identity as a labour unit;…ideal relationships and the reality of migrant and village life;…the migrants' thirst to determine their own destiny and the dry well of their alternatives" (Coplan, 1994:20-40). Coplan discusses every aspect of Basotho musical literature, taking into account historical conditions, political dynamics, and social forces as well as the styles, artistry, and occasions of performance. He engages the postmodern challenge to decolonize our representation of the ethnographic subject and demonstrates how performance formulates local knowledge and communicates its shared understandings.

Similarly, in Mozambique, sugar plantation workers were able, through satirical songs, to protest their suffering and preserve their identity (Vail and White, 1983: 883-919). During the Zimbabwean war of liberation, 'Chimurenga music', appropriated and adapted from local traditions, served to articulate 'the pressing issues of the day more eloquently than any political speech or historical treatise' (Pongweni, 1982: 64). Among the Yoruba, contemporary popular music has played a major role in the production of a negotiated Yoruba cultural identity (Waterman, 1982: 59-72). In Zanzibar, consumer tourism has shaped and been shaped in turn by the local music culture (Kirkegaard, 2007: 59).

Some if not most African governments have been encumbrances to the ingenuity of some African musicians. One of these governments was the military regime of Olusegun Obasanjo (1976-1979 and 1999-2007) of Nigeria, whose *main basse* fell on the famous Nigerian, Fela Anikulapo-Kuti in early months of 1977. Writing about this incident, Tejumola Olaniyan (2004:1) said amongst other things that:

> Fela had infinitely more and real violent visitations from the security agents of successive Nigerian governments over the course of the three decades of his musical career. One such on February 18, 1977, resulted in the invasion and sacking of his residence by nearly 1,000 soldiers. Residents—including Fela—and guests were brutally beaten and bayoneted and scores ended up with broken heads, legs, backs, shoulders, arms, and ribs; women were sexually assaulted; Fela's ailing mother, Nigeria's foremost anticolonial nationalist and feminist, was tossed from a second-floor window; and the house itself was razed—all in broad daylight, with thousands of citizens in the mostly lower-class neighbourhood watching in disbelief. The government's commission of inquiry into the cruelty by its agents acquitted it of responsibility because, it said, "unknown soldiers" committed the acts. Not even the subsequent global popularity of the phrase "unknown soldier," thanks

to Fela's musical account of the episode in the album Unknown Soldier, was able to remove the poignancy of "Arrest the music!" in my consciousness.

Olaniyan unmistakably captures his missive as "Arrest the music," as he draws and conceptually analyses how the music of Fela and the contexts of its production as well as its circulation, and consumption suggests, in a way the peculiar character of the relations which does exists between art, opposition music, and a postcolonial African state. This according to Olaniyan becomes imperative to pay or valorise Fela and his music. He maintains that:

> It is also an inadvertent homage to that part of Fela's image as a musician that is most familiar to the world: the "political." Above all, the unvarnished crudity, unhidden ill-bred megalomania, killjoy morbidity, and sheer incredibility of the unusual command speak volumes about the political order— and those who manage and protect from it—on behalf of which it is uttered. Indeed, if there is one overarching conceptual thread running through Fela's music, it is that the postcolonial Nigerian, and African, condition is an incredible one (Olaniyan, 2004:4).

Another musician who has been a torn in the political flesh of the government has been the Ugandan musician, play wright and politician, Robert Kyagulanyi Ssentamu, known by his stage name as Bobi Wine. According to the Editor, *Information Guide Africa*, Bobi Wine was born in 1982, and he currently serves as Member of Parliament for Kyadondo County East constituency in Wakiso District, in Uganda's Central Region. He also leads the People Power, Our Power movement in opposition to President Yoweri Museveni. (Editor, 2021) The country's incumbent ruler, Yoweri Museveni was again uncomfortable when in 2019, Bobi Wine announced his candidacy for the 2021 Ugandan presidential election (Editor, 2021). Unlike Fela and Dibango, Wine seems to have acquired higher education. For instance he attended Kitante Hill School, where he received his Uganda Certificate of Education in 1996. He further went to Kololo Senior Secondary School, where he graduated with Uganda Advanced Certificate of Education in 1998(Editor, 2021). With further ambition to slake his intellectual thirst he then attended Makerere University in Kampala. While in Kampala University he read music, dance, and drama and graduated with a diploma in 2003. In 2016, Bobi Wine returned to university to study law at the International University of East Africa (IUEA). It was in IUEA that he got in contact with his then-lecturer David Lewis Lubongoya, who has since become chief executive secretary of the People Power, Our Power movement (Ariba, 2012; Kigamba, 2017; Murisa, 2013).

In the Ugandan elections of Thursday 14 January 2021 Bobi Wine contested on the opposition bench. When chickens came home to roast, the incumbent, Yoweri Museveni was declared winner. Bobi Wine immediately launch a complaint. According to him, Museveni had stolen the victory by first using intimidation of the opposition candidates; refusal to use electronic voters cards, internet cuts and stuffing of voting boxes among other things. The incompetent government was swift in her action. Wine was put under house arrest. It is no longer news that most African governments have not been breathing easily with dissenting voices especially when they come from musicians. Fela and Wine are just a very few that have gone through this saga and their cases parallels that of Dibango in Cameroon. Unlike Dibango and Fela, on whom researchers and scholars have done some excellent works there is still a gap that needs to be filled on Bobi Wine. The above musicians have just been mentioned to show how musicians have not been at ease with governments in power especially those who sing with a moral tone to current dictatorial regimes. Manu Dibango felt into this category.

The Place of Manu Dibango in Cameroonian/African Music: Who is/was Manu-Dibango?

This question in this section is intentionally and interchangeably posed in the present and the past tenses. Although Manu Dibango is dead, he lives through his music. In this section, I draw heavily from "Manu Dibango: Afropolitan Musical Genius," an eulogy that Francis B. Nyamnjoh wrote on 30 March 2020 after the fall of Manu Dibango. This is also to complement information in chapter. Manu Dibango was born on December 12 in 1933 in Douala, Cameroon. His father, Michel Manfred N'Djoké Dibango, was a civil servant. Son of a farmer, he had met his wife travelling by piroque to her residence in Douala. Manu Dibango's mother was a fashion designer, running her own small business. Both her ethnic group, the Douala and his father's, the Yabassi, viewed their union of different ethnic groups with some disdain. Manu Dibango had a stepbrother from his father's previous marriage, who was four years older than him. In Cameroon, one's ethnicity is dictated by one's father, though Dibango wrote in his autobiography, *Three Kilos of Coffee*, that he had "never been able to identify completely with either of [his] parents".

Dibango's uncle was the leader of his extended family. Upon his death, Dibango's father refused to take over, as he had never fully initiated his son into the Yabassi's customs. Throughout his childhood, Dibango slowly forgot the Yabassi language in favour of the Douala. However, his family did live in the Yabassi encampment on the Yabassi plateau, close to the Wouri River in central Douala. While a child, Dibango attended Protestant church every night for religious education, or *nkouaida*. He enjoyed studying music there, and reportedly was a fast learner. In 1941, after being educated at his village school, Dibango was accepted into a colonial school, near his home, where he learned French. He admired the teacher, whom he described as "an extraordinary draftsman and painter" (Nyamnjoh, 2020). In 1944, French president Charles de Gaulle chose Manu Dibango's school to perform the welcoming ceremonies upon his arrival in Cameroon.

According to Nyamnjoh, we can conveniently understand Manu Dibango through the impact of his music in the world more than in Cameroon, the land of his birth. His music is a combination of European and African rhythms. The repressive political regime in Cameroon failed to recognize him and this led him to wander out of Cameroon to other African countries namely Zaire and Ivory Coast. Manu Dibango was not just a normal musician in the conventional sense but somehow a "musician-philosopher" so to say. It is in this light that Nyamnjoh maintains that, "Emmanuel N'Djoké Dibango — Manu Dibango — will live forever, thanks to his Afropolitan sounds, and to the fact that many artists in Africa and beyond are deeply indebted to him. He was a man of legendary generosity of spirit and talent, with an accommodating heart that sought to bridge the local and the global with creativity and innovation in song and music" (Nyamnjoh, 2020).

A Musician Beyond Borders

Nyamnjoh goes on to maintain that "His (Manu Dibango) album Soul Makossa was of such artistic genius that even a global superstar like Michael Jackson couldn't resist sampling from it to enrich his own album, Thriller" (Nyamnjoh, 2020:14). He was not only a musician but a lexicographer. According to Nyamnjoh (Nyamnjoh, 2020), "In his 1994 biography, Dibango describes himself as "Négropolitan". It's a term that would later be adopted and popularised as "Afropolitanism" by others enthralled by his idea of grounded cosmopolitanism". In a world of "incompleteness" to borrow from Nyamnjoh, Manu Dibango combined African and European instruments to produce his music. "He coined the term Negropolitan to capture his identity as Afro-European or African and European at one and the same time. He saw himself — and insisted on being seen — as "a man between two cultures, two environments". His music could not be confined to either, without losing its complexity and richness. It was the fruit of his diverse influences" (Nyamnjoh, 2020).

Colonised by France, it was always the ambition for each young Cameroonian to go to France as well as any family to send a son or daughter to France. The "…the enduring allure of modernity…" (Nyamnjoh, 2002:607) was rife in French Cameroonians. It was in relation to this that Manu Dibango's parents sent him to study in France when he was only 15 years old. In Spring 1949, Manu Dibango sailed for Marseilles. The family who was to look after him lived in the Sarthe region in the west of France. In 1950, he went to high school in Chartres, a little further south. He made friends with a few Africans, usually from good families, and was happy there, the atmosphere suiting him better than boarding school. He had however, "arrived in France bearing a gift of three kilograms of coffee from his parents, for his host."

During holidays in a camp for Cameroonian children living in France, he met Francis Bebey, slightly older than him and a jazz fan. Armstrong and Sidney Bechet were, to him, the emblems of black American jazz. The two lads set up a group in which each played his favourite instrument. This was the time he discovered the saxophone too. He started taking lessons. Music was his hobby but he never thought of earning a living from it. Thus, he took his first Baccalauréat in Reims where he attended yet another school. The following school year was marked by his weekend job in a local night club, the Monaco. Although he intended to study in a business school later, he failed his second Baccalauréat in 1956, and his father cut off his allowance. Once more, Nyamnjoh writes that, "In France he met Francis Bebey, another musician from his native Douala, with whom he formed a band and began to experiment with different modern instruments, such as the piano and the saxophone. He later relocated to Brussels where he met his wife to be, Marie-Josée (whom he would fondly call Coco)" (Nyamnjoh, 2020).

Manu Dibango's Sojourn in Belgium and How it Shaped His Career

At the end of 1956, he decided to try Brussels. Through a friend, he was hired at the Tabou, a fashionable club in the Belgian capital. He met a mannequin, Coco, who was later to become his wife. Unfortunately, after a quarrel with the owner of the Tabou, he lost his job. A few weeks later, he was offered a tour of the American bases in Europe with an orchestra. After playing the Moulin Rouge at Ostend and the Scotch in Antwerp, he signed a two-year contract with the Chat Noir, in Charleroi.

In 1960, he was hired by a Brussels night-club, Les Anges Noirs, which was very popular with politicians and intellectuals from Zaïre. At that time the town was buzzing with the independence negotiations and was full of influential people. In this atmosphere, Manu Dibango, leader of the Anges Noirs group, was playing around with real African music. Until then, he had played mostly music for westerners, cha-cha, tango, assorted varieties etc. The first music to be tried out was from the Congo, and was already well developed. It was his meeting with the great Joseph Kabasélé and African Jazz that was to trigger his music and open the doors of a world he had forgotten. After several years of exile in Europe, Manu Dibango had become a jazz-nourished musician. He rediscovered the sound of the African continent with Kabasélé, who hired him as saxophonist in his orchestra. They recorded some 40 pieces in a Brussels studio together for two weeks. Their records were well-received in Africa, and they were very successful.

With this recording success under his belt, Manu now wished to record solo. His target was "African soul", a mixture of jazz, rumba, and Latino rhythm. But even if the result was worth listening to, he did not find a producer. Nyamnjoh confirms that "It was also in Brussels that his [Dibango's] music career began to blossom through fruitful contacts. Two in particular stand out: Joseph Kabasélé and African Jazz, who introduced him to "the cha-cha and the rumba, the two breasts nourishing Zairean music", and who, in 1961, also invited him to Zaïre (today's Democratic Republic of Congo). The result was his first record, "African Soul," "a mixture of jazz, popular music, and rumba" (Nyamnjoh, 2020)

According to Nyamnjoh (2020), "Dibango's life was exemplary in its resilience, combativeness and ingenuity in mobilising his creativity to contain or at least confront political and cultural repression. His music brought him worldwide fame. But he did not feel particularly fulfilled in the land of his birth. He spent the best part of his life in a determined struggle to win recognition for music as art and musicians as artists in his motherland and else-where in Africa. These were contexts of strongman politics, personality cults and repeated frustrations by politicians, sometimes in cassock."

Granted that a prophet is never respected in his homeland, Manu was once more forced to leave Cameroon after he returned from Europe. Nyamnjoh tells us that, "Notwithstanding censorship, jealousy, penury, and repeated frustration and disappointment as an artist, Dibango refused to be deterred" (Nyamnjoh, 2020). After the blow of having to leave home again, Kabasélé (again!) gave him a second chance. He offered him a place on the African Jazz tour of Zaïre in August 1961. Manu Dibango accepted and flew to Kinshasa with his wife. Once the contract was completed, the couple took over the management of "l'Afro-Negro," a club which rapidly became successful. Two years later, Manu decided to open his own club, the "Tam Tam." He led the orchestra and they played his compositions. With no contract, he was able to play with whom he chose, thus extending his network of acquaintances. In early 1962, he started the fashion for the twist in Kinshasa with "Twist à Léo" and it turned out to be a huge success. After a long-lost reunion with his parents and on his father's insistence, Manu decided to return and set up a business in Cameroon. In late January 1963, he started up a club in Douala, also called the "Tam Tam." For six months Manu and Coco, his wife withstood police harassment, jealousy, and financial difficulty. Finally, they packed up and after a short passage in Yaoundé, returned to Paris, tired of African adventures.

Manu Dibango then started all over again, with no money. He needed more jobs in music. After one in the casino at Saint-Cast, Brittany, at the end of 1965, he returned to Paris and jobs. First he was hired by the Dick Rivers orchestra, belonging to the big sixties star, then he moved to Nino Ferrer's, where he played the Hammond organ. When Nino Ferrer discovered he was an excellent saxophonist, he made him play that, and later he led the orchestra. The tours began to accumulate and Manu found his musical soul once more. Because of his eternal love for his home "he returned to Cameroon from Zaïre in 1963, issuing the album Nasengina. This was his only piece constructed purely from the indigenous Cameroonian makossa. Dibango was appreciated by ordinary Cameroonians" (Nyamnjoh, 2020). Later on, Manu Dibango would give a sharp twist to the definition of Makossa: *"Makossa*'s not a traditional rhythm"

(Nyamnjoh, 2020), Dibango said. "It's urban music with influences from Nigeria, Zaire and so forth. Add in the Cameroonian personality, the kinds of Protestant church vocal harmonies which link us to Ghana and Kenya, all those common roots ... but then again, *Soul Makossa* is my view: something else again." (Nyamnjoh, 2020). By the following year *Soul Makossa* was in the Billboard Top 40. Motown and Atlantic labels vied to release a complete album. Dibango opted for Atlantic because "they had Ray Charles and Aretha Franklin ... much closer to my sensibilities" (Nyamnjoh, 2020)

Constructed on a purely Gallic tradition, Cameroon like other francophone states was obsessed with a spy system and anybody who said anything against the state became a *bete-noire* to the state. Manu Dibango "hated the fact that politicians kept his artistic creativity under close surveillance. He was disenchanted with authorities that did not allow people "to fantasise" and "to dream", and who forced everyone to talk "in cautious whispers" and to be "wary of everyone else" (Nyamnjoh, 2020). Therefore, "In 1964, disappointed in "this harmful atmosphere" (Nyamnjoh, 2020), Dibango closed down his club and abandoned all dreams of opening a musical conservatory or arts institute. He left Cameroon for France after barely 16 months back home. Still, he could not bring himself to give up on Cameroon entirely. He would pay brief return visits from the early 1980s onwards. Manu Dibango did not find solace in staying back in Europe but rather found a haven in Ivory Coast, "with the blessing of the then President of Ivory Coast, Houphouët-Boigny, could entrust him with the task of heading the *Or-chestre de la Radio-Télévision Ivoirienne*, while Cameroon could not even take seriously his expertise as a professional musician of world renown." (Nyamnjoh, 2020).

The Ethiopian Drought as a test of Manu Dibango's Generosity and his Love for Pan Africanism

A widespread famine affected Ethiopia from 1983 to 1985. The drought left 1.2 million people dead and produced 400,000 refugees. Another 2.5 million people were internally displaced and almost 200,000 children were orphaned. Other areas of Ethiopia also experienced famine resulting in tens of thousands of additional deaths. The famine as a whole took place a decade into the Ethiopian Civil War fought between the Ethiopian military junta communist governments and Ethio-Eritrean anti-government rebels from September 1974 to June 1991.

At the height of this drought Manu Dibango, "Together with other expatriate African musical talents in France, released Tam-Tam pour l'Ethiopie, to raise funds for famine-stricken Ethiopia between 1983 and 1985" (Nyamnjoh, 2000). He personally took the raised funds to Ethiopia. The initiative served as "proof that Africans too could take concrete action" (source) vis-à-vis their own predicaments. And he personally took the proceeds from the album to refugee camps in Ethiopia to ensure that, 'For once, the money wouldn't be misused by the government in power". Although the situation has improved significantly since the publication of his biography in 1994, Dibango's music is still much more appreciated abroad — as "world music" — than in Cameroon. Despite the government's attempts to impose creative inertia upon him in the early 1960s, Dibango was given the honour of composing the theme song of the 1972 Africa Cup of Nations football finals hosted by Cameroon.

However, as Dibango observed, "the authorities could decorate me with all the medals they liked" without doing much to stop "the descent into hell" (Nyamnjoh, 2020) for artistic creativity in a country where it is not uncommon to mobilise the military to raid clubs. Or to impose entertainment taxes with the intention of crippling artists who are perceived to be critical or unpalatable. Manu Dibango died after contracting Covid-19 at the age of 86 in Paris, where he felt "condemned to be an expatriate". Quibble as they may in Cameroon, Dibango leaves behind a towering record of Afropolitan musical genius of truly global magnitude, to feed and inspire many a generation to come. Manu Dibango does not have to be in Cameroon, in Africa or physically in the world to continue to do things of relevance. Overall, Manu Dibango's musical career can be linked to issues such as his multiple-layered or composite identity formations and performances (see for instance his proclivity for Negropolitanism, Afropolitanism and Pan-Africanism). Some of these if not all complements Chapter Two.

Chapter Synopsis

Henry Kam Kah in Chapter Two, "The Pan-African and Global Appeal of Manu Dibango's Music," contends that for over sixty years, the musical repertoire of Emmanuel N'Djoké (Manu) Dibango reflected soul searching and core pan-African ideals very dear to the people within the continent and in the diaspora. He argues that as a musician and saxophonist, Manu Dibango stormed concert houses in Cameroon, Africa, Europe and the United States with smashes or hits that both rallied people of African descent everywhere and also appealed to music loving populations across continents of the world. Although Manu Dibango was a very popular musician of Cameroonian origin, his music was in every sense Pan-African in nature. The musical compositions also drew inspiration from the musical genres of other prominent African musicians like Fela Ransome Kuti of Nigeria with whom he collaborated. Although this musical icon succumbed to the cold hands of death in March 2020, his music lives on and sustains cherished African values on the world stage. In This chapter, the musical path that he took and popularised is analysed to prove that he was a Pan-Africanist and a global star who left his footprints on the sands of time. His music consciously promoted standards so dear to Africans, their brethren across the world and also global ideals that made him a man who was in and for the world.

In Chapter Three, "Arrest the Music! The Rebel Art and Politics of Lapiro Valsero: A Pedagogical Perspective," Peter Vakunta focuses on a celebration of the vendetta of two anti-establishment songwriters in Cameroon. It chronicles the protest trajectory undertaken by Lapiro de Mbanga and Valsero, alias Le Général against the government of President Paul Biya, a cancerous regime that thrives on the rape of democracy, human rights abuses, and the emasculation of social justice. The songs analysed in This chapter constitute caustic criticisms of the inhumaneness, misgovernment and the abortive democratization process with which Cameroon has come to be identified. The leitmotif in the music of these songwriters is dystopia and protest in post-independence Cameroon under President Biya. As songwriters, Lapiro and Valsero have distinguished themselves from their peers by dint of the bravado, valiance and the audacity to speak truth to power. The underscores the critical role played by protest music in fostering post-independence revolutionary ideas in Cameroon and Africa. To do this effectively, we have revisited Vakunta revisits the songwriters' musical compositions during the 1990s, an era that marked the advent of multiparty politics in Cameroon. The overriding objective of Vakunta's paper is to propose a few dependable pedagogical paradigms that could be utilized by instructors desirous of adopting the works of these renowned songwriters for pedagogical purposes.

Chapter Four deals with Primus Tazanu's "Lapiro, the Political artist: Chronicler of Cameroonians' Precarity." In this chapter, Tazanu uses the concept of precarity to capture the lives and livelihoods of marginalized Cameroonians as portrayed in Lapiro's music. How this artist observed and most of all, depicted suffering and uncertainties of life in Cameroon was, par excellence, an unapologetic fight for human rights. For three decades, Lapiro brought to the limelight the degrading socioeconomic and political circumstances in his country, believing that he could draw the attention of the greedy leaders to these worsening conditions. Despite the hardship they experience daily, Lapiro saw Cameroonians as overcomers, as those who do not easily give up in the face of misery imposed on them. We find Lapiro eulogizing the economic feat of these strugglers and at the same time accusing the power structures of negligence and dishonesty. For the fact that through his music he fought for the downtrodden all his life, Tazanu asserts that we can describe Lapiro as a religious man because he examined the deteriorating conditions of life in his country and found himself playing the role of Jeremiah, the weeping prophet.

While Walter Gam Nkwi in Chapter Five focuses on "Female Mobility Understood through Music in Post-Colonial Cameroon: The case of François Misse Ngoh's 'U go Cry'". This chapter foregrounds music as a powerful route into the history and memory of society taking Cameroon as a case study. Nkwi interrogates how much of history is produced through music and how much of the society could be understood through music. Using a genre of music in Cameroon known as makossa, the chapter examines, Misse Ngoh's song, "U go Cry" to show the theme of prostitution and geographical mobility of women in postcolonial Cameroon. The chapter contends that much history can be produced through music, an aspect which has been glossed over by Cameroonian scholars and scholarship.

In Chapter Six, Hassan Mbiydzenyuy Yosimbom forays into Francis B. Nyamnjoh's use of popular artforms through "Singing, Dancing, Listening and Interpreting the Mimboland Unsayable and Unwritable: The Power of Music and the Music of Power in Francis B. Nyamnjoh's Oeuvre." This chapter draws on Francis B. Nyamnjoh's oeuvre to argue that in Cameroon, a country that Nyamnjoh fictionalizes as Mimboland, music is not only pregnant with questions beyond the indispensable technicians of Mimboland state power's answers, but also capable of shocking the marginalized masses out of silence and compliance. That is, the music provides an opportunity and a vehicle for characters to purge themselves of the frustrations of life at the margins; criticize the socio-economic and politico-cultural injustices forced on them by the indifference of those in power; and melt away their accumulated uncertainties and insecurities. Yosimbom affirms that the music in Nyamnjoh's works asserts the contrast between the "exaggerated superabundance" of the Mimboland Beverly Hills districts and the "bleeding ghettoes of poverty and lack" of her Swine Quarters. Through music, the downtrodden of Mimboland tell a story of how their attempts to escape from the poverty of the Mimboland Swine Quarters to the wealth of the Beverly Hills districts have failed because they are considered unwanted aliens. The paper concludes that Nyamnjoh uses music to demonstrate that Mimbolanders charged with making life better have been making life impossible and that the bandwagon of inequities and impunities has been commissioning intellectuals, politicians and moral authorities to celebrate dissemblance and appetite while ordinary folks keep subsisting the crises, hoping that one day, they will benefit from President Longstay's dripping grand ambitions.

Godwin Gham Nyinchiah, takes up "Longue Longue: History, Identity and Music and the 2016 Anglophone Crisis in Cameroon" in chapter Seven. The chapter attempts to ascertain whether Longue Longue, the Cameroonian artist, produce his art primarily to inform, educate and entertain his audience or for the revolutionary purpose of changing his society. The chapter further analyses how Longue Longue was able to capitalize on orality, and his personal terminological innovation to oppose the Biya Regime for its failure to integrate all Cameroonians into one-fold. Nyinchiah sees the attempt by the minority Anglophones in Cameroon to secede as a failure on the part of the regime that is oppressive and dictatorial. The paper posits that due to the entrenchment of capitalist/materialistic attitudes among the people in Africa in general and Cameroon in particular, revolutionary oral artists will always be needed to create awareness in the people relative to a change of mentality. It also argues that Longue Longue as an artist under reference is committed and determined to 'change his society'. The chapter further avers that the artist is a true practitioner of realism and will as long as people exist; continue to produce such songs to reflect the changing nature of society.

Chapter Eight is the way forward for further research in Cameroon with a focus on music. What is the unfinished task?

Chapter 2

The Pan-African and Global Appeal of Manu Dibango's Music

Henry Kam Kah

Introduction

In this chapter, we contend that for over sixty years, the musical repertoire of Emmanuel N'Djoké (Manu) Dibango of Cameroon reflected soul searching and core pan-African ideals very dear to the people within the continent and in the diaspora. A musician and saxophonist, Manu Dibango stormed concert houses in Cameroon, Africa, Europe and the United States with smashes or hits that both rallied people of African descent everywhere and also appealed to music loving populations across continents of the world. Although Manu Dibango was a very popular musician of Cameroonian origin, his music was in every sense pan African in nature. The musical compositions also drew inspiration from the musical genres of other prominent African musicians like Fela Ransome Kuti of Nigeria with whom he collaborated. Although this musical icon or colossus succumbed to the cold hands of death in March 2020 due to the global pandemic of COVID-19, his music lives on and sustains cherished African values on the world stage. In this chapter, the musical path that he took and popularised is analysed to prove that he was a pan-African and global star who left his footprints on the sands of time. His music consciously promoted standards so dear to Africans, their brethren across the world and also global ideals that made him a man who was in and for the world.

Cameroon is a country with great musical talent who have in different ways contributed immeasurably to African and world popular music. In the different regions of the country are several musical genres. This is a product of the blending of different traditional musical genres, resulting from cosmopolitanism. Cameroon serves as a cultural centre where music has been produced, valorised, and consumed. It is also here that African popular music has been disseminated. As 'Africa in miniature,' its popular musical genre has made it a great centre for African popular music. Among its great musicians of international recognition and fame is Manu Dibango (Fuh, 1) who gave the country a name and image both at the African and world stage. His humble beginnings and upbringing contributed to this vision of things.

Humble Beginnings and Roots of Manu Dibango's Music

As already mentioned in the previous chapter, Manu Dibango was born on December 12, 1933 in Douala to a Bassa father and Douala mother. This was during the French Mandate for Cameroon on behalf of the League of Nations which was formed to maintain world peace after World War I. His father was a civil servant and the mother a fashion designer. The names given to him at birth were Emmanuel N'Djoké Dibango. The decision by the father and mother to marry each other was not received favourably by both families because they came from different ethnic groups. This was often a serious consideration in marriage in the early years of many ethnic groups in Cameroon. Although in most Cameroonian ethnic groups one's ethnic group and identity is linked to the father, Dibango at an early age quickly forget his father's mother tongue and learnt Duala, the mother's mother tongue. Even when he did that, this was not because he wanted to confine himself to being Douala. Prove of this is when in his autobiography *Three Kilos of Coffee*, Dibango neither completely identified with the mother nor father.[1] From this early experience of Manu Dibango, one would argue that he was from the very early years a person who defied ethnic affinity for the sake of it, embraced values and identify with different people from across the world. May be if the father and mother were from the same ethnic group, this might have influenced his philosophy of life in the opposite direction. He was one who identified with different people and places within the context of a global citizen. This did not mean that Manu Dibango did not identify with his Cameroonian and African roots and on several occasions said this himself.

After completing elementary education in his village, Dibango was admitted into a colonial school in 1941 and from there to Saint Calais College in France in 1949. This was at the age of 15. It was at Lycée de Chartres still in France that Dibango learnt how to play the piano which would eventually propel him into a musical icon of no mean order celebrated the world over. While in school during the period of French Mandate and Trusteeship administration of French Cameroon, he developed great admiration for one of his teachers whom he came to describe as "an extraordinary draftsman and painter."[2] Such admiration of this teacher was certainly due to his creative ingenuity, a skill and talent Manu Dibango managed to develop at infancy that made him the great musician that he came to be. Manu Dibango proved as early as in his infant years that he could fully appreciate beauty. He went ahead to contribute in his own way to create a brand of music that is soothing to the soul of music lovers across the globe. In fact, the graphic description of his teacher by

---

[1] "Manu Dibango," https://en.wikipedia.org/wiki/Manu Dibango, retrieved on October 22, 2020.

[2] Ibid.

Manu Dibango was a great display of his God given creative imagination. This musical genius admired and was himself an epitome of creativity in his over sixty years of musical composition and presentation across the world.

Prior to his death on March 24, 2020 at 86 years old from the consequences of COVID – 19, Manu Dibango had been in music for more than sixty years. This were very long years of an intense, exceptional, and successful career.[3] He was brought up in a Protestant family which helped shaped his early musical orientation. His first musical influence thus came from the church to which he attended. He himself once said that "I am a child raised in the Hallelujah" meaning that his religious upbringing shaped his music in the very early years[4] and contributed to a wider appeal in subsequent years He was not the only Cameroonian musician whose music received a Christian appeal at the beginning of the musical career. With the advent of the church in many localities in Cameroon, many young people took to singing in the choirs which became a form of apprenticeship for those who eventually embraced music as a career.

The early basis of the music of Manu Dibango was in gospel music as he grew up in a Protestant family but also in other experiences. The humanistic appeal in his music was based on his life as a Protestant Christian in his youth. Besides, as a Cameroonian born Paris based saxophonist, composer, lyricist, and instrumentalist some of the roots of his kind of music were buried in funk, reggae, soul,

---

[3] "Cameroonian Saxophonist Manu Dibango Dies of Coronavirus," https://www.theafricareport.com/25017/cameroonian-saxophonist-manu-dibango-dies-of-coronavirus/, retrieved on April 30, 2020.

[4] "Manu Dibango: African Saxophone Legend Dies of COVID-19," https://www.bbc.com/news/world-europe-52017834, retrieved on April 30 2020.

gospel, jazz salsa, and blues among others which he had mastered over the years (Jacques 1989: 19). Such were combinations that made Manu Dibango like a few other African musicians stand out tall and a prominent musician of no mean character in Cameroon, Africa, and the world. The influence of the Nigerian Civil War of 1967-1970 and the music of Fela Anikulapo Kuti also had a profound impact on Manu Dibango especially on how he conducted himself and became famous in the musical or entertainment industry. Dibango visited Fela in the years between 1971 and 1990. From the irrefutable 'god' of Afro-beat, Dibango drew great inspiration. During this close to twenty years of his communion with Fela he listened to and examined Fela's approach in the creation of the new style of music (Igbi 175). All these experiences contributed to widen the scope of Dibango's music to become appealing to Africans of all generations and social classes.

Pan-African Appeal of Dibango's Music

The popularity of Manu Dibango's music has been endeared by the fact that it has with it the pan-African appeal in terms of lyrics and content of messages in the musical compositions. His musical repertoire prides itself with the collection of local styles and experiments which appeal to many people across the African continent from North to South and East to West. Other African musicians would always beckon on him to assist them sound African in their music. He also borrowed aspects of Afro-beat music from Fela of Nigeria which were reflected in his musical composition (Zeleza 2010: 223) and therefore appealed not only to Cameroonians but also Nigerians and other Africans from different parts of the continent. His collaboration with Fela Kuti over a long period of time made his music to have traces of Afrobeat. Dibango also successfully fussed jazz and funk with traditional sounds from Cameroon to make his music captivating.[5] In a review of his work *Three Kilos of Coffee*, this pan-African appeal is glaring. The reviewer opines that "An African sound came to mean whatever Manu Dibango was doing" (Reviews 1994). This is because the sound was a collection of lyrics and other musical elements from within the African lived environment. He was always very willing to work with young people who have the creative skills that bring about innovation. This was also to raise African standards in this domain with Cameroonian inputs. Convinced with this way of doing things, Manu Dibango once said over BBC that:

> I want to do something with nothing but African instruments ... I have already met a young man, Adama Bilorou, who plays the chromatic balafon and with whom I want to do this project. I also want to take up African standards again with a Cameroonian tam-tam player who' initiated in the transmission of messages ... And an audio-visual recording of the symphonic safari should also be made.[6]

There is therefore no doubt that Manu Dibango combined African instruments to create music that was appealing to Africans and others in different parts of the world. He worked with young people to nurture their talents and ensure continuity once he was called to the world beyond. He was very keen to place African standards by making use of local instruments like the tam-tam player. When Manu

---

[5] "Manu Dibango: African Saxophone Legend Dies of COVID – 19," https://www.bbc.com/news/world-europe-52017834, retrieved on April 30 2020.

[6] "Cameroonian Saxophonist Manu Dibango Dies of Coronavirus," https://www.theafricareport.com/25017/cameroonian-saxophonist-manu-dibango-dies-of-coronavirus/, retrieved on April 30, 2020.

Dibango composed his music therefore, he consciously and purposefully took into consideration several aspects of the African people and this explains why many Africans fell in love with his music both within the continent and in the Diaspora.

Among African men who were validated or affirmed for their black personality and way of life was Manu Dibango (Ngongkum 2017: 66) who made African music to become a way of life. He portrayed his black personality status in the musical numbers he presented. Through them he handled a wide range of contemporary social problems. In one of such sounds, Guinea was used as a perfect example of the African country facing numerous social problems. Guinea's difficulties in the struggle for independence against French stranglehold on the country, corruption, the co-existence of what was considered animism and Catholicism and unemployment among young people with university degrees were all captured by Dibango in this musical album (Ferreira 2011: 249). Under the leadership of Sekou Touré Guinea opted out of the French Union to the disbelief and revenge of the French under the leadership of General Charles de Gaulle. The Guineans paid a supreme price and were considered to be stubborn to their colonising European country France. There is literature about the Guinea and Ghana Union which eventually included Mali to form the nucleus of a United States of Africa but which unfortunately collapsed among other reasons because of neo-colonialism and double standards of the Western countries intent on maintaining a strangle hold on their former colonial possessions (DeLancey 1966; Welch Jr. 1967).

Manu Dibango also went on to address corruption, an endemic problem that has contributed to failed governance not only in Guinea but in many other African countries. Corruption is a cankerworm that has eaten very deep into the socio-political and social fabric of African countries (Agostino *et al* 2016). It has retarded development in almost every sector of national life and led to poverty, misery, unemployment, and civil strife as a few privileged persons live in opulence and the majority are in squalor. Government officials receive huge bribes in exchange for service to the public and act more or less as masters instead of as servants of the people. Teachers on their part once role models in society openly ask and collect money from students' especially female students in addition to sexual exploitation. They go on to reward these female students according to how they have satisfied them in bed. Still in the domain of education, people are promoted or appointed to positions of responsibility according to the amount of money they have given to oil the lips of those in authority or who make the decisions. No sooner have they occupied these positions that they become very irresponsible and haughty. Those who write public exams into professional schools virtually buy these exams in several African countries including Cameroon. The highest bidder and most often numskulls get admitted while the poor continue to gnash their teeth even if they are intelligent with no one to help them.

In the military sector, the people openly collect bribe on the highways like in Nigeria and Cameroon[7] and jostle for appointive positions through bribery and corruption. Tribalism has also manifested itself in promotions within the rank and file of the military thereby polarising it not only in Guinea as was presented by Manu Dibango but other sub-Saharan African countries. From the look of things, it would appear almost every sector of public and private life in many African countries is corrupt. This has resulted in the frustration of those very hardworking people who happen to come from very poor backgrounds. Life becomes unbearable for them as many resign themselves to fate. Penned up anger has often

---

[7] Eye witness account in both countries

led to civil strife in several African countries and the consequences have often been street protests, burnings, and a heavy-handed crackdown on protesters. In fact, the theme of corruption that permeates all sectors of national life which Manu Dibango addressed in his music with Guinea as a model has a pan-African appeal because. This is because it affects several African countries and is at the root of many of its myriad of problems today.

Religious differences between "animists" and Catholics in Guinea became one of the preoccupations of Manu Dibango in his musical composition. Religious intolerance was/is not only a problem in Guinea but also in several other African countries notably Nigeria and several of the Arab speaking countries of North Africa (Ogbonnaya 2012). Intolerance and extremism remain at the centre of some of these religiously motivated problems with unimaginable consequences. The Boko Haram insurgency in Northern Nigeria for example, was a result of fundamentalist Muslims describing western education as sinful and outrageous to Muslims who should abide by Arabic. This crisis is at the centre of the destruction of the ecosystem in the North Eastern part of Nigeria, Chad, Niger, and Northern Cameroon with the consequence being food insecurity. Many are in hunger because the farms are insecure and have also been rendered homeless and property less. The cost of religious intolerance to governments of countries involved is enormous which affects their ability to provide basic social amenities to the population and to rebuild infrastructure that has been destroyed.

There is also a serious religious war that has made Somalia ungovernable since the ouster of Mohammed Siad Barre in 1991. The Al Shabbab fighters want the imposition of an Islamic state in the country. As a result, this has led to suffering and untold misery not only in the country but also neighbouring countries like Kenya who from time to time suffer from serious incursions of the Islamists

(Terdman 2008). In fact, religious fratricidal wars in several parts of Africa have been a common problem which has affected not only those areas but have had multiplier effects on the entire continent and beyond because people are forced to migrate across borders. This has also led to the convening of meetings to address these multifarious problems. In fact, Manu Dibango was not blind to this when he discussed them in his music as they happened in Guinea. Many of those who listened to this music became more aware of the challenges of building a nation like Guinea which is still in problems today because of the third term in office of president Alpha Conde. It is therefore a sad thing to see leaders renege on their promises and flout the constitution with impunity and as support by their cronies.

One other thorny issue which Dibango consciously addressed in his music was the high unemployment rate among university graduates in Guinea. This is a serious problem and a time bomb which has often given ruling authorities in many African countries sleepless nights (Mohamedbhai 2015). In the university system in Africa today is what Mahmoud Mamdani referred to as the massification of education when he referred to Uganda (Mamdani 2008). This is a phenomenon across Africa because students attend universities without proper and relevant education that can address the pressing problems of the society in which they live. They graduate with a string of certificates which are not relevant. They become jobless in spite of their training and this is discouraging to those who intend to pursue formal education to a higher level. Without work, some are tempted to indulge in petty crimes like drug abuse, urban gangsterism and other social ills which are a menace to the peace of the towns and cities of Africa. Others get into menial jobs and when they cannot make ends meet, they vent their anger on their employers and on other vulnerable members of the community.

The galloping unemployment rates in Africa has created a

problem of another kind – namely migration across the Sahara to Europe or migration to Latin America through Ecuador and other countries of Latin America to find their way to Uncle Sam's country where they feel that all will be well with them. Many have died on their way to the 'Promised Land' and still others have been repatriated as was recently with some Cameroonians who left for America to seek asylum as the Anglophone crisis rages on in the country. The double frustration of being sexually exploited, abused, and tormented as well as repatriation have left many in depressed conditions and created more problems than solved them. African leaders have had to grapple with all these as they embark on half-hearted and cosmetic measures which provide no sustainable solution to the unemployment of youths. If Manu Dibango took this up in his music, it was because it is serious enough a problem with whom all Africans identify and for which reason a long lasting solution need to be found through the agency of the African Union which seems to be helpless in the face of this kind of tragedy.

All the issues that Manu Dibango handled when he was addressing the problems of Guinea are in fact African problems. Many Africans are weary of the way they are treated by government officials who offer no apology. They are also ill at ease by the conflicts emanating from religious differences, most of whom have their roots out of the continent. These are essentially foreign religious bodies which have helped to tear Africans apart. It is high time Africans retrace their roots and know that they had had a religion that was and remains noble and uniting rather than dividing people.

Africans generally fancy encounters because of their attractive power. The African popular music star Manu Dibango of Cameroon was fully aware of this when he asserted that "African music was and remains a music of encounters, in this lies its attractive power" (Mundundu 2005: 2). He also asserted that:

What is special is that Africa has a long historical relationship with sound, and a communion between sound and the visual stronger than any other culture. The sound carries the rhythm and the movement creates the images. The way an African moves compared with the environment is different from western conception.[8]

African encounter with sound is therefore over a long period of time. They create encounters with the environment to produce sound and music.

African people generally believe in the collective rather than the individual and this has made them to think and support encounters which bring them joy and shared experiences from which they learn and make progress in life. Mundundu (2005: 2) argues that these encounters are in the history of the African people, at several levels within and outside the continent. Whether in their ritual life, farming life, associative life and other forms of interaction, Africans have always been together rather than gone their separate ways. Their migration from one place to the other for trade and other activities was often in caravans or groups. These travelling encounters made them to share experiences on difficulties and successes together in the form of collective experience. There were also encounters of war between communities, of long-distance trade, of religious festivals and other performative ceremonies that brought people from different socio-cultural and political backgrounds. Such encounters have enriched the narratives of Africans whether orally or in written form. To have recognised that African music remains music of

---

[8] "Manu Dibango Obituary,"

https://www.theguardian.com/music/2020/mar/24/manu-dibango-obituary, retrieved on April 30 2020.

encounters was to recognise how it attracts many who use such spaces to share other ideas about their environment, the past, present and future. Among many Africans were those who believed and associated with the music of Manu Dibango because of this feeling of the collective through enriching encounters. Since Africa has a longer historical relationship with sound, this has also been at the centre of its appealing nature which mobilises and brings people together to encounter what the coming together offers.

His Africanness in the things he usually did manifested itself whenever Manu Dibango had an opportunity to do so. In late 1984 for instance, he brought together a group of African musicians to record *"Tam Tam pour L'Ethiopie"* (Pufleau 2014: 4). The history of Ethiopia had known high and low moments especially with regards to drought and famine of the 1970s to the 1980s (Rahmato 1988) which often attracted the sympathy of many Africans and other people of good will from within and outside Africa. The mobilisation of other African musicians to devote a record for Ethiopia in time of need was a veritable show of real concern, solidarity, and patriotism for the symbolism of the name Ethiopia to all Africans and those of African descent everywhere in the world. The very rich history of this colossus of an African country is a symbol of the pride of every African worthy of the name even if Ethiopia is always at war with itself. Besides, as seat of the African Union (AU), formerly the Organisation of African Unity (OAU), it is from Ethiopia that issues of concern to Africans is addressed by the AU. Its diplomatic importance gives the country international recognition and in some cases admiration. Manu Dibango did the right thing to rally a group of musicians for Ethiopia because apart from the historic importance of this country, music also creates greater awareness among a people about the problems they face. It soothes the soul when in distress. If Manu Dibango had Africa in mind when he produced and staged his music, he also had humanity as a whole scattered all over the world.

Global Appeal of Dibango's Music

There was no better way to express the global appeal of the music of Manu Dibango than was presented by former Ghanaian President John Dramani Mahama. During a public address at the international conference on African studies in the University of Ghana on October 24 2013 he among other things said that "Through the music of Manu Dibango, Africa seem to hold the world's attention" (Mahama 2014: 119). There was no better way of saying that the music of Manu Dibango held the attention of the world than in the speech of the President of Ghana. He captured it graphically. Reading deeper meaning into this statement one may rightly argue that Manu Dibango's music was so appealing to the world that it could not escape its attention especially the attention of the music loving people around the world. As clear prove of the global appeal of Dibango's music, the album "Soul Makossa," composed together with a musicologist Eno Belinga in the wake of the eighth edition of the African Cup of Nations football tournament in 1972 sold over two million copies in the United States of America (Ngo Nlend, 181). This was a feat never before achieved by an African musician. Thousands of people found the music appealing to them and bought copies.

As a result of the fact that the music appealed to many who secured copies, a record-breaking sale of an African musical production was established. In fact, the "Soul Makossa" album hit the New York scene with a roller-coaster different sound (Stamatescu 2017: 61). The album featured on the US top 40 (Fuh 1). The "Soul Makossa" hit became very popular in clubs and private parties in

New York and made them to become gathering spots for people at the margins of dominant culture such as homosexuals, African Americans, and Latinos (Moorsom 2011: 17). The popularity of "Soul Makossa" across cultural spaces in the global arena also made Makossa a popular musical genre in Cameroon (Brunner 51). This was really prove of how far his music had come to occupy such an important space in the musical space of New York which is a global centre of melting cultures, thanks to the fact that it is also the headquarters of the United Nations Organisation (UNO). It was still through personalities like Manu Dibango that West African music found representation in Paris or Manchester discotheque in Europe (Monnakgotla 1997: 2).

Through a collection of local styles and experiments Manu Dibango was able to develop African popular music, local styles, and experiments into a global phenomenon (Reviews 1994). It was probably this blend of local styles and experiments that made Manu Dibango to look and sound African and global, thus confusing people about where to actually locate him when it came to music. In one instance Dibango himself said of what different people who listened to his music thought he represented in the following words:

> At first people in Africa said that I made Western music, that I was black-white. I carried that around for a long time. In France, people often told me that I made American music. And when I went to the United States, the Americans thought that I made African music. It's impossible to be more of a traitor than that (Wolkerseder 2015: 12).

From this pronouncement of Manu Dibango as cited above, it therefore becomes clear that his musical repertoire was eclectic in nature and appealed to people across different cultural groups of the world. While some Africans saw his brand of music to be black-white probably because he blended western instruments with local styles, others in France instead considered him to be playing American music and the Americans believed that he was playing African music. In all of these, it was clear that if Africans saw in his music black-white, the Europeans thought but of American style of music and Americans described it to be African. If Manu Dibango was therefore associated with all these people, one can therefore argue with a degree of certainty that his music was beyond categorisation. This is more so because it caught the attention of Africans, Europeans, Americans, and people of other races.

Like other prominent African musical icons notably Baaba Maal of Mali, Hugh Mase Kella from South Africa and Youssou N'Dour from Senegal, the music of Dibango underwent cross fertilisation of ideas with those of people from the West (Emielu 136). This was because these African musical icons were essentially based abroad and acted as human agents of cross-cultural music between Africa and the West. Besides, in the thinking of Manu Dibango, music from Africa and 'black' music from the New World enjoyed the company of each other. It got to a point where these two reached a mixed audience such as in late colonial Belgium as Brussels was rapidly going through a decolonising phase (Arnault 2018: 152). Even within Africa Manu Dibango assisted Ngangura to demand a period of racial interaction which would help break down colonial barriers in the years prior to the independence of Congo (Arnault 2018: 155). Music from Africa and 'black' music from the New World actually blended to attract people from Africa and African origin as well as promote racial interaction which went beyond the African continent. This was even more so during the years before independence with the Congo as an example of a country where music appealed to people of different creeds, race, and cultures.

One thing that reflected the fact Manu Dibango's music could not be limited to Cameroon and Africa but also appealed to many music loving people across the world was due to a statement he once made concerning people's feelings about his music. In his own words he captured this by saying that "As you are African they expect you always to play African forgetting that you are not a musician because you are African. You are a musician because you are musician; coming from Africa, but first musician." [9] There is more philosophical insight to this assertion than meet the eye. In the statement one finds that Dibango did not even mention Cameroon meaning therefore that he thought and acted as an African because his music was not only Cameroonian but blended local styles from different parts of Africa which explain why he talked about African. He thought beyond Africa because he himself said that even if one was a musician from Africa, this did not automatically make him or her African. A musician and a good one at that was a global personality. Manu Dibango was essentially at ease to play music to appeal to everyone although this was not always been easy. It was therefore due to hard work and commitment that his music was played and enjoyed by many in night clubs in Paris, London, and New York among other parts of the world. This made him to have friends all over the world and to project the image of Cameroon. He was keen to add to his musical lyrics any element of local style to make his music adapted to the changing times. This explains why his music covered a wide spectrum of styles drawn from traditional African roots, jazz, soul, Afrobeat, reggae, gospel, French chanson, Congolese rumba, salsa, and solo piano. He was the founding father of funk.[10] This is made

---

[9] "Manu Dibango: African Saxophone Legend Dies of COVID – 19," https://www.bbc.com/news/world-europe-52017834, retrieved on April 30 2020.

[10] "Manu Dibango Obituary,"

possible by the fact that in 1989, Manu Dibango who was known to be a Cameroonian-Parisian musician claimed that he was African and European at one and the same time and that he founded the concept of "negro-politain" (Jayawardane 2018: 5). Like Miriam Makeba, Fela (Ransome) Anikulapo-Kuti and Youssou N'dour Dibango was a musician and singer who achieved enduring international fame (Thorsen 2004: 99).

Several of the statements made by Manu Dibango while alive and composing and presenting music left no one in doubt that his horizon had risen above his country Cameroon. Music was so much part and parcel of him that he expressed the feeling of a person who was not tied down to a specific definition in terms of his origin and musical appeal. He was quoted at one time as saying that:

> People who are curious for sounds, they seek out harmony and melody because they are curious. Your curiosity can be limited by your environment, or you can expand it to take in things from outside; a bigger curiosity for a bigger world. The extent of your curiosity should not be determined by the village, or the town, or a city in another continent. The musician moves in these circles, but he moves to break out of his limits (Garfinkel 2013: 8).

Curiosity played an important role in making Manu Dibango the person he became. It was his curiosity that led him to several experiments that yielded fruits and projected him to the limelight of Cameroonian, African and global musical scene. He exploited the African, European, and American environments to achieve greatness. This was indeed a bigger curiosity for a bigger world.

---

https://www.theguardian.com/music/2020/mar/24/manu-dibango-obituary, retrieved on April 30 2020.

Conclusion

We have in this chapter shown that Manu Dibango left his footprints on the sands of time by producing and presenting music which appealed to people beyond Cameroon and Africa. He rose to the pinnacle of music and made not only Cameroon but Africa proud in concert halls in the United States of America and Europe. Several of his hits were not only admired by many but some like Michael Jackson tried to copy some of these lyrics without acknowledging and paid very dearly for it. Manu Dibango had a humble and God blessed beginnings when he would sing in a Protestant church at a very tender age. His love for creativity took him to another level of fame beyond the national territory. He lived to train so many people, dictating talent at a youthful age and nurturing this talent to success. He also worked in collaboration with other prominent African musicians sharing his experiences with them and also borrowing from them to improve and enrich his own musical production. This musical icon was an epitome of love, patriotism, and his death at the advent of the COVID-19 was a blow to the music loving people of the world.

Chapter 3

Arrest the Music! The Rebel Art and Politics of Lapiro and Valsero: A Pedagogical Perspective

Peter Vakunta

Introduction

This chapter is a celebration of the vendetta of two anti-establishment songwriters in Cameroon. It chronicles the protest trajectory undertaken by Lapiro de Mbanga and Valsero, alias Le Général against the government of President Paul Biya, a cancerous regime that thrives on the rape of democracy, human rights abuses, and the emasculation of social justice. The songs analysed in This chapter constitute a caustic critic of the inhumaneness, misgovernment and the abortive democratization process with which Cameroon has come to be identified. The leitmotif in the music of these songwriters is dystopia and protest in post-independence Cameroon under President Biya. As songwriters, Lapiro and Valsero have distinguished themselves from their peers by dint of bravado, valiance and the audacity to speak truth to power. The purport of This chapter is to underscore the critical role played by protest music in fostering post-independence revolutionary ideas in Cameroon and Africa. To do this effectively, we have revisited the songwriters' musical compositions during the 1990s, an era that marked the advent of multiparty politics in Cameroon. The overriding objective of our work is to propose a few dependable pedagogical paradigms that could be utilized by instructors desirous of adopting the works of these renowned songwriters for pedagogical purposes.

Orature is fascinating in several respects but the aspect that captivates the attention of the audience is the performing art of the narrator. Groomed to not only entertain live audiences but also to blow the whistle on individual and collective foibles, oral performers command unquestionable respect in Cameroon and Africa at large where they are named differently depending on their provenance. In the Xhosa-speaking communities in South Africa, for instance, the *imbongi*[11] has the privilege of singing the praises of paramount chiefs and other high-ranking traditional leaders. In West Africa, notably among the Mande peoples (Mandinka, Malinké, Bambara, etc.), the role of praise-singing devolves on the *griot*. Griots are perceived as repositories of oral traditions and indigenous knowledge. By this token they are often referred to as sages. Griots are considered roving libraries on account of the encyclopaedic knowledge they possess. They have profound knowledge of the folklore, culture and mores of the people and are capable of extemporizing on current events and fortuitous incidents. Although popularly known as 'praise-singers,' griots often use their verbal artistry to chastise, satirize, and make loaded comments on traditional and political leaders in the communities to which they belong. We contend throughout This chapter that Lapiro and Valsero double as griots, entertainers and social critics in the musical compositions that constitute the corpus studied. We have not analysed all the songs written by these prolific songwriters on account of space and time limitations.

Before delving into the crux of the matter, it behoves us to shed some brief light on the philosophical believes of these prominent songwriters. Lapiro believed in the innate goodness of man but also had the conviction that absolute power corrupts absolutely. He was

---

[11] composer and orator of poems praising a chief or other traditional figurehead

noted for contending that political power creates monsters. Consequently, his entire musical career was devoted to fighting the cause of freedom for the underprivileged in Cameroon. His counterpart, Valsero, alias Le Général, with real names Gaston Philippe Abe, was born on September 12, 1975 in the city of Marseille in France. After a normal childhood in his country of birth, Valsero immigrated to Cameroon in 1987 and settled with his father in the capital city of Yaoundé. He started song writing in 1990 with his first group code-named Ultimatum, and in 2008 his first solo album entitled, "Politiquement Instable" (Politically Unstable) was released. This album had a tonic effect on Cameroonian youngsters who began to look up to him for guidance and leadership. Valsero sees himself as a political rapper and has devoted a sizeable chunk of his song writing to throwing jibes at President Paul Biya and his lame-duck governance of Cameroon. Valsero has collaborated with prominent Cameroonian singers, namely Lapiro de Mbanga, Manu Dibango, Alpha Blondy, Tiken Jah, Soprano, and Kery James. The gravel voiced rapper with his blistering looks is something of a maverick. Like Lapiro, Valsero has paid the price for speaking truth to power. He, too, has been arrested and sent to jail for being critical of government officials in his music and lending support to the leader of the opposition party headed by Professor Maurice Kamto, the Cameroon Renaissance Movement (MRC).

In Cameroon, oral performance responds to communal needs in both literate and illiterate communities. Consequently, orality and literacy co-exist as two faces of the same coin. One feeds the other. Musicians like Lapiro and Valsero no longer sing ex-tempore; they compose songs in isolation and then perform in front of live audiences. oftentimes, the raw material they utilize is culled from a communal font—folklore. Arguing along the lines Scheub (1985:16) notes:

With the advent of literature, the oral tradition did not die. The two media continued their parallel development: both depended on a set of similar narrative and poetic principles, and each proceeded to develop these within its own limits (….) 7 There is no unbridgeable gap between them; they constantly nourish each other.

Such a literary synthesis is feasible only insofar as a given number of conditions are present at the point of encounter between oral and written traditions, including especially the extent to which the synthesizing artist is well rooted in the oral forms of traditional narratives. It is in this light that we have referred to musicians in general throughout This chapter as songwriters rather than singers. As Ong (1982:2) observes in his seminal work, *Orality and Literacy: the Technologizing of the Word*, "the relationship between these two media should be construed from a historical vantage point: It is useful to approach orality and literacy synchronically, by comparing oral cultures and chirographic (i.e., writing) cultures that coexist at a certain time. But it is (…) essential to approach them also diachronically or historically, by comparing successive periods with one another."

According to Ong, a historical study of orality and literacy and the various stages in the evolution from one to the other sets up a frame of reference in which it is possible to understand better not only the pristine oral culture but also the subsequent writing culture. It is not just the profit motive that serves as a catalyst for translating orality into literacy. An equally valid reason why these artists translate orality into the written word is to preserve intellectual property that will be bequeathed to progeny. In this light, oral performers fulfil critical social functions in Africa. Their tales encapsulate the most deeply felt emotions of the people whose lives are mirrored in the narratives.

Songs suggest to members of the audience the route to wholesomeness. No wonder then that the quest for wholesomeness is the leitmotif in the musical compositions of Lapiro and Valsero as will be seen subsequently in This chapter. Many of their songs chronicle the trail of dystopia, disenchantment, and disillusionment in Cameroon. In other words, the anecdotes they tell in their songs prick the conscience of perpetrators of social anomy. These songs serve as mirrors of the very nature of Cameroonian society in this day and time. They are the prisms through which emasculators of social ideals could be seen. Most importantly, their songs constitute the means by which Cameroonians find their own connections with a world replete with unfathomable meanders.

The songs that make up the corpus studied in This chapter take readers into the innermost recesses of their consciences and, by means of luminous images, cast mind-searching light into their deepest and most secret places. As Scheub (1971:198) would have it, "storytelling chronicles our great transformations and helps us to undertake periodic transfigurations." At the explosive centre of Lapiro and Valsero's rebel art can be found our most profound hopes and aspirations, the quintessence of our own very existence as global citizens. Their songs create a continuum from the past to the present. For this reason, Scheub (2002:201) postulates that "it is the task of the storyteller to forge the phantasmagorical images of the past into masks of the realistic images of the present, thus, enabling the performer to pitch the present to the past, to visualize the present within a context of and, therefore, in terms of the past." The music of Lapiro and Valsero bridges the gap between the past and the present by juxtaposing the regimes of Paul Biya and Ahmadou Ahidjo and the ideals by which each leader stands. In doing so, the songwriters underscore the mindboggling dichotomies that exist between these statesmen and their governmental modus operandi.

Salient themes woven into songs enable Lapiro to adumbrate the concept of 'good governance' as seen in the following except from his most recent album titled *Démissionnez*:

> Trente ans de championnats
> You dong composé équipes
> Wuna dong buka ndamba for all kain stade
> Sep so soso défaite because of over boum! boum![12]
>
> I say hein wuoh, dat équipe for Lions domptables
> Wei you dong nuong for Besie for Kondengui
> Ana for Besie for New Bell
> Wei na popo you dong formé yi,
> Yes, na you be Sah for da équipe
> Nationale de shiba
> Na you di recruiter joueurs
> And na you di make dem licenses.
> Na you be sélectionneur,
> Coach and capitaine joueur,
> Na you di make classement for ndamba.

This stylistic device may not make sense to folks who do not understand the game of soccer. However, Lapiro's recourse to soccer

---

[12]Thirty years of tournament
You have formed teams
Your teams have played soccer in all kinds of stadia
Regardless, they have incurred nothing but defeat upon defeat
On account of excessive boum! Boum!

metaphors makes perfect sense to the people of Cameroon for whom football has become a national 'religion' of sorts. It should be noted that the word "wuoh" called from the native tongues of the grasslands people in the Northwest Region translates a relationship of camaraderie. However, used derogatorily as Lapiro does in this song, the word takes on a different signification—expression of contempt for the Head of State. Lapiro lambastes the Cameroonian President for his predilection for power monopoly: "Na you be sélectionneur/Coach ana Capitaine joueur/Na you di make classement for ndamba". In other words, Paul Biya is the selector, coach, and captain. He sorts out players for matches which often result in defeat! It is on this count that Lapiro describes Biya's team as "youa own sia Manchester." He reminds the president that victory in soccer requires intelligence:

Kondre man, ndamba no be boum! boum!
Ndamba na sense!
Ndamba no sense, ancien répé
No be na boum! Boum!

Lapiro's intent is to draw the attention of the public to Biya's usurpation of power from the judicial and legislative branches of government in Cameroon. Biya has silenced Cameroon's judges and Members of Parliament who remain at his beck and call. In the foregoing excerpt Lapiro contends that for thirty years, Paul Biya has failed to deliver the political goods that Cameroonians expected of him. The songwriter attributes this monumental failure to lack of clairvoyance on the part of the Cameroonian President ("because of over boum! Boum!") This songwriter seems to suggest that good governance stems from clairvoyance and the ability to connect with the populace. Other themes that are recurrent in his songs are the notions of accountability and responsibility as seen in the following excerpt:

> You wan dammer you mimba we,
> You wan souler you mimba we,
> You wan nyoxer you mimba we-oh.
> Oh Mimba we-oh, tara!
> [At table, remember us;
>   When you're having a drink,
> Remember us when you're having sex-oh
> Oh, remember us, you're our leader!][13]

Lapiro's clarion call does not stop at the doorstep of political leaders. He extends his appeal to the oppressed populace as well, urging them to stand up and fight for their rights. He believes that his compatriots acknowledge their predicament but shy away from taking the necessary action to right the wrongs of the past. They have resigned to their fate and refused to indulge in bold actions necessary to halt misgovernment. They do not want to indulge in actions perceived as criminal by forces of law and order as the following excerpt indicates:

> We no wan kick-oh
> We no wan go for ngata
> We de daso for ndengwe
> A beg mimba we-oh, yes tara.
> We no wan problème para
> We no wan go for Ndengui
> We di fain daso garri
> For helep we own family-oh!

---

[13] All translations are mine except otherwise indicated

[We don't want to steal

We don't want to go to jail

We just need to work

We beg you to think about us, boss

We are not looking for trouble

We don't want to go to Kondengui

We are only looking for a means

To help our families-oh!]

Fear of the unknown is the leitmotif in the song referenced above. Lapiro seems to suggest that Cameroonians have been rendered inactive by fear of arrest and incarceration. It should be noted that the word "Ndengui" is an allusion to Cameroon's notorious prison in Yaounde, the nation's capital city. "Mimba we" is a loaded song as it calls upon the Head of State and his henchmen to refrain from turning a blind eye to the legitimate grievances of the people they govern. Lapiro appeals to those at the helm to be mindful of the thorny problems engendered by the socio-economic morass in Cameroon. In "Mimba we" Lapiro brazenly admonishes the President against overlooking the plight of the downtrodden in Cameroon. Words like 'dammer', 'suler', 'tara' and 'nyoxer' are lapiroisms,[14] created for the sole purpose of veiling the songwriter's intent to commit what Verschave (2004:8) describes as *"crime de lèse majesté* or insult to the Head of State's honor. It is a composite language minted to underscore the metrolingual context in which Lapiro composes his songs. 'Dammer' is a camfranglais word for *manger* (to eat); 'suler' translates the standard French word *boire* (to drink); 'tara' is slang for the French word *patron* (boss or big shot); 'nyoxer' is a euphemism for *baiser* 'have sexual intercourse.'

---

[14] Neologisms created by Lapiro de Mbanga

Lapiroisms reflect the provocative attitude of its speakers and their jocular disdain for linguistic correctness, clearly revealing its function as an anti-language (Halliday 1977).

Like most protest songwriters, Lapiro drums up support from the rank and file as this excerpt clearly indicates:

> Nkoululu ah wan tok,
>
> Mokolo ah wan gi ticket
>
> Marché Central ah go troweh, heh! heh!
>
> Sauveteurs, ah chakara?
>
> [Nkoululu I want to speak,
>
> Mokolo I want to criticize
>
> Marché Central I will talk, heh! heh!
>
> Sauveteurs, I will spill the beans.]

Because he has arrogated to himself the role of mouthpiece of the underprivileged, Lapiro drums up their support in this protest song against President Biya's despotic regime. These lyrics bear testimony to the disenchantment of the songwriter. He chides the president and his henchmen for corruption, indifference to the plight of the people, and dereliction of duty. "Mimba we" is the cry of a disillusioned Cameroonian whose heart throbs for his fatherland. "Mimba we" seems to be an indictment of the dysfunctional government of Paul Biya, especially the economic crisis that has hit the nation hard:

> For dis heure for austérité so,
>
> For dis heure wey cinq no mus change position
>
> Yes, austérité da be sei dollar no mus change foot
>
> Wusai we own espoir deh no?
>
> [At this time of austerity

At this time when every dime must stay where it is,
Yes, austerity means that each dollar must be spent wisely
Where is our hope today?]

The rhetorical questions that punctuate Lapiro's lyrics are symptomatic of the singer's mental discomfort in a country that has gone topsy-turvy. He lives in a country where democracy has metamorphosed into demo-dictatorship; rigor and moralization have been transformed into reckless abandon and immorality. In 'mimba we' Lapiro underscores the fundamental ailments that have eaten into the moral fabric of Cameroonian politicians and caused the deplorable status quo that is observable in Cameroon under President Paul Biya. He notes that there is a gamut of cankers burrowing deep into the social fabric of Cameroon under the incumbent, not the least of which are corruption, dereliction of duty, double-speak and a penchant for vengeance on the part of politicians. It should be noted that Lapiro has paid the price for insubordination, including imprisonment as a result of his intention to be a political gadfly in Cameroon. Angered by imprisonment, Lapiro composed a song titled "Constitution Constipée" (2008) (Constipated Constitution), in which he describes the country's president as a senile man caught in a web of machinations that compel him to stay in power even though he is visibly exhausted. In this song, Lapiro calls for help, probably from the international community, to stop President Biya from committing constitutional rape. He states in no uncertain terms that the Head of State is burned out and ought to resign without further ado as seen in the excerpt below:

Au secours!
L'heure est grave
Les bandits en cols blancs

Veulent braquer la constitution de mon pays

Les fossoyeurs de la république

Veulent mettre les lions en cage (…)

Le coq est harcelé et menacé d'une tentative de holdup (…)

Big Katika don taya'oh!

Répé don slack'oh!

Wuna lep yi yi rest

Répé don fatigué

Yi wan go rest (…)

[Help!

Come deliver us

There is danger out there

White-collar thieves are

Bent on mutilating the Constitution of my country

The Nation's grave diggers want to

Put the Lions in the cage (…)

The rooster is harassed and shaken by threats of hold-up

The Big Boss is tired-oh!

The Father of the Nation is exhausted

Give him the opportunity to rest

Pa is tired

He needs help (…) [xi]

This song is a mix of French and Cameroonian pidgin English. It became the unofficial anthem of protesters during the 2008 youth uprising in Cameroon, and Lapiro was arrested and charged with inciting unrest. Despite this humiliation by the government of his homeland, Lapiro de Mbanga regained international renown and became even more vocal against the misdeeds of the Biya regime. During the presidential poll in 2011 he called on all conscientious Cameroonians to cast blank votes to show their disapproval of the

President's intention to run for another term. In November 2009, Lapiro was selected as the winner of the global "Freedom to Create Imprisoned Artists Prize". The jury remarked that his songs constituted a cultural megaphone by which the disenfranchised and politically endangered can vicariously exercise free speech. In 2001, Lapiro wrote a song titled "Na You" in which he sounded brazenly confrontational. "Na You" is a pidgin expression that could be translated as 'You are to Blame.' Circumstances surrounding the composition of this song are a classic example of the transformation of a social rebel into an astute and indefatigable political activist. In "Na You", Lapiro bemoans the rape of democracy in Cameroon. As he puts it, people should make a distinction between multiparty politics and democracy. He believes that what exists in Cameroon is multiparty politics, not democracy. He argues that within these opposition political parties, the attitude is the same because those with new ideas and contrary views are regarded as opposition within the house and if they insist on change they are dismissed (Sone 2009:25).In "Na You" Lapiro speaks truth to power defiantly:

> You go for Bamenda
> Abakwa boys dem di sofa.
> From north to south
> Ma complice dem di hala-oh!
> From east to west-oh!
> Free boys dem di gaz-oh!
> Na you do'am –oh!
> Na you do'am –oh!
> Na you do'am –oh! Heh! Heh!
> Na you sipoil dis kondre
> [If you go to Bamenda
> You'll find Abakwa boys suffering

From north to south
My friends are protesting!
From east to west-oh!
Free boys are farting-oh!
You are to blame-oh!
You are to blame-oh!
You are to blame-oh! Heh!Heh!

The accusing finger that Lapiro points in the face of President Biya is as provocative as his words are defiant. In no uncertain terms, he holds the president accountable for all the mess in Cameroon: "Na you do'am–oh!"/ "Na you sipoil dis kondre!" This statement could be translated as "You're to blame!" / "You have ruined this country." The rebellious songwriter does not stop at accusation alone; he enjoins the president to clean up his mess without further ado:

You mus fix'am–oh!
You mus fix'am–oh!
You go fix'am–oh!
Na you demage dis kondre
You mus fix'am–oh!
You go fix'am–oh!
[You must fix it–oh!
You must clean it up –oh!
You have to clean up the mess–oh!
You have ruined this country
You must fix it–oh!]

Lapiro insists on getting to the bottom of the matter and promises to tell the truth and nothing but the truth. It is important to note that Lapiro's lyrics amount to political commentary. His songs are tainted with socio-political reality as seen in the following excerpt:

> La vérité étant… ce qu'on ne retrouve jamais
> Aux tables des menteurs
> Je jure de chanter la vérité et rien que la vérité
> Mombo ah go brass before dem meng me
> But ah go bras daso
> Baisse de salaire na you!
> Arriérrés na you!
> Compression du personnel na you!
> Licenciement na you!
> Privatisation na you!
> Liquidation na soso you…
> Moi ah comprends sei
> Do how, do how Johnny four foot
> Go las come dammer nylon ana carton for dis kondre… [xv]
> [Truth is never… found at the table of liars
> I promise to say the truth and nothing but the truth
>   My friend, I will speak at the risk of being killed
> I will speak regardless of what happens to me
> Salary cuts is your handiwork
> Deferred payments of arrears are your call
> Employee lay-offs are attributable to you
> Privatization of State enterprises are your call
> Running companies aground is still due to you
> It is clear that in the not too distant future
> The goat will have no choice but to eat
> Nylon and cardboard boxes in this country.]

Lapiro's tone is both aggressive and provocative. In a damning diatribe, he banishes truth from the discourse of politicians: "La vérité étant… ce qu'on ne retrouve jamais aux tables des menteurs." He does not only portray politicians as liars, but he also puts on them the blame for chronic unemployment, pay-cuts, employee lay-offs, and the privatization of state enterprises. He contends that if this decline continues, there will come a time when Cameroonians will go through hard times: "Do how, do how Johnny four foot go las come dammer nylon ana carton for dis kondre." Lapiro underscores the dire consequences of this dystopia as follows:

> Consequence, boys dem dong ton na attaquant
> Nga na ninja
> Small tchotchoro for quartier dem dong begin
> Agresser man pikin for carrefour…
> Licencié na taximan
> Ala wan na bendskinneur
> BTS na secrétaire for long sitik
> Someone na bayam sellam
> GCE O/L na cuti mbanga wet cuti rubber
> Ala wan di wok na for farm banana
> Breveté na chargeur
> Ala wan na forceur
> GCE A/L na broke stone
> Someone di dig na sand-sand
> Na we dis today kondre dong fall stock…"
> [Consequently, boys have become attackers
> Girls have become ninjas
> Little girls are now sexually harassing
> Men at street corners
> BA degree holders are taximen
> Others are bendskin commuters
> BTS holders work as secretaries in offices

Others are bayam sellam
GCE O/L holders are harvesting
Palm nuts and rubber for a living
Others are involved in manual labour
On banana plantations
Brevete holders are park boys
Others are loaders
GCE A/L holders break stones
As a means of livelihood
Here we are living in a country
That has become bankrupt ...]

In a nutshell, Lapiro's oral tales are songs of resistance written with gusto and performed with zest. His songs harbour allusions, innuendos, and metaphors. They provide listeners with a new pair of lenses through which to perceive and appreciate the intent of oral narratives emanating from Cameroon. He is a gifted songwriter endowed with a gargantuan sense of self-confidence. His songs constitute a lamentation for a native land in decrepitude.

Lapiro is not a lone voice in the vendetta against the cancerous society that Cameroonians have inherited from President Biya. Valsero has followed in his footsteps with a song titled '*Ce pays tue les jeunes*'[15] in which he bemoans the fate of Cameroon's lost generation — the young college and high school graduates whose future hangs in the balance on account of governmental ineptitude:

Pour 2008 je me parle
Pour 2008 je te parle
J'espère que tu vas bien

---

[15] This country kills its younger generation

Et qu'il t'arrivera des choses bien (...)
Tous ces *diplômes chôment,*
Cette génération ne verra pas le fameux bout du tunnel
De toutes les façons je n'y crois pas,
La jeunesse crève à petit feu,
Tandis que les vieux derrière les forteresses
Se saoulent à l'eau de feu
Ce pays tue les jeunes.
Cinquante ans de pouvoir
Après ça ils ne lâchent pas prise
De bled dénature (...)
La vie est trop dure
Le système la rend encore
Plus dure, plus dure,
Ils le vivent.
A Yaoundé ils le savent
Ce pays tue les jeunes.
Ce pays est comme une bombe
Pour les jeunes à tombeau.
Faites attention quand
ça va péter ça va tuer
Tous les lambeaux
Alors les vieux, faites de la place.
Il faut pas le flambeau.
Ce pays tue les jeunes.
Les vieux ne lâchent pas la prise
De bled dénature (...)
[For the sake of 2008
I speak to myself
For 2008 I speak to you
I hope all is well with you

And I hope that good tidings
Will come your way (…)
All these graduates who are jobless
This generation that will never see
The proverbial light at the end of the tunnel
In any event, I don't believe they ever will
The youths are dying slowly
Whereas old folk are getting
Drunk in their bunkers
This county kills its youths
Fifty years in power
And yet they will not
Relinquish power peacefully
Life is too tough
The system makes it even tougher.
They experience it
In Yaoundé, they know it.
This county kills its youths
This country is like a time-bomb
For the dying youths
Watch out! When it shall explode,
It shall destroy everyone
So, I am asking the older generation
To make way for the youths
Let's avoid flames
This county kills its youth.
The old folks will not relinquish
Power peacefully (…)]

Valsero's lyrics are fiery as evidenced in the foregoing verses. The songwriter is unapologetic in his opprobrium on a regime that destroys the future generation. In fact, his diatribe against a carnivorous government seems to be the leitmotif in this song of protest. Notice the songwriter's deliberate repetition of the verse "*Ce pays tue les jeunes.*" This parallelism is intended to underscore the uncertain fate of young Cameroonians. As insinuated in the song, President Biya is compared to a mother cow that feeds on its own offspring. Valsero's reference to the year 2008 is significant given that this year constitutes an indelibly dark spot in Paul Biya's regime in Cameroon. In February 2008 Biya ordered his blood-thirsty security forces to open fire on unarmed protesters, mostly youths, who had embarked on a protest match to vent their frustration against food and gas price hikes. The 2008 protests were a series of demonstrations in Cameroonian cities, namely Yaounde, Douala, Buea and Bamenda. In reaction, the government sent out troops armed to the teeth to crack down on protesters and hundreds of Cameroonian young men and women were killed. It is interesting to note that Valsero perceives the macabre silence that hangs over the heads of Cameroonians as a time-bomb that will soon explode. He calls on the gang of kleptomaniacs hibernating in Yaoundé to decamp before it is too late to do so peacefully: "Alors les vieux, faites de la place/Il faut pas le flambeau."

Though singing in standard French, the singer infuses his lyrics with Camfranglais [16] in order to be understood by younger Cameroonians for whom his message of protest is intended. Words like 'bled', 'crève' and 'se saoulent' [country, die and get drunk)] are colloquial French words chosen with circumspection by the songwriter to translate not only meanings but also sentiments.

In a song titled '*Lettre au président*' Valsero, addresses his message directly to President Biya:

---

[16] Hybrid language created by Cameroonian younger generation

Puis-je savoir, Prési,
Pourquoi pour nous ça ne marche pas
J'ai fait de longues années d'études
Et j'ai pas trouvé d'emploi
Je te rappelle que t'avais promis
Qu'on sortirait du tunnel
On y est toujours, ce sont les mêmes
Qui tiennent la chandelle (…)
Prési, tes potes vivent au bled
Comme s'ils sont de passage
Ils amassent des fortunes,
Spécialistes des braquages
Ils font preuve d'arrogance,
Ils frustrent le peuple
Ils piétinent les règles
Et ils font ce qu'ils veulent
Ah Prési, arrête ça c'est ça ton travail
Ou inch'Allah, je jure, un autre fera le travail
Le peuple n'en peut plus, les jeunes en ont marre
On veut aussi goûter du miel sinon on te gare (…)
Prési, les jeunes ne rêvent plus
Prési, Prési, les jeunes n'en peuvent plus
La majorité crève
Dans le vice ils basculent
Et quand le monde avance, nous, au
Bled, on recule (…)
Le peuple est souverain il n'a jamais tort,
Il a la force du nombre,
Il peut te donner tort
On n'a pas peur de la mort,

Même si tes potes appellent des
Flics en renfort
Ils disent de toi que c'est toi "l'homme lion"
Mais ils n'ont qu'un rêve: ils veulent tuer le lion.
[May I know, Presi, why nothing works for us
I have spent several years in school
But still can't find work
You must remember that you promised
Bringing us to the end of the tunnel
Here we are today still marking time,
While the same people call the shots (…)
Presi, your ministers live in this country
As if they were strangers on vacation
They amass wealth
They are schooled in the art of holdup
They are arrogant, and they frustrate the people
They flout laws, they act with impunity
Oh Presi, put an end to all this, that's your job
Otherwise, Insha'Allah, I swear
Someone else will do the job in your place
The people cannot take it anymore
The younger folks are fed up
We want to have a taste of the honey too
Otherwise we will give you the boot (…)
Presi, the youths no longer have dreams
Presi, Presi, young people cannot take it anymore
Majority of them are dying
They live in vice.
We retrogress in this country
While the rest of the world progresses
The people are sovereign, they are never wrong

They have numerical strength
They can give you a vote of no-confidence
We are not afraid of death,
Even if your henchmen summon
Cops for protection
The people say you are the 'Lion Man']
But their lone dream is to kill the 'Lion.']

Valsero's interrogative missive to President Biya is incisive. Not only does he take the president to task for promises unfulfilled, he also enjoins him to perform the job for which he was elected. The song is an acrimonious diatribe that conveys the anger of the Cameroonian people frustrated with a regime that has failed them in many aspects, not the least of which is accountability. The sagacious rapper demands answers from Biya to numerous vexing questions, notably the reason for governmental dysfunction in Cameroon. Valsero's song writing reflects the sorrows, hopes and desperation of the people whose lived experiences constitute the subject matter of his song writing. As Hesch (2007:1) points out, "song writing may be the one true expression of a people's sorrow, despair and hope." He notes that the Wobblies wrote and performed songs as instruments of mobilization in the early twentieth century. Music and the American civil rights movements of the sixties became almost synonymous, as many African American musicians, from James Brown to Stevie Wonder, celebrated black consciousness and called for social change. In the same vein, McQuillar and Johnson (2010) observe that Tupac Shakur's rap songs translate the traumas experienced by Tupac himself and disillusioned African Americans. In the same vein, '*Lettre au président*' is the cry of a disenchanted Cameroonian rapper at odds with a regime that excels in arrogance, insolence, double-speak, and dereliction of duty. From a linguistic point of view, this song is more colloquial than *'Ce pays tue les jeunes.'* The reason is that Valsero is speaking on the behalf the Cameroonian younger people and has chosen to employ a lingo that is characteristic of the social class for whom he is a mouthpiece. The musician constantly culls words and expressions from figurative French as seen in the following examples: 'tiennent la chandelle' (perform a duty), 'en ont marre' (fed up), 'bled' (home, country, and village), 'potes' (friends, henchmen, comrades), and 'crèvent' (die). These words fit into the register of 'youth talk' in Cameroon. It is interesting to note that Valsero transposes foreign language words into French. The Arabic word 'Insha'Allah' is one such loan word. It should be noted that Cameroon is a multilingual country where over two hundred indigenous languages are spoken including Arabic. Musicians constantly cull words and expressions from these native tongues in a bid to fictionalize the linguistic tapestry of Cameroon. Most importantly, Valsero has had recourse to an expression to which all Cameroonians are familiar: 'L'homme lion 'or 'Lion man,' a sobriquet for President Biya. This pseudonym describes the brutality with which the president responds to legitimate complaints from citizens about governmental ineptitude.

Toward a Pedagogical Canon for Music Instructors

Interpreting music can be a daunting task, the more so because each musical composition harbours textual and non-textual elements. Arguing along similar lines, Scheub (1971) maintains:

> The problem for the translator of oral materials into a written form are enormous, some of them insurmountable except by extensive multi-media production, and even then, the impact of the original performance is diminished. The problem of developing literary

correspondences for oral non-artistic techniques is staggering, for the translation of single narrative-performance involves profound transformations which defy equivalence (28-36)

The question that arises at this juncture is the following: what are the ramifications of the foregoing discourse analysis for music instructors who are interested in teaching Cameroonian in particular, and African music in general? How could instructors utilize this information profitably in developing curricula that would enable the teaching of college level African music courses?

Given the enormity of the problem that faces the translator of African music into the written word, instructors charged with the critical task of teaching music originating from the African continent need to conceive dependable multidimensional paradigms that would guarantee not only the holistic interpretation of musical compositions but also the attainment of final learning objectives (FLOs). In the following paragraphs we have shed ample light on three tried and tested pedagogical canons that may come in handy for music instructors:

Bloom's Taxonomy

In his taxonomy, Bloom (1956) postulates that effective textual analysis could be achieved as follows:

Evaluation: making value judgments about issues, resolving controversies, assessing theories, composing ideas, and evaluating outcomes.

Synthesis: creating a unique original product that may be a combination of ideas to form a new whole, using old concepts to create new ones.

Application: using knowledge, facts, and principles to facilitate problem-solving.

Comprehension: interpreting and translating information from one medium to another, and

Knowledge: recall of information, discovery, and observation.

The framework enunciated above is germane for interpreting songs originating from Africa given the multifaceted nature of the musical compositions, the multiplicity of messages they convey, and the plethora of rhetorical devices used by songwriters. Bloom's model is particularly useful in unravelling the significations embedded in the linguistic and extralinguistic components of the songs written by Lapiro and Valsero. With the kernel of the lyrics laid bare, music instructors would be in a position to design lower-order and upper-order thinking tasks that would enable learners to achieve outcomes of learning.

Hermeneutic Model

The theory of Hermeneutics propounded by Schleiermacher (1834) underscores the importance of interpreting, not only the implied meanings embedded in a culture-rich text but also unravelling the situational dimensions that constitute the matrix in which the text is rooted. The most vital feature of the theory of hermeneutics is the concept of Hermeneutic Circle. The Hermeneutic Circle refers to the situation in which when learners encounter an oral text, they tend to make sense of it with reference to other texts. Thus, their understanding of the other text is modified by their understanding of the text they are analysing. This intertextuality is an integral part of music composed by African musicians given the correlation that exists between orality and literacy as adumbrated earlier on in This chapter. The hermeneutic circle enables learners to come to grips with the circularity inherent in the cultural, historical, linguistic, and non-linguistic components of a culture-based text. Noteworthy also is the fact that the Hermeneutic Model is particularly suited for interpreting music from Africa on account of the palimpsestical nature of musical compositions originating from the continent. Chatal Zabus (1991) defines the African palimpsest as "the writer's attempt at textualizing linguistic differentiation and conveying African concepts, thought patterns and linguistic concepts through the ex-colonizer's language." (23)

Most musical compositions emanating from contemporary Africa are calqued on oral traditions of the past. In other words, modern songwriters tend to borrow not only the themes but also the esthetics of oral performers. Scheub (2002) sheds ample light on four characteristics of oral performance that the contemporary songwriter must understand and grapple with during the course of the compositional process. These include the verbal and non-verbal elements of the performance, their structural characteristics, and the broad matrix from which individual images emerge. By "structure" Scheub is referring to the organization, arrangement, and relationship of the various parts of the oral production, as well as the nonverbal components of the narrative such as tone of voice, rhythm, facial expressions, gestures, bodily movements, particularly images created by sound, body, and the imagination. The structural manipulation of these images creates plot and reveals themes. African songwriters who borrow from oral traditions are conversant with the motifs and symbols developed on the surface of the performance. Above all, they are sensitive to the poetic use of culture-based tropes. The Hermeneutic Model is particularly suitable for teaching the protest music of Lapiro and Valsero given that it enables the instructor to interpret their musical compositions from the perspective of the Essential Elements of Information (EEIs) embedded in the lyrics—who, what, where, why, when, and how factors.

Styles-and Strategies-Based Instructional Model (SSBI)

The Styles-and Strategies-Based Instructional Model is a learner-centred approach to teaching that explicitly combines styles and strategies-based instructional activities with everyday classroom activities (Oxford, 1990; Cohen and Dornyei, 2002; Cohen and Weaver, 2006). The principle that undergirds the SSBI Model is that learners should be given the opportunity to understand not only what they are learning in the classroom but also how they are assimilating the material the way they do. Though conceived to serve the purpose of second language acquisition, the SSBI model has now become a boon for music instructors on account of the unquestionable correlation between musical and linguistic competencies. The Styles-and Strategies-Based Instructional Model is anchored on the theory of scaffolding—the idea that at the beginning of the learning process, learners need a great deal of support; gradually, this support is taken away in bid to allow students to develop a sense of self-directedness in the learning process. Cohen and Weaver describe this sense of autonomy as the gradual release of responsibility. Other facets of the SSBI model include the following: modelling, collaborative learning, activation of prior knowledge, student choices and self-initiated learning. The Styles- and Strategies-Based Instructional Model is a learner-focused approach that calls into question conventional practices and the beliefs in the lecture as an effective paradigm for engaging learners in self-empowering critical thinking and problem-based learning. It shifts the focus of pedagogy from a passive teacher-centred approach to that of a learner-centred collaborative transaction. The aspect that makes this model appropriate for teaching the music of Lapiro and Valsero is the fact that it underscores self-directed learning and learner autonomy in the performance of learning tasks.

In a nutshell, teaching the protest music of Lapiro and Valsero creatively would be a win-win undertaking for both instructors and students. Instructional motivation calls for tried and tested paradigms such as the ones discussed in This chapter. Teachers who resort to multidimensional instructional models inevitably derive immense benefit and satisfaction from the design and implementation of learning tasks that result in the accomplishment of intended learning outcomes. Instructors charged with the critical task of teaching African protest music at any level of the academic ladder should reckon with the fact that no one size fits all.

Conclusion

In sum, Lapiro and Valsero could be portrayed as talented musical virtuosos who play several roles in their song writing: entertainers, social critics, bards, humourists, counsellors, and chroniclers—all functions they fulfil with remarkable success. Given that their messages are directed at specific audiences— the powers-that-be and the wretched of the earth, to borrow words from another revolutionary writer, Franz Fanon (1963). The rationale for the musical compositions of Lapiro and Valsero is also to raise awareness in the hope of galvanizing the population into a revolution. Mandela (1994) aptly captures the quintessence of protest music when he observes that African music is often about the aspirations of the African people, and that it can ignite the political resolve of those who might otherwise be indifferent to politics. Lapiro and Valsero steer clear of linguistic sophistry. As a matter of fact, most of the time, they sing in Cameroonian lingua francas—Pidgin English and

Camfranglais. They have no compunction about resorting to profanity when they deem it an appropriate tool to properly communicate their messages and pent-up emotions. Proficiency in Pidgin English and Camfranglais would be necessary if members of the audience were to successfully decode the semantics contained in their lyrics. Words like "katika", "sauveteurs", "nyoxer", "tara", and "ngata" could be semantically challenging to those of their fans who are neither pidginophones[17] nor camfranglophones[18]. Their music is weighty and communicatively incisive. They are unfazed in their determination to tell the truth to the Cameroonian government and the governed.

---

[17] Speakers of Pidgin English

[18] Speakers of Camfranglais

Chapter 4

Lapiro, the Political artist: Chronicler of Cameroonians' Precarity

Primus M. Tazanu

Introduction

In this chapter, I have used the concept of precarity to capture the lives and livelihoods of marginalized Cameroonians as portrayed in Lapiro's music. How this artist observed and most of all, depicted suffering and uncertainties of life in Cameroon was, *par excellence*, an unapologetic fight for human rights. For three decades, Lapiro brought to limelight the degrading socioeconomic and political circumstances in his country, strongly believing that he could draw the attention of the greedy leaders to these worsening conditions. Despite the hardship they experience daily, Lapiro saw Cameroonians as resilient people, as overcomers, as those who do not easily give up in the face of misery imposed on them. Lapiro eulogizes the economic feat of these strugglers and at the same time, accuses the power structure of negligence and dishonesty. For the fact that through his music he advocated for the downtrodden all his life, we can describe Lapiro as a religious man. He examined the deteriorating conditions of life in his country and found himself playing the role of Jeremiah, the weeping prophet.

Without a second thought, my mind switched to Lapiro and his music when I was asked to write a chapter on music and society in Cameroon to celebrate Manu Dibango's achievements. I am interested in how Lapiro exposes precarious life in Cameroon in this period of neoliberalism where livelihood possibilities for the masses get harder. This hard life starkly contrasts the lifestyle of the isolated elite who *eat* government money and accrue untold wealth to themselves. Using the concept of precarity as a lived experience, this chapter shows the various ways Lapiro exposes the struggling life of the downtrodden, those who are forced, to borrow from a Fanonian critique of postcolonial state, to 'fix' (Gordon 2010:206) themselves to the oppressive conditions imposed on them by the power structure. Because he critically disclosed the socioeconomic and political implications of oppression, one cannot but describe Lapiro as an ace chronicler of life in Cameroon; he told the story the way he saw it unfold.

Both Manu Dibango and Lapiro were frustrated at the pace of change in Cameroon, though from different perspectives. Among other things, Dibango was disappointed at the politics of artistic production, promotion and the state keeping 'his artistic creativity under close surveillance', which is why he lived most of his life abroad (Nyamnjoh and Fokwang 2005:255). That he was recognized abroad much more than in his native country, irked Dibango; he worked tremendously 'in promoting artistic creativity among local musicians almost everywhere except his native Cameroon' (Nyamnjoh and Fokwang 2005:261). Lapiro sang about the plight, the suffering and struggles of the marginalized folks. Both artists were critical of the uncaring politicians who are out of touch with those they supposedly represent. For one main reason – Lapiro living and performing in Cameroon while Dibango lived most of his life abroad – the former artist was more popular in Cameroon.[19] Their

---

[19] An artist's popularity is not of course necessarily connected to his or her physical location. For sure, Dibango would be more popular in Cameroon if he

contributions to enriching *makossa* as a music genre are immense, with Dibango's version becoming jazz-like. Lapiro's music is known for its thrilling beats and sensual appeal. Accompanying these beats are his two main messages: that the masses are suffering and a categorical indictment of the inept power structure.

Music and musicians play influential roles in politics the world over. Interestingly, I started writing the first draft of this chapter at the time the Rolling Stones threatened to sue Donald Trump's campaign for using their song at campaign rallies. How music is implicated in power, power struggles and representations is deep. John Street has written about the politics of music and the music of politics, describing the various ways the political has appropriated music for specific ends. His entry point is that songs and music stimulate moods and feelings, eliciting emotional responses from the listeners (Street 2003:114). His article covers many contexts where music has been used to rouse moods and to influence perceptions. For example, he writes about the Nazis using music to whip up national sentiments in Germany in the 1930s and 40s. Also, in apartheid South Africa, the authorities tried to promote a homeland's sentiment for those lumped in the settlements, by playing Bantu music on the radio stations. Still in South Africa during apartheid, the 'urban music was censored…to create a particular sense of nationhood' (Street 2003:115). Similarly, Mobutu Sese Seko of the Democratic Republic of the Congo (former Zaire) was famous for promoting his political career through music.

These cases demonstrate that one cannot understand the meaning of music solely from the prism of entertainment and animation. It is

---

lived with the people and performed regularly as Lapiro did. The government's strategy of stifling the work of critical artists worked against Dibango who could hardly get the support of the masses because he was physically absent.

a cultural product with multifaceted functions. For example, music reinforces messages, attracts attention, hints about people's class belonging, etc. How influential music is can be seen in historical archives including the Bible. There are numerous instances in the Bible where worshippers sing and are urged to chant praises to their creator. For example, in Psalm 101: 1, the psalmist writes about singing God's mercy and justice. In other instances, it is singing praises to the Lord because He is good and pleasant (Psalm 135:3). The bible recognizes that singing and playing musical instruments require special skills (Psalm 33:39) and this perhaps explains why the production of songs was left in the hands of selected people. These artists produced songs used during deliverance, songs accompanied by prayers, songs that magnify the Lord or those used for thanksgiving. These all suggest a recognition that songs and music appeal to the hearers and that people harness music to animate courses. Additionally, we understand that music has a transformative potential; it is appropriated for propaganda, rebellion, resistance, and opposition. Street (2003:122) has mentioned that music gave hopes, dreams, and aspirations to the civil rights movement in America in the 1960s. In this way, music itself may be inherently political, for it stirs consciousness and mobilizes people to challenge the power structure. In *Music and Silence*, Glanville (2010: 3) writes about the visceral punches of music, which indeed indicates why musicians may be perceived as dangerous by the power structure:

Music is so powerful because it is a physical expression of the human soul,' says Daniel Barenboim in an exclusive interview for *Index*. 'It attacks, I would say, all the functions of the human being – the brain, the heart, the stomach, the temperament. That's what makes it so dangerous. Music is *much* more powerful than words.

Why the artist is looked upon with suspicion is specifically because s/he is bold enough to voice in public what people know but are afraid to talk in the open. It was James Baldwin who once said an artist is that person who makes us see reality again[20]. By this he meant the artist is one of the few bold people in the society who speak truth to power. In this chapter, I will portray Lapiro as an artist who speaks truth to the power structure from his position as 'President of struggling people' (Nyamnjoh and Fokwang 2005:271. See also Tangem 2016:169). Bobi Wine, the Ugandan musician-turned politician is credited similarly for being the 'president by people living in slums of Kamwokya' (Muzee and Enaifoghe 2020:196). These artists are identified this way primarily because their music is connected to free speech, ideas of identity and belonging. They sometimes act as journalists, for they report news and unfolding events. This role is vital when they operate in spaces where the state exercises tight control over the media and political opposition (Mano, 2007). Irrespective of the space they operate in, musicians 'get people singing along and to tell the news from the streets' (Shepler 2010:629).

In Africa, political music typically revolves around resisting oppression, exposing poor governance, extolling the government or the opposition, campaigning for a course, staying neutral and about national unity (see Dave 2014; Shepler 2010; Brunner 2014; Englert 2008; Nyairo & Ogude 2005). By their public appearance, most musicians are political in the sense that they use music as a form of speech to speak to, as well as, contest, power. Musicians may not necessarily declare their work as overtly political, but this does not deter other actors from appropriating the songs for political courses as has been witnessed in Kenya, Tanzania, Sierra Leone, Guinea, Cameroon, just to name but a few.. All over Africa, musicians are using their skills to tell stories in ways that position them as threats,

---

[20] James Baldwin (May 21st 1963): The Moral Responsibility of the Artist: https://www.youtube.com/watch?v=PlnDbqLNv-M (accessed on 07.10..2020).

allies, or neutral actors in the political scene. This is so because, as part of the popular culture, music is readily available to key individuals who want to disseminate political messages. Bobi Wine of Uganda and the late Fela Kuti of Nigeria are prominent examples of those musicians who have overtly tapped on their popularity to embolden ongoing struggles for power in their countries. And so are many other cases.

Shepler (2010) reports that in post-war Sierra Leone, musicians sing about elections, political parties, politicians, corruption, and the future of the youth in the country. The young musicians recognize the authority of the incumbent leaders but at the same time, they expect responsible politicians to emerge and set them free. Through music, the young artists urge the politicians to honour election promises. Failure in doing so would lead to electoral defeat for those who continue to 'act like you're [politician] deaf'. Furthermore, these musicians position themselves as representatives of disgruntled Sierra Leoneans who are prepared to 'cut your [leaders'] big bellies with a knife' (Shepler 2010: 634). This threat cannot be taken lightly considering that the young men had been instrumental in the war, both in their own right and as puppets of 'powerful political forces outside their control' (Shepler 2010:630). A fragile atmosphere that followed the war provided a space for the young artists to use music to issue threats to those in power, reminding the leaders that their authority depended on the voters but more importantly, through music, they claimed entitlements to better lives and education. This would guarantee that they became responsible citizens.

Over in Tanzania, a country known for its socialist inclination, a particular kind of music genre has played an influential role in projecting new political actors in the country. These are the youth who 'challenge the conventional, hierarchical ways of Tanzanian politics which used to be dominated by the older generation' (Englert

2008:71). At the beginning of the 21st century, politics was dominated by old people in this country. Things began to change when the Bongo Flava music genre, through its critical lyrics, shaped the consciousness of young people; they realized that they could achieve youth agenda by participating in politics. The youth's possibilities of good life were compromised, if not frustrated, by the deteriorating socioeconomic conditions arising from structural adjustments. They realized their lives would be worse than that of generations before them. Unlike in some African countries, the young people in Tanzania did not resort to violence; they simply became more politically active. Bongo Flava has been instrumental in instilling assertiveness in the young people who want to be politically visible (Reuster-Jahn 2014). Owing to its popularity, Bongo Flava is played at campaign rallies and young radio presenters who popularized this music genre gained fame and were voted into the parliament where they fight for the voice of the younger generation to be heard (Englert 2008).

Music would mean different things to different people most often depending on where they position themselves in relation to the existing power structure. Here, we are talking about what meaning music has for the various audiences. In Kenya, Gidi Gidi Maji Maji's popular song, *Unbwogable*, occupied a centre-stage around the elections taking place in that country in 2002. The song was appropriated back and forth by the different political parties primarily as 'a symbol of resistance and determination' (Nyairo and Ogude 2005:227). Because of its message of liberation, *Unbwogable* was banned from playing on the national station and a presenter was fired for playing the song. This song was produced against a backdrop of economic hardship facing an average Kenyan youth. That *Unbwogable* was appropriated by the various political parties tells just how politicians are ready to tap into music to foster their course. In

Cameroon, Anne-Marie Nze's popular song, *Libterte*, has been used by various political parties even as it was sung to celebrate the decolonization of Cameroon. Following the reintroduction of multiparty politics in Cameroon in the early 1990s, both the government and opposition parties appropriated *Liberte* to pass messages of freedom in the new dispensation. The song's message tipped in favour of the opposition who wanted the country to be liberated from the Biya regime characterized by economic crisis and its inability to redistribute resources (Brunner 2013:42).

In all these cases, we realize that an uneasy relationship between music and politics plays out mainly in times of economic uncertainties. Put in other words, a deteriorating socioeconomic condition in a country often inspires artists to do political commentary through music. To understand this connection between music and politics in periods of insecurity, I turn to the concept of precarity as an ontological experience and as a labour condition.

Conceptualizing Precarity

In Africa, music permeates nearly all activities – funerals, sports, weddings, church services and politics, just to name a few scenarios. As such, we hear music emitting from houses, alleyways, street corners, markets, and bars, religious and educational precincts. It is actually in such spaces that hardship can be observed: market women haggling prices of food items, street vendors selling their wares, churches where people sing and wish for heavenly miracles (Tazanu 2016, 2018), bars where some drink themselves to ecstasy and temporarily forget their daily predicament (for the last theme, see Ndjio 2005; Nyamnjoh & Fokwang 2005). These are just a few cases of people responding to socioeconomic and political breakdown. Precarity captures these conditions at the level of livelihood and being. This concept has been used extensively in the West to describe post-industrial working conditions resulting mainly from neoliberalism (Masquelier 2019). Some aspects of its definition aptly capture the precarious conditions and experiences of those Lapiro portrays in his music as strugglers and sufferers. Precarity has always been the norm in the global South (Millar 2017:6; Fuh 2020). It is thus not solely a Cameroonian experience. Pierre Bourdieu (mentioned in Millar 2017) has used the concept to describe insecure employment. It was later associated with poverty. As a labour condition, precarity is uncertain work that is 'characterized by job insecurity, temp or part-time employment, a lack of social benefits, and low wages' (ibid, 3). Because those working under these conditions lack protection and stable income, they may harbour anger against the authority (Millar 2017:3). Tsing (2015: 2. Quoted in Millar 2017:4) goes further to describe precarity as 'life without the promise of stability' (see also Fuh 2020).

As in most countries in the Global South, most Cameroonians are small independent entrepreneurs. They work in what is commonly classified as the informal sector. Even though they constitute a majority of the labour force, their marginalization means they are structurally positioned to receive or access few resources compared to the elite. What does precarity do to these people? How do they experience life as marginalized citizens? These are important questions, considering that the neoliberal economic creed forces countries such as Cameroon to liberalize their markets and to cut down on government intervention in the economy. As we will see later, Lapiro's music cuts into these themes of capitalist development, dissecting this in ways that only academics, and to an extent, politicians, have been able to do. But there is a difference which keeps Lapiro at an upper edge when compared with the academician and the politician: he has a larger audience, his songs carry thought-provoking messages, and the beats of his music stir good feelings and entertain an oppressed people. Before analysing his music, let us look at who Lapiro was.

Lapiro: A Short Biography and Direct Political Involvement

From the mid-1980s right up to his death in 2014, Lapiro was among the pantheon of the greatest musicians Cameroon has produced. Lambo (La) Pierre (pi) Roger (ro) was born in 1957 in the small town of Mbanga to a Duala mother and Bamileke father.[21] That he advocated for the struggling and marginalized urban hustlers is both intriguing and interesting. Lapiro's biography offers a fascinating revelation on why he originally sang for *mbokos* – 'conmen, swindlers, thieves plying their trade in public areas' (de Mbanga and Brown 2010:127). Sone's (2009: 20) description of Lapiro's childhood vividly highlights why he dedicated his songs to *mbokos* and other downtrodden folks:

> In spite of his rich and comfortable background, Lapiro alias Ndingaman drifted into delinquency in his early life. He made friends with streets urchins and together they engaged in pick pocketing and other petty crimes. Like most juvenile delinquents in urban setting, his misdemeanours landed him in prison. The time he spent behind bars gave him the singular opportunity to experience at first hand the deplorable and precarious living conditions of the wretched of the earth.

Lapiro came to prominence in the 1980s, reaching the pinnacle of

---

[21] The Duala people are found primarily in the Littoral Region of Cameroon. The Bamilekes inhabit most of the Western Region. In anthropological studies, the Bamilekes are classified as people from the Eastern Grassfields.

his career around 1991. This was a period of political turmoil, revolt, violence, and uncertainty. On the economic front, Cameroon started experiencing a downturn after a boom in the preceding decade. The global economic and political shifts arising in part from the end of the Cold War further aggravated the situation. On the political front, due to sustained pressure from within the country, the one-party state was dismantled, and this was followed by violent protests in major cities. In this atmosphere of power and counter power, opportunism of all sorts emerged. Because of anger, frustration and greed, people resorted to destroying private and state property, revolted, smuggled goods, and engaged in all sorts of activities considered as illegal by the authorities. One particular form of revolt that defined the political chaos at the time was the Ghost Town – a phenomenon characterized by violent clashes with the police.

Lapiro decided to actively engage in politics and was one of the recognizable faces in the Ghost Town protests in 1991. Ghost Towns were a strategy adopted by the political opposition to force the government to institute reforms. Concentrated mainly in the West, North West, Littoral and South West Provinces and lasting for six months, the scheme involved reducing transportation – to make the cities look ghostly, closing shops and offices, 'street demonstrations, market and other economic boycotts' (Takougang and Krieger 1998: 127). These tactics aimed at, and in fact succeeded, to 'drastically reduce the 1991 state revenue base' as well as 'stretched security forces' (Takougang and Krieger (1998: 131).[22] Distancing himself from the Ghost Town after a rift between him and other organizers, Lapiro argued that the protests harmed the livelihood of the

---

[22] See also Robert M. Press (Oct 1991): Cameroon 'Ghost Towns' Rouse Public Resentment (https://www.csmonitor.com/1991/1001/01051.html). (Accessed on 26/7/2020)

common man in the street.[23] His standpoint was instantly contested by those who accused him of turning against his people. Because he used the state media to condemn the Ghost Town, people believed his message was sponsored by the government. Rumour further flew around that Lapiro received a bribe of 22 million FCFA from the government. It is an accusation he refuted all his life. At one point he ridiculed the bribery allegation, saying the amount was too small to buy him over (Nyamnjoh and Fokwang, 2005:272). Unsurprisingly, going against the popular rebellious zeitgeist sanctioned Lapiro to marginality; he went into oblivion in the next decade. As punishment for condemning the Ghost Town, his house was burnt down, and he was scorned by those Cameroonians who accused him of betrayal.

In the intervening years before he resurfaced in 2001 with *Na you* (It Is You [who is to blame]), in which he accuses the president of incompetency, the government in place had worked hard to entrench its authority in the country. The strong opposition that emerged in the 1990s had dissipated in part because of internal struggles and the ingenious strategy of the government to split those opposing the regime. Additionally, more power had moved to the executive branch of the government. The ruling party appeared stronger, more so due to the prebendal practices of those attached to the ruling party. Also, within this scenario, the opposition could not keep in constant touch with the grassroots due to limited resources. One notices in Lapiro's song that he was infuriated by what he saw as complete disconnect between the rulers and the ruled. He would go on to criticize the political structure, individual politicians, and the international financial institutions he believed connived with the Cameroon government to indebt Cameroonians. From 2001 up to his death, he had become uncompromising and daring, condemning the

---

[23] ibid

government for not fulfilling its contract with the people. Lapiro knew what he was getting into which is why he openly predicted that speaking truth to power would lead to his death.

Central to all his music-message is the struggling Cameroonian who is forced into precarious living in an increasingly tough country. In this sense, Lapiro was *produced* by the changing realities of his society; he was a product of the society in which he found himself. It is this society that provided him with the material he used to reflect on the socioeconomic and political conditions of Cameroonians. Lapiro sought not just to entertain with rhythm and beats; how he wrapped socioeconomic and political messages in his songs is ingenious which is why one could – drawing on Marshall McLuhan (1964) – reiterate that this artist knew his medium was, in fact, the message. In 2007, he contested the mayoral seat in Mbanga, under the ticket of the then main opposition party, the Social Democratic Front (SDF).[24] Additionally, Lapiro was a traditional chief in District 12 in Mbanga (de Mbanga and Brown 2010:126). He was imprisoned in 2008 primarily because of his song, *Constitution Constipée* [Constipated Constitution]. After leaving prison in 2011, Lapiro emigrated to USA the following year and died of cancer in Buffalo, New York in 2014. He was 56.

Lapiro: A Religious Chronicler of Precarious Life in Cameroon

The economic depression starting in the late 1980s and the political upheavals in the early 1990s radically influenced how Lapiro

---

[24]Joe Dinga Pefok (May 7th 2007) Lapiro De Mbanga Picks SDF Ticket For Mbanga Municipality,

https://www.postnewsline.com/2007/05/lapiro_de_mbang.html (accessed 27/07/2020) positioned himself as a chronicler of change in Cameroon. Ferdinand A. Mbecha chronologizes Lapiro's music career into three stages: he sings about the economic feat of the bullies/thieves (*mbokos*), the strugglers (*sauveteurs*) and then, politics[25]. To this must be added, emphatically, his songs about the implications of global neoliberal economic policies on Cameroonians. Lapiro operates in a milieu where he is one of the few people who are bold enough to publicly indict the power structure of ineptitude. To this end and bearing in mind his deep commitment to speak the truth at all cost, we can describe him as a religious man. Being a religious man simply means he is dedicated to the course for which he fights. Through his music, he consistently commented on the socioeconomic and political malaise in the republic.

In the lively and entertaining *No Make Erreur* (1986) and *Kop Nie* (1988), Lapiro identifies those he represents in his music. Just as in Mbecha cited above, Tangem aptly defines this calibre of people as 'the *buyam sellam*, ambulant petty traders whom he [Lapiro] refers to as *sauveteurs*, the motorbike riders, park boys and even prisoners whom he often refers to as his "complices" or partners' (Tangem 2016:169). Over the years, Cameroonians seized all available hustling opportunities that came their way, leading Lapiro to expand the list of those he advocates for, including the call box operators (airtime salespersons. See Tazanu 2012:124-129), rock crackers, sand diggers, but more crucially, labourers working in slave-like conditions in multinational agriculture farms (de Mbanga and Brown 2010:127). It was to these people that he owed his legitimacy. It was also on them that he depended for his security – physical, financial, and moral.

---

[25] Dr Ferdinand Awunglefac Mbecha's unpublished paper titled *Lapiro De Mbanga, Mboko Subculture and Political Consciousness in Cameroon* (personal communication).

When the economic crisis set in, he was one of the few artists to bring this to public attention via *Mimba We* (Remember Us [Think about Us]), his 1989 hit song that still speaks to the reality of life in contemporary Cameroon. Delivering his message in Pidgin, French and English, Lapiro deploys *crude* humour and vitality to tell about the economic transformation occurring in the country. It is a song in which he tells those in authority to think about *us*. He is, of course, part of *us*.

You wan dammer you mimba we,	At [the] table, remember us;
You wan souler you mimba we,	When you're having a drink,
You wan nyoxer you mimba we-oh.	Remember us when you're having sex-oh
Oh Mimba we-oh, tara!	
(Vakunta, 2014, p. 45)	Oh, remember us, you're our leader!

A more accurate translation of the message conveyed in this song's title is an appeal for the politicians to *think about us;* it is reminding the politicians about the neglected Cameroonians. Lapiro starts the song by asking the downtrodden if they do not deserve attention from the leaders. They affirm they want attention. With this mandate he launches an appeal that the leaders should think of the marginalized when they (leaders) are eating, drinking, and having sex. As noted by various scholars, be it about the politics of the belly (Bayart 1993) or (often male) sexual pleasures (Mbembe 2001:126-127; Nyamnjoh 2005a; Fuh, 2011), people in position of power in Cameroon often arrogate to themselves the privileges of bodily satisfaction using state funds. But as we see through Lapiro, the marginalized are aware of, or at least, they suspect the leaders rarely compromise when it comes to satisfying their voracious sensual appetites (Nyamnjoh 2006). At this stage, Lapiro's message is just a friendly reminder that the leaders should think of redistributing the national resources. As we will see later, he became more outspoken and direct when these leaders turned deaf ears to his friendly calls. In the late 1980s, Lapiro signalled the politicians that because of deprivation and the urge to stay alive, the marginalized are forced to engage in *nonconventional* economic activities. We find him appealing to the leadership not to penalize the downtrodden for struggling to feed their families even though the strugglers' economic activities may not necessarily conform to the rules stipulated by the government:

We no wan kick-oh	We don't want to steal
We no wan go for ngata	We don't want to go to jail
We de daso for ndengwe	We just need to work
A beg mimba we-oh, yes tara.	We beg you to think about us, boss
We no wan problème para	We are not looking for trouble
We no wan go for Ndengui	We don't want to go to Kondengui[27]
We di fain daso garri[26]	We are only looking for a means
For helep we own family-oh!	To help our family-oh!
(Vakunta, 2014, pp. 45-46)	

Not wanting to portray the oppressed as folks who are completely

---

[26] Garri is the cheapest food in the urban area. It is a powder made from cassava. In Cameroonian Pidgin, and in the context of Lapiro's music, garri also means an uncertain source of income as well as an insignificant/struggling person (e.g. garri boy).

[27] Kondengui is a notorious maximum-security prison in Yaounde. In Cameroonian imaginary this prison symbolizes torture, isolation, pain and vindictive punishment.For more on this prison see Albert Mukong,s *Prisoner Without a Crime: Disciplining Dissent in Ahidjo,s Cameroon (*Mankon, Bamenda: Langaa Research Publishing and Common Initiative Group, 2009)

beaten and hopeless, Lapiro, in *Mimba We*, leads us to a joyful atmosphere where he and his *complices* smoke and share cigarettes. He is saying they too love to enjoy life, just like the leaders who eat, drink, and have sex. Through this interjection, he lightens the weight of the more serious things he is raising in the song. For example, after the scene where they enjoy cigarettes, he turns to the audience in the crowded market space – people probably emboldened by the cigarette fire and puff – and asks the strugglers if he should break loose and spit fire (*sauveteur*, I chakara?). They urge him to go ahead (go before, go before, go before). Having received the *sauveteur's* approval (motion, motion, motion [of support]) he then hints them that it is not only in South Africa that people face precarious lives (No be daso for secteur for Pieter Botha[28] wey yi bad eh), which is his way of introducing the situation in his own country. He reveals that things are getting bad here at home (moyen no dey for ngola). This was at a time few people understood the impending catastrophe of economic downturns. At this point, the government and the international financial institutions were already talking about austerity measures. Lapiro knew the burden of the austerity would fall more on those who were already suffering, those with dampened hope (wusai we own espoir deh no?):

For dis heure for austérité so,	At this time of austerity
For dis heure wey cinq no mus change position	At this time when a dime must stay where it is
Yes, austérité da be sei dollar no mus change foot Wusai we own espoir deh no?	Yes, austerity means that each dollar must be spent wisely
(Vakunta, 2014:47)	Where is our hope today?

---

[28] He was singing at the time Pieter Botha was the president of South Africa, a country where many people were suffering the scourge of apartheid.

While acknowledging tough times in periods of austerity, Lapiro is particularly interested in how the strugglers would be impacted by the economic crisis. He spells out the vulnerability of the marginalized, describing them as people who do not need certificates to qualify for hustling, they do not anticipate retirement, they do not need diplomas and five years of working experience to hustle and, lastly, they do not write competitive exams into *strugglehood*. And to show how dire the situation is, he reminds leadership that those with high school certificates and degrees cannot find jobs; they would eventually join the bandwagon of the strugglers.[29] Throughout his musical career, Lapiro constantly reminded the world that he was uneducated but this is not evident in the ways he understands and dissects transformations in socioeconomic and political structures in Cameroon.

Over the years, he became more frustrated and started pointing fingers directly at those he believed should be held accountable for the suffering Cameroonians. It was through songs like *Na You* (It is You) and *Lefam So* (It is Enough) in the early 2000s that convinced most Cameroonians that Lapiro had not changed camps, for he foolhardily indicts the president, his close associates and corrupt Western institutions for bringing doom to the country. In *Na You* (2001), he does not veil who he is referring to; he categorically blames the president for dragging the country into a quagmire. Before arriving at this direct accusation, Lapiro outlines the hardship Cameroonians go through, using the metaphor of farting to convey

---

[29] The desperation in Cameroon that was/is partly resulting from the structural adjustment programme imposed by the International Monetary Fund saw many graduates going to the street to earn a living by all means necessary. Some became cab drivers, others became petty traders.

this suffering. We can understand it this way. We are all too familiar with that gas we expel from our rear opening when lifting a heavy load. The introduction of the song reveals that if you venture to every corner in Cameroon – from north, south, east, and west – you would realize that everyone is farting and suffering. It is this nation-wide anguish that makes him tell the president that 'na you spoil this contri' [you are responsible for destroying this country].

You go for Bamenda	If you go to Bamenda
Abakwa boys dem di sofa.	You'll find Abakwa boys suffering
From north to south	From north to south
Ma complice dem di hala-oh!	My friends are protesting!
From east to west-oh!	From east to west-oh!
Free boys dem di gaz-oh!	Free boys are farting-oh!
Na you do'am –oh!	You are to blame-oh!
Na you do'am –oh!	You are to blame-oh!
Na you do'am –oh! Heh! Heh!	You are to blame-oh! Heh! Heh!
(Vakunta, 2014:52)	

By 2001, Lapiro was no longer that entertainer who calmly appealed to politicians in *Mimba We*; by 2001, he was an outright critic of the government. He critiqued and criticized policies, institutions, and politicians. If one were to sample the popularity of those who speak out against the government, Lapiro would rank at a higher echelon when compared to other political actors such as writers and organized political opposition. More concretely, one must locate the difference between Lapiro's intrepid music and political opposition at the level of popular appeal and the audience he garners. A criticism coming from within the political circle easily runs out of steam with time but political music, even when censored, still has its way of permeating down to the grassroots where it entertains and stir people's consciousness. It reaches a wider audience both in the urban and rural areas, it is played and sung in the streets, verandahs, markets, homes, and nightclubs (Brunner 2017; Shepler 2010; Rathnaw 2010). In short, it is everywhere, it enlivens people's moods as they sing, shake their bodies, and are entertained. As they sing and dance to the beats of the music, they hear Lapiro forcefully telling the president to repair the damage he has done to the country:

You mus fix'am–oh!	You must fix it–oh!
You mus fix'am–oh!	You must fix it–oh!
You go fix'am–oh!	You have to fix it–oh!
Na you demage dis kondre	You have ruined this country
You mus fix'am–oh!	You have to fix it–oh!
You go fix'am–oh!	You have to fix it-oh!
(Vakunta, 2014: 53)	

Lapiro's patriotic lamentation is reinforced by the supporting singers, those representing the people, chorusing 'you mus fix'am oh'. This call-and-response is a trademark of his music whereby he interacts with his supporters, asking them what next to do before launching punch lines. He never mutes the voices of the masses. It is in part because of these supporting voices that Lapiro finds himself playing the role of Jeremiah, the weeping prophet in the bible. He weeps for the nation and knows where to place the blame. First, he sees mendacity within the presidential circles and promises to tell the truth, even at the cost of his own life. When asked if he was 'not frightened of the consequences of being so frank', Lapiro responded that it was 'all part of my struggle. If I was the scared type I would never have started singing in 1985. I am not going to start getting scared after all these years' (de Mbanga and Brown 2010:123). And there is plenty of evidence in his music testifying that he kept to these words. In *Na You*, before enumerating the misfortunes the president is responsible for, Lapiro brazenly says he will speak the truth:

La vérité étant… ce qu'on ne retrouve jamais	Truth is never… found at the table of liars
Aux tables des menteurs	I promise to sing the truth and nothing but the truth
Je jure de chanter la vérité et rien que la vérité	My friend, I will speak at the risk of being killed
Mombo ah go brass before dem meng me	I will speak regardless of what happens to me
But ah go bras daso	Salary cuts is your handiwork
Baisse de salaire na you!	Deferred payments of arrears is you
Arriérés na you!	Privatizing state enterprises is you
Compression du personnel na you!	
Employee lay-offs is you	
Privatisation na you!	
(Vakunta, 2014:52-53)	

Lapiro accuses the head of state for the many economic disasters facing the country. He has a litany of proofs to demonstrate that the state is collapsing. For example, people employed in the public sector are no longer sure of their salaries, the money owed them by the state and even the security of their employment, is at stake. Because of liberalization, the state companies have been handed over to the private sector, usually transnational companies, whose unfettered quest for profit often means laying off workers – Cameroonians; the Cameroonian workers in these companies are expendable, so to speak. In an interview in which he accused one of these foreign companies of exploitation, Lapiro describes Europeans investors as exploiters who underpay Cameroonians working in slave-live conditions in plantations in his hometown of Mbanga:

You have to see Mbanga to understand what misery is about here. We offer very cheap labour to anyone who wants it. That's why the Europeans have invested in the palm and banana industries here. People earn 20€ a month for 30 days of work on the banana plantations. They start at 5am and finish at midnight. All for 20€! People are suffering. How can they send their children to school on that salary? (de Mbanga and Brown 2010:127)

Recall that following the 2008 nation-wide uprising which was partly inspired by his song (*Constitution Constipée* [Constipated Constitution]), Lapiro was accused of inciting the youth to burn and loot a banana plantation in Mbanga. According to the authorities of the banana plantation (partly owned by the French), Lapiro participated in destroying property belonging to the plantation. One would understand this farm attacks as arising from the frustration of those who experience exploitation. To say workers in these plantations finish work at midnight is a hyperbole but this conveys the message that the labourers are abused beyond comprehension. What is also important here is that the government connives with the foreign companies to exploit the desperate Cameroonians; Cameroon does not protect the interests of its people in the face of these abusive multinational firms. This leaves the people defenceless as the country is 'stuck in the tunnel'. Cameroon's excessive debt and financial quagmire leads the International Monetary Fund to classify the country as heavily indebted. Lapiro rather sardonically describes this as a 'privilege'. The irony in this *privilege* is that the debtor is heavily indebted to the creditor, so, it is not a privilege at all. It is unalloyed thraldom on the part of the debtor. Sadly, despite the international financial loans, the average Cameroonian continues to suffer economically. For example, the dire economic situation makes it hard for parents to send their children to school, leading to a poverty-stricken environment where 'boys become gangsters' and girls as young as fourteen involve themselves in sex work.

Na we this today, kondre dong bouke for inside tunnel	Look at where we are today, the country has been stuck in a tunnel
So, we don batta go heben statu particulier for member privilegie PPET, Pays Pauvres Très Endettés	We have been granted the special status of the privileged member of HIPC, Heavily Indebted Poor Countries Initiative
Situation no ham, repé dem no fit assurer education for dem muna dem again	The situation has seen no change, Parents cannot still send their children to school
Consequences; boys dem dong turn na attacquants, nga dem na ninja.	Consequences: boys have become gangsters, girls are ninjas.
For sika over efraim small chochoro nga for quartoze ans dem dong begin agresser man pikin for Carrefour.	Because of poverty underage fourteen year old girls are already hanging out at road junctions, harassing men.[30]

The fact of the matter is that Lapiro provides evidence after evidence when telling his audience that Cameroonians live in precarious conditions imposed from above. Further in *Na You*, he reveals that Cameroonian certificates have become useless with graduates working as commercial motorbike riders, food sellers, palm nut harvesters, migrant labourers in the Middle East, etc. His conclusion is that people are left to fend for themselves and this echoes the appeal he makes in *Mimba We* that the strugglers should

---

[30] Thanks to Dr Ferdinand Awunglefac Mbecha for this text.

not be penalized for engaging in unconventional economic activities. Lapiro uses music in this sense to shine light on the economic reality in the country; it is a country where, because of economic crisis, people are desperate to do all types of work irrespective of their certificates. In fact, as mentioned earlier, one does not need a certificate to be admitted into the life of the *sauveteur* or the struggler.

Lapiro sees Cameroon an extremely sick country that niggerizes its people. In *Lefam So*, he describes Cameroon as a country that has attempted all remedies to its problems without luck. With every new medication, the situation gets worse. Considering that Cameroonians have not witnessed any improvements in their standards of living despite the huge loans from the World Bank and IMF, Lapiro asks how much loans the country has received, how much has been repaid and how much debt Cameroon still owes these institutions. Acting as a whistle-blower, he addresses the collusion between the powerful financial institutions and the Cameroonian leadership, revealing that every citizen contributes to repay the debt when in fact, only those at the top have squandered the money. He sees the IMF-Cameroon relationship as gangster-like and without mincing his words, he describes those in charge as master con artists [*grand frere for fey*] (see Ndjio, 2008, for Feymania) who insolently flash money around; they engage in conspicuous consumption. Since huge amounts of money has been borrowed, Cameroon's great grandchildren are already indebted for they will contribute to repay these debts after a hundred years. Presently, the state collects taxes to repay these loans by placing its foot on the neck of everyone, including the strugglers. In 2010, Lapiro painfully observed that 'the state forces them [the common man] to pay taxes. They are lumped with all the duties and none of the rights. They pay their taxes and get nothing in return. Informal when they work, formal when they're fleeced' (de Mbanga and Brown, 2010:128). The artist is here talking about the borderline between the formal and informal sector, mediated by the state; the state, through taxes, forces the *sauveteurs* to participate in the formal economy even as these strugglers get nothing in return.

Lefam So is just one of the many melancholic messages about Cameroonians losing hope in their country. It is wrapped in humour with Lapiro saying what people know, but for various reasons, are afraid to speak out publicly. This musician is indeed a religious man for his uncompromising commitment in denouncing state corruption and oppression. This calls for a critical reading of Lapiro within the context of human rights and the political context he found himself in.

A Critical Reading of Lapiro

Music usually paints the sociocultural reality in a country. Or so it may be. In postcolonial Cameroon, popular music and media tended to invent a version of reality that was in line with the ideals of national unity and identity (Nyamnjoh 2005b; Rathnaw 2010). It is in this sense that Brunner (2017, 2013) talks of musicians contributing to create an image of a cohesive postcolonial Cameroon. Cameroon's first president exercised tight control over the country and instituted a centralized system of governance, fearing national disintegration. Knowing the importance of music, he did all he could to turn this media into a tool of education with a stress on national culture. After gaining independence in 1960/61, the Cameroonian government under Amadou Ahidjo discouraged civil society organizations and critical voices to the extent that the musicians who sang political songs did so in praise of the government. Otherwise, their messages were apolitical, focusing on love, pain, culture, development, etc. Popular musicians such as Anne Marie Nzee aligned themselves with the state and this came with huge financial benefits (see also Dave,

2014, for a similar case in Guinea). Generally, because of the censorship, musicians refrained from signing in ways that portrayed the state negatively. This was one of the key reasons why Manu Dibango never returned to Cameroon to continue his music career.

According to Tangem (2016:160), artistic creativity improved in Cameroon under Paul Biya who came to power in 1982. He further says the changes witnessed under Biya are either by design or forced on the regime by popular movement. As of the time Ahidjo ruled the country, Cameroon was experiencing an expanding economy, which is also one of the reasons why opposing the government in such good times was portrayed by the state as an attempt to destabilize the country. The economy started contracting in the mid-1980s, leading people to talk about the hardship they faced in daily life. Lapiro must be credited as one of the few artists who started talking about a *schizophrenic economy* (economie don craze) right back in 1988 in *Kop Nie*. This was a year after the government acknowledged the economic crisis. What is important here is that Lapiro told the public what economic crisis meant and went further to predict its consequences. It was at a time the government was reticent in providing details about the IMF/World Bank economic prescriptions and conditionalities.

Once more, we see Lapiro not waiting or expecting the ethical voice of the political to unpack the implications of the crisis on Cameroonians. He basically reveals to the public what he has examines. Lapiro is aware that the power structure preys as well as thrives on ignorant citizens. In other words, this artist considers it a duty to inform his people that which is concealed from the public. This is very Socratic in that he thinks life in Cameroon must be examined. But for Lapiro, an examined life in Cameroon is painful particularly in the period of neoliberal economic practices where international financial institutions have a stranglehold on the country's economy. The Cameroon government, under pressure from the IMF and *World* Bank, embarked on liberalizing, privatizing state corporations and utilities companies which basically meant, as mentioned before, handing these companies over to western firms. The state cut investment in the public sector and devalued the currency. Lapiro is singing at a time when the neoliberal economic practices ensure that resources are sucked up from bottom to the top, where political leadership is more answerable to corporations and international financial organisations. How pervasive neoliberalism is can further be seen when countries such as Cameroon must comply with the dictates of the World Trade Organisation, a Western market platform that opens non-Western markets for unbridled exploitation by Western corporations.

Under these conditions, Cameroonians have had to 'fix' themselves to the oppressive conditions (Gordon 2010:206). Fixing is a deep analytical concept that describes people's adjustment to discomforts. Both Franz Fanon and WEB Du Bois have talked about this in relation to oppressed folks. In classic Fanonian (1967) view, these *sauveteurs* experiencing all forms of precarity are located in zones of non-being; a zone where their humanity, livelihood, and all forms of human characteristics are of no significance to the power structure (they may be valued in times of cosmetic elections). Their lives parallel that of the elite whom the singer describes as first class epicurean con artists. They live in spaces where Fanon (1967) describes as zones of being, zones where their humanity counts, and they have all forms of security. In Lapiro's music, we see primarily an urban and semi-urban space where precarity is normalized. In other words, they have made peace with the socioeconomic uncertainties. The singer, in an unforgiving way, holds leadership responsible for the hardship in zones of nonbeing.

Lapiro had an authoritative voice, as a social commentator, to make these accusations. One only needs to look at his proximity to the downtrodden to see why. Emblematic in his music, as mentioned earlier, was the participation of *sauveteurs* during his public performance. He would be seen dancing with them in the streets, roundabouts, and markets. These are spaces where the *sauveteurs* struggle to earn a living. It is within these spaces that he taps into the anger and disappointment of these people who lack political representation. In a sense, he performs the role of a lobbyist in a political setting characterized by mauvais foi or bad faith on the part of the leadership. Politicians prefer to ignore the ugly reality of the suffering masses, Lapiro's *constituency*. He speaks on behalf of those whose voices often do not count. They are not voiceless as one would often hear the marginalized portrayed in most literature. To me, voicelessness conveys non-agency on the part of the subjugated, but the reality is that those Lapiro speaks for actually have a voice. The fact of the matter is that these voices do not count unless they resort to some form of violence, rebellion, or protest as witnessed in the March 2008 strike where Lapiro was caught and accused of inciting violence.

Lapiro understands music as a site of resistance and sees the young people as those who can transform the political landscape in Cameroon (see also Shepler 2010; Englert 2008; Nyairo & Ogude 2005). The titles of his songs are telling: *No Make Erreur, Mimba We, Na You, Lefam So, Constitution Constipée,* just to name a few. Every Cameroonian would fairly guess the meaning of the songs without listening to them. How he uses humour to present serious topics on politics and the precarious lives of the majority is ingenious. In his own words 'the most serious things in humanity must be said with a laugh and not with bitterness…When you laugh, things stick in your mind…Cameroonians listen to me…I'm the one who takes the microphone into the public when they are demonstrating' (de

Mbanga and Brown 2010:127). By this, Lapiro knows he is, to use a social media term, an influencer.

Conclusion

This book is meant to celebrate the achievements of late Manu Dibango. In his long career spanning six decades, he projected the image of Cameroon and Africa in many ways. One of his greatest disappointments was that he was never given the recognition he deserved in his own country. For Dibango, the state stifled artistic creativity when politicians promoted only those artists who conformed to the dictates of the state. One can easily find a link between Dibango and Lapiro; they were both disgruntled at the government. They both loved Cameroon. In this chapter, I have described Lapiro as a religious chronicler of precarious life in Cameroon. His music carries messages of protest, care, corruption, exploitation, etc. He was a man who refused to be subdued; he did all he could to be heard. It is for the love he had for his country and his people that he exposed the struggles and suffering of Cameroonians through one of the most potent platforms. It is out of love that one would criticize his or her country but from the standpoint of those in power, people who call on the leaders to be responsible are by default enemies of the state. For telling Cameroonians that their country could be better than what he witnessed, Lapiro paid many prices – he was jailed, his house was burnt down and most of all, he went into exile where he finally died. He was not born into a poor family which means he could have chosen to live a good life. His class privileges did not blind him to the realities of the society he found himself in. Lapiro understood music is a powerful media, which is why he combined this medium and his popularity to project the precarity of life in Cameroon.

Chapter 5

Understanding Female Mobility in Post-colonial Cameroon History through François Misse Ngoh's U go Cry

Walter Gam Nkwi

Introduction: Biography of Misse Ngoh and the Objectives of the chapter

This chapter foregrounds music as a powerful route into the history and memory of society taking Cameroon as a case study. It draws its inspiration from the fact that music the world over is the form of recording and preserving history as well as using it to understand history. In a broader perspective ,music such as Australia's "Waltzing Matilda", England's "London Bridge is Burning" and Quincy Jones's, We are the World (from the album *USA For Africa*) remind us of certain historical moments . In most societies of eighteenth Century and post-colonial Africa music is an arsenal of history if critically exploited. The pith and kernel of This chapter is to interrogate how much of history is produced through music? How much of the society could be understood through music? Using a genre of music in Cameroon known as makossa, the chapter examines, Misse Ngoh's *U go Cry* to show the theme of "prostitution"[31] and geographical

---

[31] I used the word in quotation marks because I am still not convinced that prostitutes existed in colonial Africa. Colonial officers as well as their ancillaries,

mobility of women in post-colonial Cameroon. In other words what kind of Cameroon society can be understood from the song of Misse Ngoh? The data for the chapter was harvested from the archives and secondary material from university libraries in Cameroon and Europe. From the sources, the chapter contends that much history and the mobility of women can be produced through music, an aspect which has been glossed over by Cameroon scholarship.

The song *U go Cry* by François Misse Ngoh, reflects female mobility and prostitution in post-colonial Cameroon. It x-rays the lamentation of one Mary the protagonist of the song who is purported to be an *akwara*, a derogatory terminology of a prostitute who is the mirror of prostitutes in post-colonial Cameroon. The music further epitomizes the growth of urban joints and the mobility of women who are portrayed in the music as prostitutes. Prostitutes were a thing which the British and French colonial administration considered to be loathsome (Nkwi 2016). Through this song one could appreciate the economy of Cameroon in the 1980s and the spilt over which was devaluation of the currency and the hardship which resulted there from in Cameroon second Republic (1982-till present).

Although there are various accounts and counter accounts about the origin of the state of Cameroon, there is overwhelming evidence which suggest that Cameroon is a child born out of the congress of Berlin which took place in 1884 and for the next thirty years became a German protectorate (Mbembe, 1986; Ngoh, 2001; Johnson, 1970;

Native Authorities were very quick to brand single women as prostitutes. In certain areas traditional rulers were sent to round up women in cities and bring them back to the rural backyards. For more see Nkwi and Walker-Said, "Undesirable and Unwanted Women: Female Mobility and "Prostitution" in the British Cameroon Province and French Cameroon, c.1928-1959" (Forthcoming, 2021).

Ardener, 1967).Using outright force, the Germans succeeded to create what became in western jargon as a "modern Cameroon", after containing all the dissenting voices. Their brief stay came to an end with the First World War in which the Anglo-French and Belgian forces succeeded to push them out of Cameroon (Elango, 1987; Fanso, 1989; Ngoh, 2001). However, the Germans had succeeded to introduce Cameroon to the "international economy" (Ardener, 1967). She had introduced a plantation complex in which many cash crops were cultivated which included cocoa, coffee, rubber, palm oil and also started a modern transportation network (Rudin, 1938).

The First World War rendered Cameroon an international orphan. From 1916 Cameroon became "two Cameroons"-the English and French Cameroons which were administered as separate entities first, under the League of Nations Mandate and later on under the United Nations Trusteeship. This has been elaborately captured in the literature of Cameroon historiography (Ardener *et.al.* 1960; Ardener, 1967: 285-337; Johnson, 1970; Rubin, 1971; Joseph, 1978; Kofele-Kale, 1980; Fanso, 1985: 23-43; Mbuagbaw *et.al.* 1987; Chiabi 1989: 170-199; Njeuma, 1989; Ebune, 1992; Ngoh, 1996 and 2001; Milne, 1999; Mbile, 2000; Awasom, 2004: 86-116).

The years 1914 to 1916 was the *interregnum* and the France and Britain attempted a joint administration of the territory which later on collapsed even before it ever took off the ground. (Elango, 1987; Fanso, 1989). That notwithstanding, France and Britain resorted to the partition of the territory as a war booty and to administer it under the mandate of the League of Nations between 1919 and 1945 and from 1945 to 1961 under the United Nations trusteeship. While Britain took 1/5 of the territory and administer it as part of the Southern Provinces of Nigeria France took 4/5 and administered it as part of French Equatorial Africa. The post Second World War Africa experienced a wind of change and most of the colonies were demanding for independence. French Cameroon took the lead and on 1st January 1960 she obtained her independence from France while British Cameroons gained independence through a UN organized plebiscite and reunification in October 1961.

The two territories which had been under different colonial administrations became the Federal republic of Cameroon which lasted from 1961 to 1972 (Fanso 1999; Kale 1967). In an organized and hasty referendum, the federal structures were superseded in its place and the United Republic of Cameroon was born (Fanso 1989; Chem Langhee 1995; Bayart 1993). Ahmadu Ahidjo, its first president resigned in 1982 and power changed hands to his constitutional successor, Paul Biya. Meanwhile, there were lots of developmental structures in terms of roads, railways, urbanization, industrialization which were relatively achieved under the First Republic. Five years into Biya's Presidency, the economic crisis became quite pronounce as the prices of the prices of raw materials soured in the international market, life became difficult and women crisscrossed the length and width of the national territory in search for greener pastures. The ramifications were evident. It is within this broad understanding of the political, economic, and historical-social context of post-colonial Cameroon that the song of Misse Ngoh could be well understood.

The chapter is divided into the following parts: After the abstract and an introduction, the chapter examines methodology, significance, and literature. This is to stake the various methods which were used to gather the data in the work and also to show the significance of the chapter. The next section examines prostitution in colonial and post-colonial Cameroon and the fourth section examines historical nexus of François Misse Ngoh's *U go Cry* in Post-Colonial Cameroon. Several methods were used to gather data for this essay. Being a secondary school student in the 1980s I observed several themes that are reverberated in this song. I felt the souring economy which was encapsulated in the devaluation of the Franc CFA, the intervention of the Bretton Woods institution (IMF) and the layoff of workers. Life became unbearable. As a young man I was also a lover of makossa, the genre of music produced by Misse Ngoh. Apart from living the experience, I also got accessed into the "hotbed of historians", which is the archives. Apart from the my personal experience and using the archives, I also used the internet and dicographs. Internet was relevant as little or no written documents existed on Misse Ngoh. It was through the internet that I trooped into the lone article written by Enongene Mirabeau Sone and Ngade Ivo Ntiege Mesumbe titled "Moralising female identity in Cameroon in the 1990s: female prostitution and the song "you go cry"" (2014:103-115). They write from sociological and Anthropological perspective. This chapter diverts from them by focusing on the same author but taking historical approach to understand Misse Ngoh,s music.

In the song, Misse Ngoh has raised several themes which could be best appreciated within the context of socio, economic and political context of post-colonial Cameroon. To a very large extent this explains why historical sources including the archives have been used in the chapter to understand the music. The National Archives, Buea was quite relevant. Furthermore, I confronted the secondary literature on music, mobility, and prostitution.

Historical Nexus of François Misse Ngoh's *U go Cry* in Post-Colonial Cameroon

According to sources which I gathered from the internet and (Sone & Mesumbe 2014: 105-106), François Misse Ngoh was born on the 17th July 1949 at Mbonjo, Moungo division in the Littoral

Region of Cameroon. His father died when he was only nine months old. His mother had to struggle hard to bring up the little man and his other brothers and sisters. After his elementary school he continued his education in Yaounde where he enrolled in accounting and shorthand typing. During these years he taught himself the basics of guitar playing. In 1967 the young François Misse Ngoh graduated as a stenographist. He left school and started to work because his mother was not able to pay his school fee any longer. From that moment François spent every free minute to improve his guitar playing skills. In 1970 he joined *Los Calvinos*, the band founded by Nelle Eyoum and some former members of the disbanded *Uvocot Jazz*. In 1972, he released his first 45 rpm under the leadership of one *Jico*, a Nigerian producer who was based in Douala (Sone & Mesumbe, 2014: 107). The title was so successful that Misse Ngoh became the informal leader of the group though the others were much older than him in the profession. It was not long that the group was renamed François Misse Ngoh and Los Calvinos. The successful band became the household name band of the Mount Cameroon Bar and surrounded by Manfred Nyamsi *(Bass Guitar)*, Esso Job *(Solo Guitar)*, Edward Ebongué *(Drums)*, Freddy Komé Ngosso *(Vocals) and Gustave Ebelle (Rhythm Guitar)*, Misse Ngoh entertained the customers till dawn with his spicy Makossa rhythms. But, entertaining the visitors of the Mount Cameroon Bar and other venues was not enough for the ambitious Misse Ngoh. It was in 1975, that the young artist decided to contact the *Sonodisc* record company in France to record his first album. The answer was immediate and two months later he was invited to come to Paris. To solve this problem, Misse Ngoh convinced producer Mathias Njocka to join him to give him the money in exchange for the production of the album. The risk was not in vain, since this debut album released on the Sonafrica label and entitled *Ngon'a Suza*, becomes a true success.

Sonodisc was very content about the cooperation with the promising young artist and until 1982, they released six more LP's of Misse Ngoh on their *Disques Esperance* label . Together more than 100.000 copies were sold. His biggest hit was the LP with the Ivorian band *Bozambo of Jimmy Hyacinthe*, of which 35.000 copies were sold. In 1978 he part ways with Los Calvinos and continued his career as a solo artist. He became one of the most gifted guitarists of his generation and one of the most influential innovators of Makossa (Sone & Mesumbe, 2014: 106). With his international exposure and also singing at a time which the Ahidjo, the President of Cameroon was craving towards national unity, he decided to title his song, u *go cry* in the language understood by the common man, the Creole pidgin language. There is also speculation that he learnt this language through *Jico*, a Nigerian producer based in Douala. He might have also been influenced by Prince Nico Mbarga and Eko Roosevelt who both made highlights in their music by singing them in the Pidgin English.

The music has been produced here in its original form and then transcribed.[32]

You go cry o
You go cry o
You go cry o
You go cry o
My baby (4x)

Which kind man be tell you say akwara di get money?
Which kind man lie you say akwara di get money?

---

[32] I am very grateful to my wife, Akeambom Felicitas for transcribing the music as it appears here. To her I remain forever grateful

Sote you go leave your husband you go waka akwara
You go leave your husband you go waka akwara

You go cry o
You go cry o
You go cry o
You go cry o
My baby

Johnny eehh make you no cry
Johnny eeh eeh make you no cry
You must to sabi say outside di strong o
One day by one day monkey go chop pepper
One day by one day Mary go come back

And she go cry o, she go cry oo
She go cry o, she go cry o
She go cry o, she go cry o, My baby
She go cry o, she go cry o

You go find am but you no go get am
Money palaver don ton na ginger (2x)
Eh! Eh! Eh! Eh! Eh! Eh! (4x)

You go find am but you no go get am
Money palaver don ton na ginger (2x)

Huh!
Mary, na so dem don go lie you; your kombi dem don go fool say road ei fine
You go take Mbonjo, go for Missaka, Missaka you go for Mudeka,

Modeka you say na for Tiko

Tiko, you say na for Limbe, Limbe you say na Kumba hehe

Now wey you don reach sote for Bamenda, you don see weti?

Outside too e don strong now

Money no dey

Caca don go down

Café too e no dey again

Mary you go do how?

E don bad oo Mary

Monkey go chop pepper

You go come back, Mary

You go come back

Hahahahahahaha

Ashia Mary

You go find am but you no go get am, Money palaver don ton na ginger(2x)

She go find am but she no go get am, Money palaver don ton na ginger (2x)

Eh eh eh (4x)

Mary, eh eh eh

Ei don bad, eh eh eh

Money don run, eh eh eh

No one dollar no dey again, eh eh eh

Caoco too e do go down, eh eh eh

Café no di give no no thing, eh eh eh eh

Na plantain di give am? eh eh eh eh

Eh eh eh eh

In Misse Ngoh's lead album of the mid 1980s he begins with the lamentation *'u go cry o'* and repeats it as chorus throughout the song. This lamentation suggests the ills of the profession in which 'my lady' has indulged in, which is prostitution. The next stanza that follows is a set of questions

> Which kind man be tell you say akwara di get money?
> Which kind man lie you say akwara di get money?
> Sote you go leave your husband you go waka akwara?
> You go leave your husband you go waka akwara?

(Who advised you that prostitutes are wealthy until you left your husband and went into the profession, who told you a lie that prostitutes make a lot of money until you abandon your husband).

These questions show the social and economic context of Cameroon which triggered in prostitution. Some women took up the profession because they were advised by their peers that it fetched money. Others abandoned their husbands and went in for the profession in other to become bread winners. Mary was one of the women who abandoned the husband and took up the profession. This suggests that economic factors were partially at the root cause of prostitution. The economic causes of prostitution have been well established in the literature. For instance, Naanen (1999) noted the economic factors and maintains that prostitution thrives because there is a market for it. He draws on Victorian England to demonstrate that although it had all its modesty of civilize values it had a soft underbelly as far as sexuality was concern. Some anthropological literature has also suggested that women achieved happiness only when they escaped traditional strictures, perhaps by leaving villages for the city and for the job of prostitution (Boserup 1970).In Cameroon drawing from my previous work on prostitutes' geographical mobility between Accra and Lagos in the colonial period abundant evidence shows that prostitution was a profitable venture (Nkwi 2016c). While writing in 1941, His Excellency, Governor B.H. Bourdillon said: there can be no doubt that the profits from trafficking of women prostitutes are considerable and the case is quoted of one of these harlots who returned recently from the Gold Coast with no less that eighty pounds in her possession.[33]

Socially, Misse Ngoh therefore takes up the next lines by consoling Johnny who purportedly is the husband who has been abandoned by Mary for the sake of prostitution.

>Johnny eehh make you no cry
>Johnny eeh eeh make you no cry
>You must to sabi say outside di strong o
>One day by one day monkey go chop pepper
>One day by one day Mary go come back
>
>(Mr. John do not regret; you must know that things are very difficult outside there. A time will come when the monkey, zoologically known as *Macaca Fascicularis* will eat pepper).

Social, cultural, and economic issues are at the basis of such a consolation. Thus, John should not be crying because times are difficult. By difficult times it means the economic blizzard or crisis of the mid-1980s. This led to the high rate of unemployment, inflation, and the devaluation of the *communate Francaise Argent*, the

---

[33] File Sf(1941)4 , Letter No. 360051, prostitutes in Accra and Lagos

Cameroon currency since 1916 (Williame 1986). It was because of these difficult times which people had to device new and creative ways to cope with life. Metaphorically, monkey will not eat its usual food. The diet of monkeys includes fresh fruits like mangoes, apple, papaya, grapes and above all bananas which is the most favourite. It also eat fresh vegetable like carrots, cucumber, fennel, onions, tomatoes, cooked vegetables like peas and green beans, boiled eggs, yoghurt, cooked meat like chicken and turkey. But in this context it has to eat chili pepper. In short people have to go out of their way to cope with the hard situation. Money has become so scarce such and those who even worked for a salary do not see the money. Thus, *you go find am but you no get am; money palaver don ton na ginger* (You will work but you will not have the money). This is because devaluation had caused the currency to lose its value. Put in colonial perspectives, prostitution in Cameroon indicates that it was also with the complicity of some of the husbands.

For instance, some of these women after selling their bodies sent back money to their husbands advising them on how to spend it. Broadly speaking as I argued elsewhere (Nkwi 2015) although focusing on prostitutes in Lagos and Accra one can have a glimpse of how prostitutes were encouraged by some of their husbands. The letters of the prostitute Selina Rowo, who lived and worked in Sekondi, Gold Coast, clearly illustrate this situation: In the letter of 14 March 1943, she informed her brother at Ediba that she had remitted "20 pounds to her husband to build a comfortable house for her. She also sent 10 shillings to her brother to assist in the upkeep of their daughter ….In another letter dated 27 July 1943 she reminded her husband , Eze Aji of her previous remittance to him and that he should keep the rest of it until it was enough to build a house. In Eji's letter of 23 July 1943 to his wife , he gave a breakdown of the expenditure of 22 pounds from her Part of the expenses: 2

pounds for the 'native doctor' for the medicine Rowo requested for her mysterious sickness; 10 shillings for juju consultation and an unspecified amount given to Rowo's brother Johnny Ikpa Onyi while Eji himself used 10 shillings for out of pocket expenses; 13 shillings went for legal fees as a result of litigation initiated by Rowo's relatives against Eji"The business was good. Female prostitutes became the breadwinners of their families following their professional migration from Nigeria to the Gold Coast. While writing in July 1941, His Excellency, Governor B.H. Bourdillon said: "there can be no doubt that the profits from the trafficking of women are considerable and the case is quoted of one of these harlots who returned recently from the Gold Coast with no less than eighty pounds in her possession' Bourdillon's letter further lends credibility to the profitability of prostitution. The District Officer Mamfe, wrote to the senior resident Buea, Cameroons Province on 29 January 1942 saying that prostitutes who had been to Gold Coast and had then retired displayed wealth. He said: "The women of Okuni (Ikom Division) who have retired from the profession of prostitution in the Gold Coast have built themselves splendid houses ...it seems that they succeed well enough to be able to refund their own dowries to their husbands and to provide male members of their own families with wives' All these led to the conclusions that prostitution was profitable and generated wealth although the colonial state never kept any financial records and so far the prostitutes who were moving from one city to another in Cameroon has no records in the archives.

Misse Ngoh further, elaborately and emphatically re-echoed the economic situation in the following words: *outside don strong; money no dey; cacoa don go down; café no dey again* (Times are hard; there is no money; the prices of cocoa have gone so low; coffee is not there again). It is widely believed by Cameroonians and non-Cameroonians as well, that Cameroon for several years experienced an economic boom especially during the country's First Republic under Ahmadu Ahidjo (1961-1982). This was from sectors which included the exportation of agricultural products (Coffee, cocoa, and cotton) and petroleum which was later discovered in Victoria in early 1980s. During this period, it is also widely believed that the per capital income was high and Cameroonians had better access to health and educational facilities. The country's Second Republic under President Paul Biya, was a continuation of the First Republic, although the change from Ahidjo to Biya may be seen as constituting what the political scientist Gramsci called "quantitative Caesarism" where there is not a passage from one type of state to another but merely an evolution of the same type along unbroken lines (Geschiere 1986: 32).

However, they were few better days in Biya's first two years of his reign which soon dashed and Cameroon economy was caught up in global whirl wind that stretched the economy into its elastic limits entering into the first decades of the 21st Century. The global world crises struck Cameroon economy from the spinal cord. With it came a downturn in world prices for primary products, Cameroon experienced serious crisis (Ngu 1989; Jua, 1991). After its budgetary year of 1985-1986, its economy went into serious complete downturn. An evaluation during this period revealed that the economy had experienced a brutal drop in revenue from exportation. This drop went further to affect petroleum as well as other primary products that were exported at the time. This drop was estimated at about 329 billion FCFA, estimated at about 8.2 % of the Gross Domestic Product (GDP). The dilapidation of the economic sector was further exacerbated from 1986 to 1987 due to the persistent drop in the prices of the main products exported such as Petroleum, coffee, cocoa, and cotton. From 1985 to 1988, exchange rates plummeted by more than half (Jua 1991).

The Biya government did not only sit watching. To cope with this crisis, the government first put in place a policy of internal adjustment in which salaries of civil servants were reduced and other costs of production. The diminution in the standards of living and the influence of the state in the economy did not seem to be making the situation any better. Economic gauge did not stop emitting negative warning signs. A continuous decrease in revenue induced a 40% drop in consumption per Cameroonian between the years 1985 and 1986 and 1992 and 1993. External debts incurred, increased from less than half to more than three quarters of the GDP between 1984 and 1985 and 1992and 1993 (Sikod, 2006). The investment rate decreased from 27% to less than 11% of the GDP (Jua 1991). To cope with the situation marked by rising tensions at the treasuries, the government opted for salary cuts in the civil service in 1993 again. The salary cuts affect the man-on the streets negatively as well as the man in the office. People found it very difficult to cope as they could not sponsor their children in schools, pay hospital bills as well as feeding. To add insults to injuries, government forced the students of the lone university, the Yaoundé University to start paying fees, something that was not hitherto done since the opening of that university in 1962 (Williame 1986).

The economic downturn did not go on *sine die* . From 1994, new economic policies based on monetary adjustments were put in place; leading to a gradual change but not remarkable positively in the trends. Astonishing changes were made at the level of exportation as well as on the general scenario of government's budget (Jua 1991). The government, however, continued to suffer from the inability to cope with internal and external pressure, coming from debts that could not be paid. Relations with foreign partners equally turned to a stalemate. Two new programs of structural adjustments concluded with the International Monetary Fund (IMF) as all the agreements ended up "in smoke" alongside with the preceding ones. Furthermore, all attempts to solve internal and external debts at the time failed completely willy-nilly (Baye and Amongwa 2002; Sikod 2006). It was only later in August 1997 that the government was able to come to terms with the IMF after successfully going through a reference program followed up by this institution. An accelerated structural adjustment plan was put in place in which the IMF gave full support for an economic and financial program which had to be realized within a period from 1st July 1997 to 30th June 2000.

The execution of this program came alongside a voluntary action staged by the government to portray a better image of credibility of Cameroon abroad. This was done by paying back about 05 billion dollars of debts owed to foreign creditors. The government also went ahead to closely associate with the private and public sector towards the evaluation of a three-year economic and financial program as well as negotiating on a financial agreement with the IMF (Sikod, 2006). These moves led to a better adhesion of economic operators and the civil society to policies of adjustment and reform. The governments financial and economic program for the period stretching from 1st July 1997 to 30th June 2000 was satisfactorily executed, with the needed support from determinant International financial bodies like the IMF through its structural adjustment facility, the International Bank for Reconstruction and Development codenamed (World Bank), through a third loan for structural adjustment, the European Union, the African Development Bank and the Paris Club (World Bank 1981;1984;ARB 1988).

From 1996-1997 to 1999-2000, the mean annual growth of the GDP stood at 4.5% and inflation, measured by the index of the final price of consumption by homes was redressed to less than 1% (Sikod 2006). The situation with public finance greatly improved, and this was also thanks to a better mobilization of funds and a rationalization of national expenses. Success on the macroeconomic scale did not necessarily mean an amelioration of living conditions amongst common Cameroonians. In effect, living standards dropped considerably during the ten years and beyond over which Cameroon experienced economic crises. The availability and access to basic social services provided by the state were seriously affected during this period and very little could be done at the time (Sikod 2006). Road infrastructure also degraded seriously due to lack of maintenance. The construction of new road was totally stopped. Water and electrification programs also experienced serious drawbacks especially in rural area due to lack of financing. As concerns employment, the restructuring of enterprises of the public and private sector, which led to the closure of some companies on the one hand and the freezing of recruitment in the public service on the other hand led to increasing unemployment (Sikod 2006). During the period between 1984 and 1991, the level of employment soured by 10% and reached 17% in 1995 (Sikod 2006). This mostly affected the youthful population as well as women, thus leading to a rise in the informal sector. In 2001, unemployment affected more than 12% of the active population, 16% in urban areas and 8% in rural areas; with record heights in Douala and Yaounde that registered 18% and 14% respectively (Sikod 2006). The situation may at times seem to get better due to an involvement of people in the informal sector, yet most of such employment is precarious and unstable (Nkwi 2015; Mokake 2013).

The government took up palliative measures and launched a series of measures through the National Employment Fund which were aimed at ensuring transparency in the job market and encouraging unemployed citizens through trainings and workshops on how to create small private micro projects. The government also created a National employment and professional training observatory

(Onefop) in order to ameliorate its knowledge about the job market (Sikod 2006). These measures were relevant and important to move the economy ahead because hitherto now employment opportunities were based on tribalism and *godfatherism* rather than merit. The "petite bourgeoisie" had brought into play the politics of social justice where merit was sacrificed at the altar of mediocrity, favouritism, and tribalism as far as job employment was concerned (Jua 1989). Other strategies which were also put in place included: the creation of a platform for dialogue between organizations/companies and training centres/universities and between the government and private sectors through a ministerial committee enlarged to include the private sector and other frameworks of dialogue (Jua 1991). In the educational sector, the drop in the budgetary envelop allocated to education was manifested by an insufficiency of hosting structures due to a halt in the construction of classrooms; a decrease in the teacher to student ratio, due to the lack of recruitment of teachers; insufficiency of didactic materials and other teaching and learning auxiliaries; an absence of equity and inefficiency in the management of the whole system. The consequences of all these were a net corrosion of the educational system, which was marked by a high rate of repeat cases in classes and finally abandonment. It was also marked by disparities in the access to education according to gender and geographic region; disparity in the creation of schools and degradation in the quality of teaching and learning and finally a highly centralized management of the educational system.

Identical problems were encountered in the domain of health. Till today, the health system is still seriously affected by the halt in the construction and acquisition of health training equipment. There has also been a perennial halt in the recruitment of health personnel in the public service and insufficiency in the quality and quantity of health personnel as well as a low distribution of health services throughout the country and its low output due to the drastic cuts of salaries and the loss of motivation by personnel. The ratio of patients to personnel is very weak; one doctor for 10 000 inhabitants, one nurse for 2250 inhabitants and one hospital bed for 770 patients. The degradation of the health system coincides with the appearance of new challenges in the health sector. The most remarkable is HIV/AIDS and malaria which accounts for 40% to 50% of consultations and 28% of admissions. Unfortunately, these diseases mostly affect the active population who normally should have been indulged in the economic development of the country. Hence, the life expectancy still remains low (59%), infant mortality very high (77%) and death of mothers at birth estimated at 430 cases in every 100 000 births (van de Walle 1989).

The next stanza in the music of Misse Ngoh illustrates road transport and urbanization in colonial and post-independence Cameroon. He sang in the following words:

Huh!

Mary, na so dem don go lie you; your kombi dem don go fool say road ei fine

You go take motor go for Mbonjo, go for Missaka, Missaka you go for Mudeka,

Modeka you say na for Tiko

Tiko, you say na for Limbe, Limbe you say na Kumba hehe

Now wey you don reach sote for Bamenda, you don see weti?

(Mary is that how they confused you that the road is good? You have travelled from Mbonjo to Missaka and to Mudeka; from Mudeka to Tiko; and from Tiko to Limbe and to Kumba until you have reached Bamenda. What have you seen?)

The literature on women's geographical mobility has shown how this form of migration came much later than that of the male. Clifford, (Clifford 1992: 183), observes that 'Good travel (heroic, educational, scientific, adventurous, ennobling) is something men should do. Women are impeded from serious travel. *Some of them (women) go to distant places but largely as companions...*' In other words, women were always believed to have travelled in conjunction with men. There is evidence, however, that European women, at least, travelled alone as far back as the 19th century. Thus, the geographical mobility of African women sketched here suggests a different picture. The mobility of women as independent agents as demonstrated by the prostitutes resonates with other women in Africa and has occupied some space in research landscapes. For instance, Barnes (Barnes 2002: 87) studied the migration of women in Southern Africa, especially between South Africa and Zimbabwe during the colonial period. She employed statistical, documentary, and oral evidence to critique the dominant paradigm that women were silent observers of migration in colonial Southern African historiography. She stated that 'when historians follow the dominant model and consider mobility, travel, and migration *a priori* as male preserves, African women are automatically consigned to mass immobility. They are barred from centre stage and frozen in perpetual economic childhood'.

In the light of the music of Misse Ngoh, it is relevant to understand the inter-urban and transport history of Cameroon so we can better read meaning into the song. Cameroon has over the years experienced a rapid urbanization, greatly spurred up by rural exodus. Rural-urban migration has been a frequent theme in colonial Africa and in Cameroon it was not exemption. Urban nudges became magnets where people especially women sought for comfort and modernity. Thus, according to available statistics, more than half of the population of the country have moved into and lives in towns. The average growth rate of the country is 5% in urban areas, with Yaounde and Douala having rates of 7% and 6.4% respectively. It is estimated that the populations of these towns doubled by the year 2015. A combined effect of poorly managed urbanization and economic crises is the proliferation of phenomena such as urban ghettoes, insecurity, traffic jams, poor hygienic conditions, unemployment, multiplication of homeless people, street children, prostitution, mental illnesses, psychological stress Just to name but a few (Steedman 1986).

Sone and Mesumbe (2014), have done an excellent job by showing the growth of cities in colonial Africa. They draw from Abdoumaliq & Abdelghani (2005: 1) in their *Urban Africa: changing contours of survival in the city* to analyse why there was a sudden disintegration of urban public life, as well as the "intricacies of sustaining traditional modes of sociality through periods of economic and political crisis" in Africa. However, the Cameroon cities mentioned by Misse Ngoh has a deeper history. The cities of Bamenda, Mbonjo, Missaka, Mudeka, Kumba, Tiko, Limbe (Victoria) were founded in colonial French and British Cameroons. Bamenda played a key role in the German and British administrations and thus became a veritable administrative hub. British Southern Cameroon was consequently administered as part of Nigeria it suffered considerable economic and political neglect under the British administration. This was largely because it was found at the periphery of the British colony of Nigeria. The situation did not improve significantly, in the independence period. However, the earliest written documents on Bamenda can be traced to colonialism. The Germans annexed Cameroon in 1884 but it was only by the end of that century that they pacified the hinterland people by outright force (Rudin 1938). After blood pacts with the Bali chief the Germans with the help of Eugene Zintgraff moved and first established a garrison at Mendakwe, the area from which the name Bamenda derives.[34] The establishment of the Medankwe garrison was simply due to its strategic location as opposed to Bali. Medankwe is on a hill and Bali is on a plain. Consequently, Bamenda became the *Berzirk* of German administration in the Grassfields area in the beginning of the 20th Century.

The German administration lasted about thirty years and the British and French then partitioned the territory. Bamenda fell under the British and the entire region with its neighbourhood was generally lumped up by the British Administration as the Bamenda Province, with Bamenda itself being the administrative capital. The administrative and commercial services during the British colonial administration caused many people to migrate into the area either to work in the colonial administration or carry out commercial activities. There is also strong historical evidence in colonial reports that some-ex-service men returning from the First World War and who were also newly converted into Christianity were not comfortable going back to their villages. They preferred to stay on in Bamenda (Nkwi 2011).

In 1949, the Bamenda Province was re-organised and Bamenda under the new dispensation remained the capital but was consists of Wum, Nkambe and Bamenda itself. Out of a total population of 264,790 of this division in 1953, 10,000 lived in what was known as Abakwa, the former original name of Bamenda.[35] This area continued to attract more and more people it hosted commercial firms like the United Africa Company (UAC), John Holt and

---

[34] File Cb/1916), Confidential Report Bamenda Province, 28th February 1916 by G.S Podevin, National Archives Buea

[35] File Cb(1953)1, Bamenda Province Annual Report by Acting Resident, A.B. Westmacott,NAB

Hollando and Barclays Bank International. The UAC and John Holt specialised in buying coffee and palm kernels from the indigenous farmers. These companies' also retailed assorted materials like umbrellas, bicycles, buckets spoons and zinc[36]. With the attainment of independence in 1961 these companies were forced to leave Bamenda and Cameroon as a whole. Bamenda remained without a major industry to serve its growing population, yet the urbanisation of the area attracted may women who came in to enjoy the niceties of the city.

Mbonjo is the hometown of Misse Ngoh which is situated in Moungo division of the Littoral province. If the saying goes that "charity begins at home" was something to by, then Misse Ngoh had no other option than to put the place of his birth in his music. Mbonjo did not hold any significant economic importance in French Cameroon except that rural farmers who cultivated cocoa came to settle there. Unlike Mbonjo, Missaka is along the Mungo River and inhabited by Ibibio farmers who are well known for their poultry, cocoa, and yam cultivation.

Mudeka was very important fishing market throughout the British colonial administration and far into the post-independence period.[37]. Kumba became the hub of commercial activities in colonial Southwest Cameroons. This was because of the influx of Ibos from Nigeria and also because the climate was very suitable for the

---

[36] see File Cb/1958/1, Annual Report for Bamenda Division, 1957 by Senior District Officer for Bamenda, Mr. R.J. Elkerton, NAB

[37] File Ba (1938)1, Cameroons Province : Notes for the League of Nations Report 1938 (National Archives Buea henceforth cited here as (NAB); File Qc (1960) Kenneth E. Berill to J.O. Fields, The Economy of the Southern Cameroons: A Report Submitted to J.O. Fields Commissioner of Southern Cameroons 25August 1960 (NAB).

cultivation of cocoa and rubber and coffee. When Southern Cameroons gained independence in October 1961, Kumba became a railway terminus. The railway line which radiated from Douala to Mbanga was extended to Kumba in 1969. Ahidjo justified this railway line on the basis that the trade which was flowing into the Cross River region of Nigeria would be diverted into the Cameroon republic.

Tiko gained prominence as a commercial area beginning with a port which the Germans used to export bananas and other produce. But before the Germans, Tiko was a trading area and named after trading in the mpoke language as keka. With the German plantations of rubber and bananas opened in the area and the factories, hospitals Tiko gradually became a cosmopolitan area with people who have migrated from the hinterland as well as west African coast (Nkwi 2017).

Limbe which was the new name for Victoria also had colonial beginnings. Arguably, the foundation of Victoria could be traced to the London Baptist Missionaries who were led by Alfred Saker who bought the land at the cost of £18,000 for his missionary activities. After the abolition of slave trade in the British Empire in the early 1830s some emancipated slaves from Jamaica pressed for an evangelical mission to return to the African homeland. In England the religious motive was complemented by a search for scientific and economic goals geared towards the opening up of more lands in Africa. In 1841, the Niger Expedition was launched with the primary goal of opening up modern day Nigeria to British traders, missionaries, and scientists. The Committee of the London Baptist Missionary Society (LBMS) took advantage of the abolition of slavery and the slave trade in the British Empire as well as the Niger Expedition and decided that an effort be made to give the light of life to the Dark continent and also to atone for the crimes that English greed had for centuries committed by proclaiming in Africa itself the glad tidings of divine liberty from on high. Consequently, the missionaries left England on 13 October 1840 and reached Fernando Po (Present day Equatorial Guinea) on January 1841. While in Fernando Po they were given an introductory letter by the former Governor of Fernando Po, Lt. Colonel Nicolls. In 1845, the Spanish Consul, General Don Carlos Chacon, arrived in Fernando Po with instructions to send the Baptist Missionaries away unless they agreed to stay in a private capacity only (Nkwi 2016). They refused they were allowed to stay unmolested until after 1856 when the Spanish Catholics in Fernando Po made things quite difficult for them. In May 1858 the Spanish Jesuits arrived on the island and proclaimed Catholicism the main religion. Thence, Alfred Saker decided to move with his followers in Fernando Po to the mainland opposite the island. This area was Bimbia but after he acquired it, he named it Victoria in honour of Queen Victoria of England. Saker's expulsion from Fernando Po had different but contrasting motives. He was expelled because of religious and, to a lesser extent, economic motives. His decision to found Victoria was also due to religious and economic motives. Writing about this view, Saker's biographer, Edward Bean Underhill said *inter alia:*

I (Alfred Saker) need a home for our people where a trade may be created and to which commerce may be drawn. I searched for a landing only....Here if Her Majesty's Government sanction and sustained our efforts, can be put, coal stores, provision stores, building yards and every other essential for commerce. Here too a highway may be made into the interior and the native produce be shipped in smooth water for Europe. It will be essentially a religious enlightened colony (Underhill 1958:56) .

Saker's words suggests that there were already ingredients of a city in Victoria as early as 1858. It also shows that, the foundation of Victoria was due to economic and social factors. No records so far have shown that there was any resistance in the founding of Victoria. Neither has there been any documented evidence that natural rulers played any significant role in the acquisition of Victoria. Consequently, the beginnings of Victoria could be traced to the 1880's when the Germans annexed Cameroon. That ambition was well executed when volcanic soils which are often fertile for agriculture led to the opening of plantations both in Victoria and coastal Cameroon. These plantations cultivated various agricultural products such as palm oil, rubber, bananas, pepper, and cocoa (Nkwi 2016). Conversely the cities in the post-colonial Cameroon which were created by the colonial administration were mostly located in the littoral quadrant of the country. The two major cities started as ports. These were Victoria which later became Limbe and Tiko. Satellite city like Kumba was a railway terminus which radiated from Douala. The railway line was constructed under the German colonial administration known as *mittelandbahn* and Kumba was also a commercial hub. Mudeka and Tiko also came to limelight following commercial activities and fishing. These administrative and commercial notches all symbolized modernity and thus attracted considerable number of single or unmarried women who moved into them either individually or following their husbands. Cities had modern facilities which were lacking in the rural suburbs. Electricity, beer and chicken parlours, modern dressing habits all signalled.The urban thesis in the geographical mobility of women who later became branded as 'prostitutes' have been well illustrated by Aderinto (2010). The author maintains that in most parts of Africa and the world over, prostitution has been an aspect of 'social urbanisation and that consensual sexual labour seemed inevitable in a colonial urban centre which was characterised by youthfulness and cultural heterogeneity and anonymity' (Aderinto 2007: 22). In his other work, Aderinto, traces the dynamics of prostitution. He analyses the causes of prostitution amongst which were the socio-cultural and economic changes which colonialism brought to bear on Nigerian cities.(Aderinto 2007). The situation in the post-colonial Cameroon was different. 'modernity" and went a long way to attract young women from the rural backwaters. Other women who were going through hardship in their marital life saw the city as areas which symbolized autonomy and freedom.

Conclusion

This chapter has essentially examined the mobility of women in post-colonial Cameroon because of the economic hardship which led these women from moving out to the city. Misse Ngoh captured this aspect in one of his songs, *U go Cry*. From a humble beginnings in the village of Mbonjo, François e Misse Ngoh acquired very little education because of the demise of his father he was forced to drop out from School. He then tries a hand at Stenography, a technology that accompanied the typewriter but more fruitful to him was music. As an apprentice under a Nigerian musician in Douala he took up his vocation. He sang in the language best understood by the subalterns- the creolised pidgin English. Through the music of Misse Ngoh we can capture the development of cities in colonial and post-colonial Cameroon, the mobility of women and the economic hardship that hit the Cameroon state so hard in the mid-1980s. By doing so the chapter has added an important feminist perspective to what would have been an overwhelmingly masculinist volume. More crucial to this chapter, is the fact that a lot of history lies below music which further needs to be excavated. Misse Ngoh is well known by musical fans as the best guitarist of his time.

Chapter 6

Singing, Dancing, Listening and Interpreting the Mimboland Unsayable and Unwritable: The Power of Music and the Music of Power in Francis B. Nyamnjoh's Oeuvre[38]

Hassan Mbiydzenyuy Yosimbom

Introduction

This chapter draws on Francis B. Nyamnjoh's oeuvre to argue that in Cameroon, a country that Nyamnjoh fictionalizes as Mimboland, music is not only pregnant with questions beyond the indispensable technicians of Mimboland state power's answers, but also capable of shocking the marginalized masses out of silence and compliance. That is, the music provides an opportunity and a vehicle for characters to purge themselves of the frustrations of life at the margins; criticize the socio-economic and politico-cultural injustices forced on them by the indifference of those in power; and melt away their accumulated uncertainties and insecurities. The paper affirms

---

[38] I acknowledge that this research was funded by the Andrew Mellon Foundation through the African Research Universities Alliance (ARUA) in collaboration with the University of Ghana, Legon under the Project, "Mobility and Sociality in Africa's Emerging Urban" and also by the Centre for African Studies, University of Cape Town under the Project, "Entanglements, Mobility and Improvisation: Culture and Arts in Contemporary African Urbanism and its Hinterlands".

that the music in Nyamnjoh's works asserts the contrast between the "exaggerated superabundance" of the Mimboland Beverly Hills districts and the "bleeding ghettoes of poverty and lack" of her Swine Quarters. Through music, the downtrodden of Mimboland tell a story of how their attempts to escape the poverty of the Mimboland Swine Quarters to the Beverly Hills districts have failed because they are considered unwanted aliens. The paper concludes that Nyamnjoh uses music to demonstrate that Mimbolanders charged with making life better have been making life impossible and that the bandwagon of inequities and impunities has been commissioning intellectuals, politicians and moral authorities to celebrate dissemblance and appetite while ordinary folks keep subsisting the crises, hoping that one day, they will benefit from President Longstay's dripping grand ambitions.

The fight against resilient colonialism, neo-colonialism and authoritarianism has given the plot of the African novel the mood of a narrative song: lamentation, lullaby, dirge, work song, ritual song, revolutionary song, anthem, just to name but a few. Besides sounding like a song, the African novel has been the site of enormous, long, and ongoing creativity in relation to the use of the theme of music as a vector for producing social life, religious and cultural beliefs and the constant constituting and reconstituting of the African society, political ideology, and aesthetics. If music is a language which has a crucial role in the production and reproduction of African society and the re(situation) and re(imagination) of diverse ontologies and epistemologies, then, within the African novel, it is often a language embellished with the performativity of the body and enacted in both public and private spheres either as protest against, or as praise for the *status quo*. African novelists concur with Nyamnjoh and Fokwang's assertion that "much remains to be known about the relationship between music and politics, and on how musicians, politicians and political communities all strive to appropriate each other in different ways and contexts; [that] most African musicians tend to limit their overt participation in the political sphere through the medium of their songs" (2005:253). In other words, African novelists use music "to contest taken-for-granted and often institutionalised and bounded ideas and practices of being, becoming, belonging, places and spaces" (Nyamnjoh 2015:6). African novelists also use the genre "to investigate not only the ways in which musicians have used their songs in order to achieve personal and collective identities that are of political significance, but also the ways in which political power in Africa has responded" (Nyamnjoh and Fokwang, 2005: 253). In line with Ardono's assertion, "[s]ince the mid-nineteenth century [Mimboland's] music has become a political ideology by stressing national characteristics, appearing as a representative of the nation, and everywhere confirming the national principle. Yet music, more than any other artistic medium, expresses national principle's antinomies as well" (1988:68).

This chapter argues that Nyamnjoh's thematization of several forms of Cameroon music (Makossa, Bikutsi, Asiko, Bendskin, just to name a few.) affirms the peculiar character of the relationship between oppositional music and the postcolonial Mimboland state. Nyamnjoh's characters ensure that the musical power of the peoples' music penetrates the stone walls of Mimboland Beverly Hills districts and force them to listen to the Swine Quarterians. The pragmatic indestructibility of music's performativity, as well as its uncontrollability and its characteristic fierceness, have transformed it into a supreme art that both challenges status quo and inspires the masses. Singing, dancing, listening and interpreting the Mimboland unsayable and unwritable refers to Mimboland music's ability to communicate that which cannot be said or written because of the fear of the *commandement*; the power of music nurtures the potency of Mimboland music's critical capabilities; and the music of power designates the absolute corruptibility that has rendered absolute power a national song, an anthem, that the powerless are expected to sing as a sign of reverence.

Thus, the paper asserts that the overarching conceptual and a thematic thread running through the Makossa, Bikutsi, Asiko and Bendskin in the novels is, to borrow Olaniyan's description of Fela's music's depiction of the Nigerian condition, an "incredible" one because like Fela's it inscribes "that which cannot be believed; that which is too improbable, astonishing, and extraordinary to be believed; [that which] is not simply a breach but an outlandish infraction of 'normality' and its limits" (2004:2). Inspired by Olaniyan's description of the incredible, the paper argues that if Mimbolandian "belief, as faith, confidence, trust, and conviction, underwrites the certainty and tangibility of institutions and practices of social exchange, the [Mimbolandian] incredible" that Nyamnjoh captures through music, "dissolves all such props of stability, normality, and intelligibility (and therefore of authority) and engenders social and symbolic crisis" (Olaniyan 2004: 2). Evident in the Makossa, Bikutsi, Asiko and Bendskin thematized by Nyamnjoh and in his scholarly and fictional works, therefore, is a gigantesque will to articulate, to name, Mimbolandian socio-economic and politico-cultural incredibility and thereby inscribe its vulnerability. Given that the expressed objective of the musicians whose music Nyamnjoh thematizes is the shellacking or at least the emendation of the Mimboland reign of the incredible, both Nyamnjoh and the musicians obviously envision its deciduous dominance as a transition, an interregnum.

The paper further acknowledges that although Nyamnjoh traces the operations of power – social, economic, political and cultural – through the medium of music and through his characters' discussions about, and interpretations of music, he does not make an irrefragable claim for the power of music itself to persuade, coerce, resist, or suppress Longstaycentrism; rather, he addresses the uses to which music is put, the controls placed on it, and discursive treatments of it. Like Fela's music discussed by Olaniyan, the Makossa, Bikutsi, Asiko and Bendskin exertions, in all "their recalcitrant multidirectional sprawl, are best seen as meaningful confrontations with a presupposed interregnum that increasingly threatens to become [a Mimboland] norm, a norm with a rapidly consolidating hierarchy of privileges feeding on and dependent on the crisis for reproduction"(Olaniyan 2004: 2). To sing, dance, listen to and/or interpret the Makossa, Bikutsi, Asiko and Bendskin referenced in Nyamnjoh's novels is to listen to a musicalized socio-economic and politico-cultural chronicle of the crisis-ridden life of the postcolonial Mimboland state. To borrow once more from Olaniyan's discussion on Fela's music, the chronicle delineates "the relationships between oppositional music and the state; (dis)empowerment; cultural identity and the refashioning of new subjectivities; authenticity and hybridity; popular culture and the (im)possibility of radical politics; cultural imperialism; and cosmopolitanism"(Olaniyan 2004: 4). The paper concludes that Nyamnjoh's characters are critical singers, dancers, listeners, interpreters and sometimes composers of the unsayable and unwritable elements of Mimboland socio-economic and politico-cultural life. That is, in Nyamnjoh's oeuvre, music in plainspoken, direct, and crude language constitutes a realm within which political ideas and social identities are contested, navigated, and negotiated. To flesh out this hypothesis, the paper will borrow its conceptual framework from Olaniyan's idea of the social, economic, political, and cultural incredible.

Interdependencies Between the African Novelist and the African Musician

Throughout the history of the African novel, the novelists have used music as a medium through which their characters record, dance, listen to and interpret history, moments, and memories, and to sing the unsayable and unwritable. For instance, in *Things Fall Apart,* Achebe uses Unoka, Okonkwo's father, a feckless and impractical flutist, incapable of taking care of his family and of achieving quintessential Igbo personal socio-economic and cultural status to lampoon the western tradition of the bohemian artist and to affirm that the African or Igbo artist does not share in that worldview. As a corrective view, within the presentation of Unoka's personality, Achebe interjects the description of another musician:

> Okoye was also a musician. He played on the *ogene*. But he was not a failure like Unoka. He had a large barn full of yams and he had three wives. And now he was going to take the *Idemili* title, the third highest in the land. It was a very expensive ceremony (1958:4).

Ngugi and Ngugi's *I Will Marry When I Want* thematizes revolutionary songs that carry explicit protest messages meant to stimulate political awareness and revolutionary action. In Ngugi's *Devil on the Cross* the peasants and workers of Njeruca use revolutionary songs to protest neo-colonialism. Nyamnjoh and Fokwang remind us that in *The Poor Christ of Bomba*, Mongo Beti captures the missionaries' delusional attempts at policing Africa's expressive lyrics and dance forms which they consider obscene and diabolical through an episode in which

> Father Dumont, who considers the local Bikutsi music of colonial Cameroonian forest dwellers 'heathen', proceeds on one

occasion, in a mad rage, to pounce on the xylophones and knock down the tam-tams of a village that had stubbornly insisted on singing and dancing to their own music on the first Friday of the month (2005: 652).

Other African novelists such as Camara Laye, Ayi Kwei Armah, Nuruddin Farah and Yambo Ouologuem have thematized music through the use of griots (characters who tell their stories through music, using accompanying instruments such as the *balafon*, *ngoni* or the *kora*) to demonstrate the important and multifaceted duties of African musicians as genealogists, advisers, teachers, interpreters and historians, responsible for preserving the ancestral records of entire communities through oral storytelling.

The failures and successes of the dream of Africa's real independence which, in many guises and names, has again and again excited the African novelists' imagination has been captured adroitly through a thematization of music as a socio-economically and politico-culturally committed African art form. Drawing on Achebe's description of Igbo worldview and art, one could say that the African novelists demonstrate that the neo-colonial and authoritarian African world "is an arena for the interplay of forces; a dynamic world of movement and flux" (1989: 62) and African music "reflecting this worldview [is never] tranquil [but] mobile and active, even aggressive" (Achebe 1989: 63). The "need and the striving to come to terms with a multitude of [socio-economic and politico-cultural] forces and demands [gives African] life its tense and restless dynamism and its [music] an outward, social and kinetic quality" (Achebe 1989: 63). Thus, in most African fiction the musical and written modes exist interpenetratively and interdependently because the music is often provocatively present in the written and so the characters usually live, idiomatically, as musical beings in the episodes through which they are delineated. Their musically imbued diverse questing intellectualities and discernments are nurtured by recollections of musical anecdotes, apologues and kinsfolk perceptiveness imbibed from the musical cultures of their diverse origins and childhoods. To paraphrase Derek Wright's discussion on Nuruddin Farah's novels, one could say that most major characters in African fiction are garrulously musical creatures, given to torrents of musicalized talk and intoxicated with the sheer sound of words (1991:87). That is, African novelists affirm Nyamnjoh and Fokwang's submission that African music "has historically been appropriated by social actors with a variety of interests" and that the way music is produced and appropriated in Africa, "by whom and how, is inseparable from power relations: political, cultural, economic and gendered" (2005: 253).

In Nyamnjoh's novels especially *A Nose for Money* (*ANFM*), *Souls Forgotten* (*SF*), *The Travail of Dieudonné* (*TTOD*) and *Married but Available* (*MBA*), the interconnections and interdependencies between all-walks-of-life characters, tetraglossic linguistic blends, thematic diversities, multiple layered plots and philosophical structures give the works either the tone and tempo of a Felaian symphony and cacophony. Nyamnjoh thematizes virtually all forms of Mimboland music. The dynamics of the complex relationships between music, musicians and political power is visibly present in these novels. He examines "the relationship between musicians and political power in Cameroon [Mimboland] in order to make a case for understanding the dynamics of agency and identity politics among musicians" (Nyamnjoh and Fokwang 2005: 653). Nyamnjoh seeks neither to rehabilitate national musical forms nor to discredit and repudiate them but rather to show how indigenous Mimboland music has been implicated in the new political tribulations and terrors of the independent Mimboland state. These four novels provide a space where through Nyamnjoh's use of music the dark is tempered by the light, despair by hope, the past by the future and the individual's ambitions by the collectivity's determinations. Nyamnjoh's characters make music from congealed history and underscore the capacity of music to reinvent identities and to transform realities. To borrow from Achebe Nyamnjoh affirms that music facilitates the Mimbolander's "constant effort to create for himself a different order of reality from that which is given to him; an aspiration to provide himself with a second handle on experience through his imagination" (1989: 95-96). *ANFM, SF, TTOD* and *MBA* resonate with Nyamnjoh and Fokwang's idea that politicians in Mimboland appropriates musicians and their music to seek to maintain themselves in power, and musicians react variously to such invitations: "Some musicians criticize and ridicule those in power [while] others [use such] invitations as an ideal opportunity to attain greater social recognition and respectability. Some try to straddle both worlds, serving politicians while at the same time pursuing their creative art in the interest of other constituencies" (Nyamnjoh and Fokwang 2005: 253).

ANFM, SF, TTOD and *MBA* are set in a Mimboland (Nyamnjoh's pseudonym for Cameroon) world in which power has run amuck. The country is ruled by a power-drunk megalomaniac elite led by President Long stay (Pidgin English coinage for president for life). In the Mimboland world of *ANFM, SF, TTOD* and *MBA*, President Long stay is presented as a prototypical oligarch. His activities and ideologies remind one of Joachim Fest's (1963: 25) telling description of Adolf Hitler. Like Hitler and his *Third Reich*, Longstay is the ruling party's organizer, creator of its ideology, tactician of its campaign for power, rhetorical mover of the masses, dominant focal point, operative centre, and, by virtue of his fetishized charisma as *l'homme* lion, the ultimate and underived authority: leader, saviour, redeemer. He is the one to whom the Mimboland masses look up to in their hunger for faith, their longing for self-surrender, and their aversion from responsibility. The country is under the suffocating grip of Longstay's regime of force, drummed-up successes, and down-played failures. In the Longstaycentric world of these novels, the idea of struggle is totalized: the stronger, the more able Mimbolanders, always win, while the less able, the weak, always lose. Longstay's collaborators ignore their national culture, despise their skin colour, pretend to be white, speak English or French with Oxbridgean and Parisian accents respectively.

In another of Nyamnjoh's novels, *The Disillusioned African (TDA)*, Moungo tells us that the Mimboland leadership suffers from "a delusion of superiority and a bizarre nose for red herrings" (Nyamnjoh 2007b:26). They are childishly elated to "have houses in Europe or America where they can afford to live better than the middle-class white that stubbornly claims to be superior to them" (*TDA* 2013: 26). During every Bank Holiday, Longstay's and his ministers' wives jostle with middle class housewives in giant supermarkets in Oxford Street where they have their hair retouched. These leaders buy designers' rights for dresses in order to stop other women from dressing like their wives and mistresses who boast of a thousand pairs of shoes, rings of ruby, diamond, and sapphire. Mimboland leaders know nothing about their countries' problems, but they know American, English, French and Western histories. They excel in Elizabethan literature, uphold Victorian values, recite Shakespeare, chuckle at Chaucer's tongue-in-cheek humour, praise Dickens' plume, criticize Racine's sentimentalism and agree with Corneille's fanatical commitment to "La Patrie" (*TDA* 2013: 27). The colonial schools taught, and the neo-colonial ones have continued to teach them to make passing or footnote references to their people or ethnicity. The leaders and the elite know what they do not need and need what they do not know. At the same time, economically, they encourage the production of what they do not consume and consume what they do not produce. Granted the multidimensionality of Nyamnjoh's setting, This chapter asserts that *ANFM, SF, TTOD* and *MBA* resonate with the Lukácsian idea of great art because they "provide a picture of [Mimboland] reality in which the contradiction between appearance and reality, the particular and the general, the immediate and the conceptual, etc., is so resolved that the two converge into a spontaneous integrity ... the universal appears as the quality of the individual and the particular, reality becomes manifest and can be experienced within appearance (Lukács 1970: 34).

Musical Conceptualizations of the Mimboland Social Crisis and Postcolonial Transgression

This section draws on Nyamnjoh's *ANFM* and *SF* to argue that the music thematized therein acknowledges the existence of a Mimboland social crisis and calls for social transgression; movements from one social domain to another, the testing and challenging of fetishized social limits, the mixing and intermingling of Mimboland heterogeneities, cutting across social expectations and boundaries, providing unforeseen pleasures, discoveries and experiences. The music in *ANFM* and *SF* tests and challenges social limits by reflecting the emotional content of the lives of Mimbolanders, essentially their struggle to deal with and rise above their unfulfilled lives and lifestyles. The music is a safety-valve through which characters like Prospère (*ANFM* 2011) and Patience and other passengers (*SF* 2008) release the tension and pressure precipitated by daily trials. The cathartic songs purge anxieties born of separation, loneliness, love affairs gone sour. The music may not possess a transcendent resolution, but it strikes an emotional chord, generating hope even in the darkest moments. The section concludes that granted that the music is sad, sometimes mad, at times glad, and funny, too, Nyamnjoh invokes it in order to compose a different voice, (an)Other, a resurgent social language for the renaissance of the Mimboland downtrodden.

In *ANFM*, we are introduced to the first dose of music through Prospère, a truck driver for the Mimboland Brewery Corporation (MBC). The narrator references him on his way back from West Mimboland to Sawang (Nyamnjoh's pseudonym for Douala), listening to his favourite programme, *La Variété Musicale* (Nyamnjoh, 2011:53) over his truck's radio. We are told that Prospère loves music because it makes his journeys less tiresome. When a familiar Makossa, Asiko, Bikutsi or Bendskin tune is played, he sings along; but when it happens to be a strange tune, he listens keenly for a while, and then starts to hum, once he has got the right beat (*ANFM* 2011: 53). He enjoys Manu Dibango most and Dibango's *"L'Ennemi Ne Dort Jamais"* (French for "the enemy never sleeps") is his favourite single. It is a song that touches on all aspects of life, and that has an unforgettable meaning for him. Even politicians "are said to love it, because of what they claim to be its relevance to the politics of rancour and backstabbing that has poisoned the entire atmosphere" (*ANFM* 2011: 53). Referencing Prospère further, the narrator tells us that the music suddenly ceases to play and is replaced by the signal tune for the one o'clock news bulletin. We are told that the news signal tune is "part of a song written by a patriotic musician urging the President to unite rather than divide, to make rather than mar" (*ANFM* 2011: 54). However, part of the song that has been adopted by the powers that be as the news signal tune is that which least brings out the composer's intended message thereby incriminating its author as a political praise-singer and not a committed patriot (*ANFM* 2011: 54).

L'Ennemi Ne Dort Jamais and the news tune variously affirm the social crisis, the incredible, that has bedevilled Mimboland and the attendant attempts at transgression thereof. They are songs of indirect social protest used by Nyamnjoh to provoke the transformation of consciousnesses in Mimbolanders. Through Dibango's *L'Ennemi Ne Dort Jamais*, Nyamnjoh establishes the fact that Mimbolanders are living in a very strange world of enmity, confronted with all kind of enemies. Nyamnjoh uses Dibango's song to remind us that in postcolonial societies such as Mimboland, the term enmity is slowly becoming a concept which captures the unfamiliarity of everyday encounters which bring Mimbolanders into regular contact with distant others, while at the same time estranging them from those who would conventionally be considered as neighbours/friends. In Mimboland, at least from Prospère's perspective, there seems to be a degree of consensus that enmity designates societal conditions in which neighbours are enemies and Mimbolanders are all a little bit enemy to one another (and to themselves). The idea of the enemy never sleeping captures the incredible that denotes a situation where it is no longer meaningful to identify (a small number of) others as enemies: enmity is a condition of the social and is permanently enveloping all Mimbolanders. The song's title affirms that enemies are not necessarily those we are wont to easily position in terms of us/them and inside/outside dichotomies, contemporary figures of the enemy, the song supposes, occupy an indeterminate place in society because enemies are emerging rapidly into a Mimboland social world whose citizens are striving to remain totally anonymous.

For instance, the powers that be are an anonymous enemy of the artist who composed the song from which the news signal tune is derived because they have successfully misappropriated the aims of the artist's composition thereby turning him/her from a committed patriot and the people's friend to a political praise-singer and the people's enemy. The capability of a song's content to stretch its composer's identity between a political praise-singer and a committed patriot affirms that musical forms are important means of identity creation; that identities get represented and affirmed by music; and that identities have not only been asserted through musical contents that denote political leanings but have also been questioned and reconstructed through those very contents. Nyamnjoh's demonstration of the government's ability to appropriate critical music for its propagandist agenda reminds us that transgression demands that Mimbolanders (like the composer of the distorted song) go beyond the bounds or limits set by the *commandment*, or law or convention; that is, a recuperation or restitution of the true meaning of the song would require that Mimbolanders violate or infringe shady laws/conventions because transgression is that conduct which breaks rules or exceeds boundaries. The coexistence of praise-singing and commitment within the same song asseverates that transgressive behaviour does not deny limits or boundaries, rather it exceeds them and thus completes them. To borrow from Jenkins, one could argue that such coexistence demonstrates that every musical piece just like "[e]very rule, limit, boundary, or edge carries with it its own fracture, penetration or impulse to disobey; [that] transgression is a component of the rule" (2003:7). Seen from this perspective, any move (either by the composer or the public) to recover, recalibrate and domesticate the true composite meaning of the song would be a dynamic force in cultural reproduction that would ensure stability by reaffirming the right rule. Thus, transgression would not be the same as disorder; it would initiate meaningful chaos and remind Mimbolanders of the necessity of order while at the same time ensuring that Mimbolanders know the collective musical order and recognise the musical edges in order to better transcend them.

Another exemplification of the Mimboland incredible captured in Dibango's song is achieved through Nyamnjoh's delineation of Prospère's paranoid and near psychopathic lifestyle. Throughout the novel, Prospère exhibits an unprecedented siege mentality; a pathological fear of the unknown that intensifies when the fraudsters, Jean-Claude, and Jean-Marie, die in a ghastly accident, leaving behind 200 million francs that Prospère inherits and flees to Nyamandem. Prospère's mood keeps swinging between utopianism and nihilism. As a character and as a person, Prospère exhibits morbid fear for nearly everything and everyone; he lives a life bereft of trust and always equates strangeness to the threatening difference associated with the Other. His fear of the unknown explains why he always consults witch doctors and fortune tellers such as Seng to know what the future holds for him if he leaves Sawang (where he thinks he has uncountable enemies) to Nyamandem (which he considers a more enabling society). His consultation of Seng ties in with what Nyamnjoh has elsewhere described as "technology of self-activation and self-extension – something that enables [Prospère] to rise beyond our ordinariness of being [such as enemies that never sleep], by giving [him] potency to achieve things that [he] otherwise would fall short of achieving, were [he] to rely only on [his] natural capacities or strengths" (2019:4). Prospère's consultation, his technology of self-activation and self-extension is an act of transgression that makes him a Camusian (1971:29) rebel. It is also a form of metaphysical rebellion, the means by which Prospère questions his condition of the Mimbolandian incredible and the whole of creation. It is metaphysical because Prospère disputes the ends of man and creation and protests the deplorable human condition in general; his consultation is a declaration that he is frustrated by the Mimboland universe. Through his paranoia we find an assessment of Mimboland values in the name of which Prospère the rebel refuses to accept the condition in which he finds himself. Given that Seng concurs with Prospère's decision to leave Sawang for Nyamandem and that while in Nyamandem Prospère rises to become one of the richest Mimbolanders, one could argue that Prospère's change of city, just like his consultation of Seng, is an act of transgression that challenges fetishized social limits; cuts across social expectations and collapses the boundaries between the absolute rich and the absolute poor. As Nietzsche has rightly put it, "[w]e have Art [such as music] in order that we may not perish from Truth" (qtd. Auden 1962:x).

The public spheres, Tonton Bar (run by an experienced prostitute), *Les Capables* (a nightclub nicknamed '*Les Coupables*' or 'The Guilty' by the poor) and Eldorado Bar, where Mimboland music is played and danced add some meaning to the Mimboland incredible. Tonton Bar is a notorious hideout for "the unemployed young men and women who smoke cannabis and drown themselves in alcohol in their quest for happiness" (*ANFM* 2011: 144). Politicians support these bars' selling of beer with exceedingly high levels of alcohol because they believe that "a clear- and critical-minded populace; a sober population is a recipe for political nightmares and headaches" (*ANFM* 2011: 59). *Les Capables* is the centre for sensuous overindulgence "frequented by the truly well-to-do, such as Minister Ngomnsong who dances Bikutsi "with bedevilling agility." It is also a place where Ngomnsong comes "to wriggle to everything in skirt" by taking advantage of "desperate upward-seeking beautified young girls" (*ANFM* 2011: 144). Women have nicknamed Ngomnsong "the virus" because "he does not distinguish between teenage girls, students, married women or widows, his sister's children, and his own daughters (*ANFM* 2011: 145). Nyamnjoh's description of these bars and their denizens especially Ngomnsong, resonates with a transgression that reveals the disgust, fear and desire which inform the excesses of bourgeois culture and the contradictory political construction of Mimboland bourgeois leadership. Also, that the music finds space and meaning in bars for the rich (*Les Capables*) and those for the downtrodden (Tonton Bar) affirms Jervis's argument that "[t]he transgressive is reflexive, questioning both its own role and that of the [hegemonic] culture that has defined it in its otherness. It is not simply a reversal, a mechanical inversion of an existing order it opposes" (1999: 4). In other words, "transgression, unlike opposition or reversal, involves hybridization, the mixing of categories and the questioning of the boundaries that separate categories" and this explains why the music appeals to Mimbolanders of all walks of life. Thus, the Mimboland downtrodden's decision to rename *Les Capables* (The Capable) as *Les Coupables* (The Guilty) is Nyamnjoh's way of reminding us that spaces of music are as important as the lyrics; that the borders and borderings of musical spaces have been moving from the margins into the centres of social life and vice versa; and that the bordering of musical spaces are redefining contemporary notions of Mimboland citizenship, identity and belonging, constructing hegemonic minorities (such as the Ngomnsongs) as well as affirming marginalized majorities (such as the Prospères) in their everyday lives while creating growing exclusionary grey zones nationally.

From another perspective, one of the musical pieces referenced in *SF* is a famous composition by Tala André Marie titled "I'm Going to the Land of Milk and Honey"; a song that Radio Mimboland International has adopted as the signature tune before every news bulletin. When this song is played on board the bus that Kwanga boards from Nyamandem to Zingraftstown, the song sparks diverse commentaries and interpretations among passengers. A self-proclaimed bilingual gendarmerie officer who assumes graduation "from the regime of obeying without questions to the civility of interpretation" (Nyamnjoh 2008:204) condescendingly offers to translate the song from Muzungulandish (French) to Tougalish (English). To the gendarme, Tala asks an elegantly dressed farmer, a well-kempt student with a triumphant look, a young woman, and a driver where they are going, and they respond that they are going to the big Great Capital City to look for a better life (*SF* 2008: 204-5). The gendarme concludes that at the end of the song, Tala urges the farmer, student, young woman, and driver to freely seek the land of their dreams, look for their betterment in daily life (*SF* 2008: 205). In a second song, "a real celebration of the power, privilege and comfort of the chosen and insensitive few in the political landscape of Mimboland" (*SF* 2008: 332), interpreted in Muzungulandish by another passenger, President Longstay has just appointed a young man's brother to a high position of authority and the young man envisions his brother's appointment changing his life in several ways: stopping him from trekking, eating sandwiches and boarding overloaded taxis and giving him the wherewithal to start riding in an air-conditioned Mercedes, winning dubious tenders; living in beautiful residential areas; traveling to Muzunguland; and shopping in hard currency. The third reference to music is captured through Kwanga's dream that during the launching of an opposition party by President Longstay's tribe's man in Longstay's village, five different songs were sung by five unidentical groups of musicians. In the president's native tongue mixed with Muzungulandish, they describe Longstay as someone who has ironically reciprocated their support with callous indifference to their plight (*SF* 2008: 348); express "their disillusionment with a son of the soil who has promised without fulfilling, and who has used them to fight his sterile battles for selfish power" (*SF* 2008: 348); compare Longstay "to his predecessor, President Habas, during whose leadership money was available, and peasants were at least sure to sell their crops, feed themselves and keep their children in school" (*SF* 2008: 350); and ask Longstay "to tell them where he has kept the country's money" (*SF* 2008: 351). They then summarily identify Longstay as "that person in folklore who had cried wolf time and again in vain, to the point that his people had lost faith only to fall prey to him as the real wolf" (*SF* 2008: 348).

The above three instances of music, especially the first, with its dreams of the big Great Capital City with a better life, the Mimboland "Land of Milk and Honey," ironically project Nyamandem as a bareface sample of the excruciating problems of 21st century urbanization challenges; what Professor Moses Mahogany refers to as Nyamandem's "cosmetic appearance" which "is likely to deceive the foreign tourist, but not the native who has learnt to distinguish between gold and golden, and who knows that no one ever makes any valid judgement about a country from a flying plane, from within a luxury car, or through the windows of a five-star hotel" (*SF*, 2008: 12). Through the expectations of the farmer, student, young woman and driver, Tala's song reminds us of the squalor that has stubbornly survived urban reforms and exacerbated socio-economic and politico-cultural problems such as corruption, embezzlement, prostitution, and robbery. Nyamandem ironically happens to be a quintessence of what W. H. Auden describes in his poem, "The Capital," as "Quarter of pleasures where the rich are always waiting,/Waiting expensively for miracles to happen,/O little restaurant where the lovers eat each other,/Café where exiles have established a malicious village" (1979:78).

Also, the baroque ambitions of the young man who does not have access to power even by proxy is what Kwanga refers to earlier in the novel as Nyamandem's change "from a garden of blooms to a jungle where the able preached one thing and did quite another, and where corrupt practices were kept from public scrutiny because of the 'civilised' belief that it was only normal for a goat to eat where it was tethered" (*SF* 2008: 12) Furthermore, the reference to the five songs of Kwanga's dream is Nyamnjoh's way of telling us that within the Mimboland social world high (President Longstay and his cohorts) and low orders (the masses) have an antagonistic relationship; both struggle for recognition and supremacy and the possibility of one depends upon the necessity of the other and they are fatefully locked in an absolute contingency. Granted that the five songs are sung by groups disgruntled Mimbolanders, the songs are classic examples of singing and dancing the unsayable and unwritable. They constitute singing the truth to and dancing the truth before power. The journeys undertaken by the farmer, the student, the young woman, and the driver from their various localities to the Great Capital City symbolize physical crossing of the social barriers.

Nyamnjoh's delineation of the foreigner-treatment meted out to Kwanga at the University of Asieyam is a way of asserting that the Mimboland authorities often treat physical crossing as a dangerous pollution and polluters like Kwanga referred to as "*éléments dangereux* by the popes of power" (*SF* 2008: 5), become doubly wicked objects of reprobation, first because they cross the line and second because they endanger others. Through the three songs, Nyamnjoh variously contends that the Mimboland experience of social life is a series of compartmentalizing compartments, each unadulterated on the inside and sequestered around the margins; that the spaces between these compartments are dangerous and threaten not just the marginalized individual but the whole Mimboland social system. The songs are like Bakhtinian carnival laughter; universal in scope; directed at all and everyone, including the [song's] participants; the entire Mimboland world is seen in their droll aspect, in their gay relativity; they are ambivalent; they are gay, triumphant, and at the same time mocking, deriding; they assert and deny, they bury and revive (1968: 11–12).

The comparison of Longstay to the "cry wolf" story shows how

Longstay's lack of value for truth has been transformed into a Mimboland narrative about Longstay being a mischievous political trickster who has been warning about a danger that does not exist. Through the songs, singers reject Longstay's pained and discombobulated assimilationist, universalistic and identity politicises. The songs are, therefore, Nyamnjoh's call for a Mimboland transversal politics (Cockburn and Hunter 1999; Yuval-Davis 1997, 1999); a Mimboland politics of solidarity across social boundaries. Unlike Longstay's failed identity politics, transversal politics, according to Yuval-Davis, Wemyss and Cassidy (2019: 168-169), would ensure that participants in dialogue would not be seen as representatives of their collectivities but rather as advocates, and there would be "recognition of the fact that people who share similar socioeconomic positionings and membership of particular collectivities [could] still differ widely in their identifications, in their social attachments, and in their normative value systems". Such Mimboland transversal dialogues would be supported by processes of rooting (respect of personal positionings) and shifting (respect of others' positionings) that would imply that everyone would be listening, empathising, and trying to imagine the situation as experienced from the others' different standpoints. Even though transversal politics would not assume that dialogue would be without boundaries or that every conflict of interest would be reconcilable; it would garner its optimism from Pettman's affirmation that there would almost always be "possibilities for congenial or at least tolerable personal, social and political engagements" (1992: 157). It would affirm that compatible Mimboland values would cut across social differences in positionings and identity and assume what Assiter calls "epistemological communities" (1996: 79).

How the Grand Canarians Use Dissident Tunes to Sing and Dance Against the Official History of Beverly Hills

Drawing on the image of multitudes of rats and cockroaches celebrating impunity used to describe the inhabitants of SQ (in *TTOD*) as a fitting metaphor for the fight against denigration and a symbol of the nonconservative history that the inhabitants of SQ use as a weapon against the inhabitants of BH who have adopted a hegemonic *weltanschauung* that identifies them as masters and views those in SQ as servants, this section argues that in *TTOD*, Nyamnjoh's characters use music to challenge the stereotypes of Mimboland orthodox history as misrepresentative, and present the complexities of African societies, with the masses' attempts to write alternative histories that will help them to regain belief in themselves and combat years of denigration and self-abasement. The music played, sung, danced, and interpreted in the Grand Canari (GC) and other spaces, focuses on the mindboggling contrasts between Beverly Hills (BH) and Swine Quarter (SQ) (literally a pigsty).

While BH (an imitation of the BH in the US), home to privileged Mimbolanders and expatriate whites, swims in the niceties of life ("every comfort in BH seemed exaggerated in its superabundance"), SQ - home to the underprivileged Dieudonnés and Dieumercis - is a "bleeding ghetto" reputed for its "muddy meanders of footpaths and shacks whose walls were delicately sustained by ant-infested wood, human excrement, dog shit ... multitudes of rats and cockroaches that celebrated impunity" (Nyamnjoh 2013: 20, 149). Dieumerci conjectures that "[e]ither God had been waylaid, attacked and his generosity taken to BH, or his sense of creative balance had fled him altogether when it came to deciding what to make of BH" (*TTOD*, 2013: 20). The section asserts that the music thematized in *TTOD* affirms that while the BH of the novel symbolizes "authenticated" history, a place brimming with the niceties of life, the SQ stands for "unauthenticated" history.

TTOD, and the dwelling spaces of BH and SQ, are therefore a musical rendition of a microcosm of the socio-political goings-on in Mimboland but it could also easily represent any African country in the throes of underdevelopment, bad governance, and economic morass. The section also contends that the multilingual musical competences of the characters in *TTOD*, especially Dieudonné, who sings in French, English, Pidgin English, and Arabic, affirm the contribution of the Grand Canarian music Babel to Mimbolandian apocryphalism and heteroglossia. Heterolingual music confers on the apocryphalist the task of a facilitator of contact among different experiences, ideologies, knowledges, and aspirations, for Mimboland social justice and democracy. The diversity (Makossa, Asiko, Bikutsi and Bendskin) and apparent fragmentariness of the music in the novel does not correspond to a Nyamnjohian validation of the fragment and is not even Mimboland fragmentariness at all. Rather, the fragmentariness of the songs represents a call for an inclusiveness which attempts to pay heed to the many-sidedness of Mimbolandian lives which suggest that for one Mimbolander's story to be told musically, many Mimbolanders' stories must be composed and sung and told.

It also suggests that Mimbolanders are all so variously connected that one person's musicalized story is always already the other peoples' unsayable and unwritable stories. This section concludes that the music in *TTOD* testifies to the exclusion, marginalization and peripheralization of the Mimboland masses, a majority group in a subordinate position in wealth, power, and prestige (status), by its leadership, a minority group in a superordinate position in wealth, power, and prestige (status). That is, the content of the songs reveals the existence of a Mimboland system of national apartheid that is emerging because President Longstay's Mimboland national village is dichotomized into what, to borrow from Tehranian (2002: 33), one may call "castles inhabited by the [Mimboland] lords of the manors, protected by moats of electronic surveillance, and surrounded by teeming, restless [Mimboland] peasants living in panoptican societies monitored by the watchmen armed with electronic surveillance systems, from remote sensing satellites to video cameras."

The GC, the space of and for Mimboland musicalized apocryphalism is a marginalized, peripheral urban space physically disconnected from Nyamandem, located outside of Nyamandem's canonical history, and tacked on as an afterthought, considering available city services. The GC is at the same time inside and outside, but being tainted by the touch of the outside, of the other, it loses all claims to being inside the city. The music sung and danced by the denizens of the GC specifically and SQ generally emphasizes musicalized space as a factor of Mimbolandian human relations. Every time the inhabitants of the GC compare their miserable socio-economic conditions to the luxury of the inhabitants of BH, they musically decry Mimboland's broken fluidity and call for a Mimboland network of society that connects all groups and cultures into a conglomeration of heterotopian spaces. The narrator tells us that like the "multitudes of rats and cockroaches that celebrate an impunity of survival against all [SQ] odds," the inhabitants of SQ use the GC as a music site from which they challenge the conservative history of BH (*TTOD*, 2013: 149). By placing SQ (the margin) and BH (the centre) side by side, the music argues that there is an interdependence among Mimboland heterotopian spaces, knowledge, and power. However, it is important to remember that one's musical/social location on the SQ side of Nyamandem power relations does not automatically mean that one is thinking and acting from a subaltern epistemic location. There are characters

(Chopngomna for example) who are musically and socially located in the GC, but circumstances sometime force them to ape the thoughts and actions of those in BH. Thus, using dissident tunes to sing and dance against the official history of BH is not a claim to an unassailable nonconservative history of liberation where any history sung and danced in the GC is automatically hallowed and unorthodox. Rather, the argument is that in *TTOD*, musicalized histories are located either in the dominant or the subaltern side of the power relations of Mimboland.

During one of their bacchanalias at the GC, Dieudonné asks the Canarians "Qui est le type qui a chanté 'no condition is permanent'" (*TTOD* 2013: 63)? In an attempt to answer his question, they introduce us to Mimboland musicians and the diversity of the themes they engage in their songs: Tchana Pierre, "the Salsa King of Mimboland"; Manu Dibango, "the King of Soul Makossa"; Sam Fan Thomas, "Auteur for Makassi"; Tala André-Marie, "Le Roi du Bendskin"; Prince Nico Mbarga, "Père for Sweet Mother"; Lapiro de Mbanga, "l'homme de petit peuple, le president des sauveteurs, whose music is like fire in the backside of big men"; Petit Pays, "un avocat defenseur des femmes"; Sustain Parole, "l'auteur compositeur chop die fait moi bien"; Joli Bébé, "Man for 'L'amour n'as pas de compteur, love does not have a meter"; Bébé Mbonbolono, "the golden voice of modern Makossa who sings "Quelqu'un ne peut pas être quelqu'un sans son quelqu'un quelque part… No one can be someone without her someone somewhere"; Anne-Marie Ndze, Queen Mother of Bikutsi; and Sally Nyollo, l'ambassadrice du genre (*TTOD* 2013: 63-64). These citations confirm that "two principal genres of music have dominated the urban landscape, namely, Makossa, which emanated from the Douala area, and Bikutsi, principally from Beti ethnic group, whose prominence is linked to the emergence of the Biya regime" and that "Makossa and Bikutsi, the respective musical forms of the indigenous Douala and Yaoundé (Sawa and Beti) populations" (Nyamnjoh and Fokwang 2005: 254) have dominated the Cameroon musical scene since independence.

The descriptions of Lapiro de Mbanga as "*l'homme de petit peuple, le président des sauveteurs*, whose music is like fire in the backside of big men" and Bébé Mbonbolono as the singer of "no one can be someone without her someone somewhere" are quite telling. Just as Mbonbolono's idea that "no one can be someone without her someone somewhere" obliquely refers to all forms of favouritism, the qualification of Lapiro's music as fire reminds one of the conflicts between the power of Lapiro's music and the music of President Paul Biya's regime. As Nyamnjoh and Fokwang rightly point out, "Lapiro made a name in the Cameroonian musical scene from 1987 onwards. He was highly appreciated by common people for the use of Pidgin English in his songs but loathed by pro-government politicians for his attacks on President Paul Biya" (Nyamnjoh and Fokwang 2005: 269) because his songs reflected a failing economy and growing social disillusionment. The reference to Lapiro also reminds us that in several multilingual albums such as *Kob Nyé* (Pidgin English expression for "come and see"), *Surface de Réparation* (French expression for "Penalty Area"), *No Make Erreur* (Franglais for "Don't be Mistaken"), and *Mimba We* (Pidgin English for "Remember Us"), *Na You* (Pidgin English for "You are to Blame"), Lapiro challenged orthodox history – represented in the GC by President Longstay's picture with the inscriptions: "'L'homme lion, l'homme des grandes ambitions'.... 'Le Guide Eclairé', 'The Enlightened Guide of Mimboland" (*TTOD*, 2013: 3) – thereby writing apocryphal history from the SQ of musical studios that extended from Cameroon to Nigeria and Benin.

His anti-establishmentarianism was so undaunting that in 2008, Lapiro criticized Cameroonian President, Paul Biya, in the song titled

"Constitution Constipée" ("Constipated Constitution"); denouncing the proposed erasure of the constitutional clause which limited presidents to two seven-year terms. The government responded by banning "Constitution Constipée" from the airwaves. However, thousands of Cameroonian students later used the song as an anthem as they rallied and rioted in the streets in February 2008 in protest against the proposed constitutional change, which would allow Biya to run for a new term in 2011. On April 9, 2008, Lapiro was arrested and charged with complicity in looting, destruction of property, arson, obstructing streets, degrading public or classified property, and organizing illegal gatherings. Two days later, the Cameroonian parliament adopted the new "constipated constitution" and on September 24, 2008, Lapiro was sentenced by the Tribunal de Grande Instance (TGI) to three years in the New Bell prison after a trial that he referred to as "Kafkaesque," saying that his fate had been "decided in advance," despite the utter lack of evidence against him.

By referencing Lapiro's music as that which is like fire in the backside of big men, Nyamnjoh intertextually offers a contrasting panoramic vista of the unauthenticatedness and shantiness of the GC bar and the authenticatedness and affluence of BH. The latter is home to big men such as colonial settlers and the leaders of Mimboland while the former is a ghetto for the downtrodden majority of Nyamandem (Yaoundé). Although Nyamandem is a deeply divided city and the maintenance of an apparent hierarchy and distance between the "rich" and the "poor" is central to its epistemo-ontological existence, Lapiro's music asserts that the experiences of the two groups are connected. While the bar is the ministry of enjoyment for the powerless, BH is the Eldorado of Nyamandem reeking with extravagant luxuries (*TTOD* 2013: 2, 3). For those who drink at the GC, BH is the poor man's idea of paradise (*TTOD* 2013: 3). The intertextuality between Nyamnjoh's *TTOD* and Lapiro's music asseverates the stark contrasts between the wealth, centre, and power of BH and the poverty, margin, and powerlessness of the GC.

These contrasts point to four postcolonial concerns that Lapiro addresses in his music: the demographic and geographical consequences of French and British colonialism; the material and economic realities of colonialism that enabled the colonizer and subsequent-Mimboland leaders to amass vast fortunes; the distinctions between the leaders who are the beneficiaries of colonialism and the disenfranchised natives who are the losers; and the persistent influence of the colonial experience on Mimboland. This is because the BH-centre versus the GC-periphery and the BH-power versus the GC-powerlessness binaries are reminiscent of colonialism's the colonizer versus the colonized, the metropolis versus the empire, the civilized versus the primitive structures. The BH versus GC binaries thus represent the continued survival of a colonial hierarchy that accommodates BH's impulse to exploit and civilize the GC. Such staggering differences explain why upon his release from prison on April 8, 2011, Lapiro returned to the stage on July 13, 2011, in Lille, France and during the Summer of 2011 he also played in Lausanne, Brussels, Paris, Barcelona and at various venues in the United States, Canada, and Britain.

Another episode where music is used for apocryphalism is seen when Dieudonné sings Remmy Ongala's song, "No Money, No Life" (*TTOD* 2013: 84). The song, whose lyrics Dieudonné has mastered, is a message that a city dweller sends back to his grandmother and grandfather informing them of his/her city duels. In the first part the singer urges his/her young brother "to take [his/her] greetings back home/Tell my grandmother that/I am still sweating in town/Tell my grandfather that I am still sweating in town" (*TTOD* 2013: 85). In the second part he/she sings that "[l]ife in town needs more money/If you don't have money you will suffer; you will never sleep; you can never eat; you won't wash your clothes/Everybody needs money, more money/Life without money is like punishment/Life without money no respect" (*TTOD* 2013: 85). By exposing the reality of city life especially in SQ, by scanning the field of the socio-economic possible in which the Mimboland "real" occupies merely a tiny spot and plot, Ongala's song, a shard of "unattested" history, paves the way for a critical attitude and activity which alone can transform the present predicament of Mimbolanders. The contemplation of alternative solutions to the festering problems of Mimboland's present reality of socio-economic morass is therefore a necessary condition for historical change. By exposing the overwhelming financial demands of city life, Ongala and by extension Nyamnjoh, explores the dynamism of poverty and how the downtrodden of Mimboland cope with their condition of desperation and helplessness, revealing at the same time the resilient side of Mimbolanders who keep hope alive against all odds (Nyamnjoh, 2013:20). The songs content alludes to the BH-SQ asymmetry, thereby testifying that, as Madina Tlostanova argues, "the colonial city is a playful space of mimicry, a non-identical copy of the metropolis, where recognizable signs of colonization shaken the stability of the original imperial capital" (Tlostanova, 2013: 25). *TTOD*, Tlostanova continues, captures the postcolonial urban space of Nyamandem undergoing Nyamnjohian "interpretations in the frame of the fantastic, the magic, the metamorphing, giving birth to imagined hybrid cities, particularly [because] the time aspect of the [Nyamandem] chronotope corresponds to the moment of disintegration of empire" (Tlostanova 2013: 25).

"No Money, No Life" is Dieudonné's way of asserting that instead of simply tracing the scars of a Francophonized or Anglophonized history of aggressive capitalism on the faces of different Mimboland cities such as Nyamandem (a distorted pronunciation of Yaounde) and Sawang (a disguised reference to the town of Douala and its predominantly Sawa inhabitants and culture), Nyamnjoh's unorthodox transcultural chronotope rehabilitates spaces – the GC, the "bleeding ghetto" and the shanty – and their denizens (Dieumerci, Dieudonné, Tsanga, Precious, Mamelle) and gives them a new musicalized impetus to live and not just to survive. The GC becomes a utopian urban space for sweating out poverty and lack, an imagined parallel world that engenders what Walter Mignolo identifies as a universal that is a pluriversal (2000:16–17). Thus, a concrete Mimboland universal in the Mignoloian sense would include all the iconoclastic musical (Makossa, Asiko, Bikutsi and Bendskin) particularities towards a nonconformist socialization of power. The principle of hope sustained by the sweating Canarians is important in *TTOD* because it focuses our attention on concrete moments in Mimboland history that point the way towards an actual transformation of the Mimboland material world. The luminous aesthetic quality of *TTOD* derives from the fact that these concrete moments, such as the singer's undaunting sweating, even though they are fragmentary, allow Mimbolanders to realize what is not yet but can become; for example, a Mimboland society not dominated by orthodox history and its aggressive capitalism. Insofar as *TTOD*'s musical ("No Money, No Life") formulations illuminate what is missing and might still come, they instil hope in the Canarians and provide the impetus for individual and collective change from the dogmatic tendencies of a rigid bureaucratic system. Thus, "No Money, No Life" just like the GC where it is sung, is not only a clarion call for change but also a challenge to orthodoxy.

Perhaps, the most committed musical episode in *TTOD* is the band set up by the proprietress of the GC, Madame Gazellia Mamelle, to promote a new form of Bikutsi dance style called *Pédale* (to cycle). To the narrator, Bukutsi offers the Canarians an opportunity to scream with their feet and "once a moving Bikutsi piece is played [in the GC], dancers crush together on the circular floor at the centre of the gigantic wooden block, shaking in frenzied trances, intoxicated with physical and emotional pleasure, yearning to purge themselves of the frustrations of life at the margins" (*TTOD*, 2013: 183). Threatened by "death induced by poverty, plagues, disasters and the indifference of those in [power]" the Canarians use each vibrant song to melt away their "accumulated uncertainties and insecurities" as they "cycle away intensely" deriding "those who have made it a habit of poking fun at ordinary lives" (*TTOD* 2013: 183). Thanks to the band, Dieumerci's girlfriend, Precious, "has risen to ghetto stardom with "Swine Quarter", her debut album" and "even the rats, lizards and cockroaches on the rafters and in the crevices of [GC] seem to sing along when Precious appears on stage" (*TTOD* 2013: 184). Upon release of the album, Precious has become known as "SIDA (salaire insuffisant difficilement acquis)" (*TTOD* 2013: 188) – insufficient salary difficult to acquire. As an apocryphalist who knows where the shoe of SQ life's uncertainties pinches them the most, Precious sings the Mimboland masses' plight: "'Le Seigneur regarda notre travail et en fut content. Il vit notre salaire, se retourna et pleura amèrement. (The Lord looked at our work and was pleased). He looked at our salary, turned around and cried bitterly" (*TTOD* 2013: 188). She concludes that, "'some days [Swine Quarterians] have work, some days [they] don't; but the price of bread must always be met'" (*TTOD* 2013: 188). We further learn that the lead song of Precious' album, *Tremblement des Fesses*, "has been banned from the national radio and television by the authorities whom *radio trottoir* says "adore the tune in the privacy of bars and nightclubs with the help of the bottle and have been known to keep their mistresses busy with the new dimensions of resting inspired by Precious" (*TTOD* 2013: 189). But like most acts of apocryphalism, the ban "has made her music more popular even among the high and mighty [Beverly Hillsians], who regularly use it at private parties and health fitness clubs that promise long life through 'le confort du sport'" (*TTOD* 2913: 189).

The wordings of Precious' music unequivocally capture the spirit of Mimboland in all its mind-numbing contradictions. Hers is the quintessential music of that condition of botched decolonization and ambiguous modernity known as democratization. In his discussion of Fela's music cited earlier, Olaniyan recalls how "Retired General Olusegun Obasanjo, during his first session as dictatorial head of state of Nigeria, once accused Fela of 'destroying the lives of Nigerian youth" and how "Fela, who cannot be defeated in rhetorical combat, retorted that Obasanjo had 'destroyed the lives of an entire nation'" (*TTOD* 2013: 83-84). Even though Precious' music laments the fact that President Longstay, just like his Nigerian doppelgänger, has destroyed the lives of the entire Mimboland, the leadership of Mimboland has ironically banned Precious' song because, to them, like Fela did with his Afrobeat, Precious is using hers to destroy the lives of Mimbolandian youth. What the ban implies is that Precious, through her music, has successfully exposed to young Mimbolanders new, rebellious, and impatient aspirations that are pushing out of their hearts and minds any affection for the leadership and the state. As a composite phenomenon, she is helping to democratize socio-economic, political, and cultural Mimboland thinking by constantly transgressing and pushing the boundaries of what can be thought and imagined especially through provocatively unorthodox song titles such as "Tremblement des Fesses" and "Dear Monsieur Kondom." The leadership may be right, after all: Precious is destroying the Mimboland youth, but only the kind of mindless, pliant youth that Nyamnjoh has portrayed elsewhere (Marxy Wang (*SF* 2008), Marie-Claire, Marie-Louise, Chantal and Monique (*ANFM* 2011) and Fanda Yanda (*Mind Searching* 2007a)), a dictator, craves. Precious' music may not overthrow the government, but her overall contribution is much more far-reaching: her music's potent detachment of the power of truth from any putative hegemony that the Mimboland state might continue to profess.

Precious' lyrics about the Lord looking at the work of Swine Quarterians and smiling and then looking at their salaries and weeping profusely reminds one of Fanda Yanda's poem in which he contrasts Briqueterie and Bastos: "There were compounds sad and dark/Which I passed onto the park/Men that smiled day and night/Lived a life without light/In these compounds sad and dark/But, towering high and bright/Stood a lone house, mad with light/Light on hedges, grasses, tress/Made a man live in peace/Here, towering high and bright" (*Mind Searching* 116). The narrative of this poem like that of Precious' lyrics lingers in the public mind as a guide for postcolonial socio-political action and an obstinate reminder of the never-plugged gap between the promises of the likes of President Longstay and the reality of SQ. Precious' experiences and the promptings they give her to critique Longstaycentrism mythically conjure an image of a future and better Mimboland which, like a utopia, is still unfulfilled but whose foundation has been laid by the courage that Precious' music has given her fans: "Like all ordinary Mimbolanders in bleeding ghettoes like Swine Quarter, her fans have refused to give the powerful the pleasure of leading them away in handcuffs. They insist on their share of life's delights with such spontaneous exclamations as: 'Qu'ils ne nous tiennent pas par le ventre'" (*TTOD* 2013: 189) Such a Mimboland world is perceived as desirable as a BH world not so much bound to come as one which should come to SQ. It is also a world involved with a measure of hazard and it seems that a better world will come to pass only if fostered by the deliberate collective action of the Mimbolanders. Most importantly, lyrical narratives such as Nyamnjoh's, with their nonlinear plot, point out that the days when contemporary life was frequently likened to a journey characterized by progress and enlightenment through time, and with an itinerary drawn in advance by a destination he/she wanted to reach, are gone.

The Talking Drums of Black & White Nightclub and the Musical Names of Gender Hegemony

This section draws on the sexually suggestive expression "perpendicular expressions of horizontal desires" that Bobinga Iroko uses in *MBA* to describe Saturday-evening-nocturnal activities at the Black & White Nightclub, Sakersbeach, to argue that one of the major conduits of Nyamnjoh's condemnation of gender oppression and misrule is the clubbers' grotesque response to a music that forces customs, bodies and self-presentations to succumb to grotesqueries. That is, the music is considered talking drums that musically delineate genderized rules thereby naming gender hegemony at the club where the dancers and their actions are caricatured through distortions or striking incongruities in their appearances, shapes, or mannerisms. Bodacious fantasy and the bizarre become mainstream and studied conspicuousness the order of the nights. The world of the club and its imagery project Mimboland men and women as nymphomaniacally eccentric, strange, ridiculous, and absurd. This is affirmed through Bobinga Iroko's incommensurable detailed interpretations of the songs and the dance steps of the young girls; the sheer cacophony of their (mis)demeanours, the hellish maelstrom of their flexible agitations and their absolute commitment to wanton bodily gratification. The section concludes that Nyamnjoh uses the grotesque dance steps of the nightclub's nocturnal carnivals to generate both a logic and an aesthetic, a transgression that affirms the distinctions between humans or men and animals or women and between classes of Mimbolanders and their mannerisms.

On their way to Black & White, Iroko and Loveless pass by "young and old women of all shapes and sizes, dressed in skimpy attire and headed in the same direction" (Nyamnjoh 2009:81). Iroko tells Loveless that "the younger of them" are going "to the nightclub, but the older ones are heading for the bars, chicken parlours and other popular spots. All of them are fishers of men" (*MBA* 2009: 81). The songs played variously affirm profanities and ribaldries like "there's no such thing as love"; Mimboland men suck inspiration from women's breasts; "Man is the belly and the under belly"; "The husband of another is sweet and the wife of another is sweet"; girls' perfume "smell like grilled fish"; and Mimboland women die for a man's "Stick of Authority" (*MBA* 2009: 81, 82, 83). The club's DJ prioritizes playing songs of the rawest, crudest, most uninhibited musician, Petit Pays, whose songs are very popular because they are luring in their provocativeness and irresistible obscenity. Though he describes himself as "the defence lawyer for women," he proceeds to invite men "to 'inject', 'pump', 'pierce', 'drill', 'fill up', and, like the praying mantis, 'kill this evening' and 'finish off' the very same women he loves and protects" (*MBA* 2009: 84). His songs affirm "phallocracy or 'the dictatorship of the penis' stretching from the helm of state through universities and schools down to the ghettoes and villages" (*MBA* 2009: 84) They celebrate "the pride that [comes] with having 'an active penis'" as Mimboland men champion their pleasure through subduing women (*MBA* 2009: 84). Loveless remarks that the club "'is pregnant with desired meaning and the meaning of desire'" and Iroko concludes that "[w]hat rules this land of Mimbo is not the Longstays who keep re-inventing sterility. What rules it is the Mimbo in all and sundry or what you see on the dance floor: ambitions of the body and the body of ambition" (*MBA* 2009:

85). Listening and dancing to Mimboland's rich and fascinating music on social virtues (love, honesty, hard work, etc.), social ills (jealousy, corruption, prostitution, etc.) and power relations between men and women and at various levels of society is a subtle way by which Nyamnjoh introduces elements of the carnivalesque because the music creates a mood that subverts and liberates Mimboland assumptions of the dominant style or atmosphere through the humour and "chaos" generated by the singing and dancing.

Granted that the carnivalesque has always aimed at subversion by standing in opposition to the sacred, and that governments have always viewed the carnival as a profane organ, Nyamnjoh's introduction of it is a subtle way of castigating the Mimboland leadership's pretentiousness. The music played and danced at the club is, therefore, a form of transgression perpetrated in thought, word, and deed within the confines and conventions of the Mimboland gender system. The musical festival both permits and ensures the exposition of the licensed mayhem of Mimboland men over women. This explains why, just like carnival practices, the singing and dancing gestures of the musicians (such as petit Pays) and dancers (such as the young girls' perpendicular expressions of horizontal desires) respectively, are rude, provocative, shocking, and offensive to Mimboland genderized morality. Nyamnjoh uses the grotesque ribaldries and movements on the dance floor of the GC to critique the Mimboland dominant ideology which has set the terms designating the masculine gender as high and feminine gender as low. In line with Stallybrass and White's discussion on carnival, Nyamnjoh's use of singing and dancing in this manner is a way of contesting "the most powerful ruses of the dominant [groups] that critique can only exist in the language of 'reason', 'pure knowledge' and 'seriousness'" (Stallybrass and White 1986:43). Thus, as Stallybrass and White further explain, "[a]gainst this ruse [there is] . . .

the logic of the grotesque, of excess, of the lower bodily stratum. This logic could unsettle 'given' social positions and interrogate the rules of inclusion, exclusion and domination which structured the social ensemble" (Stallybrass and White 43). Through the musical festival, Nyamnjoh affirms that there has been a Mimboland recurrent pattern where the masculine gender has continuously attempted to suppress the feminine gender for reasons of phallocratic prestige and status, only to discover, not only that it is in some way frequently dependent upon that feminine-Other (in the classic Hegelian master-slave dichotomy), but also that the masculine gender includes that feminine gender symbolically, as a primary eroticized constituent of its own fantasy life. The result of that pattern is what, to borrow from Stallybrass and White, one may categorize as "a mobile, conflictual fusion of power, fear and desire in the construction of subjectivity: a psychological dependence upon precisely those Others which are being rigorously opposed and excluded at the social level. It is for this reason that what is socially peripheral is so frequently symbolically central" (Stallybrass and White 5). Even though the music repeatedly tells us that the Mimboland feminine-Other is despised and denied (even by those who claim to be "the defence lawyer for women" (*MBA* 2009: 84) at the level of political organization and social being, "it is instrumentally constitutive of the shared imaginary repertoires of the dominant culture" (*MBA* 2009: 6). Granted that Black & White just like the music festival "is pregnant with desired meaning and the meaning of desire", this section affirms Iroko's mantra that "What rules this land of Mimbo is not the Longstays who keep re-inventing [genderized] sterility. What rules it is the Mimbo in all and sundry or what you see on the dance floor: ambitions of the body and the body of ambition" (*MBA* 2009: 85).

Conclusion: Giving Peace a Chant and Chanting Peace a Gift

Drawing on Nyamnjoh's thematization of music, This chapter has demonstrated that tyrannical leadership, political misconduct, flagrant disregard for rules and entrenched nepotism are the currency of official transactions in Mimboland, thereby affirming the paper's argument that Mimboland is Cameroon in miniature. It has also affirmed that social virtues (love, honesty, hard work, just to name but a few), social ills (jealousy, corruption, prostitution, etc.) and power relations between men and women and at various levels of society are some of the components of postcolonial Mimboland that catalyse Makossa, Bikutsi, Asiko and Bendskin. Nyamnjoh or most appropriately the musicians in Nyamnjoh's works seem(s) to be exasperated not so much with the crises as with their seeming permanence, their normalization, their totalization and fetishization. Nyamnjoh portrays Mimboland popular music as a stimulus for consumer desire; a site for the iteration and reiteration of Mimboland dominant values; a galvanizer of commercialized leisure that provides distraction and diversion rather than fulfilment; and an emplacement where ruling ideologies are simultaneously articulated and disarticulated. In Achebe's *Anthills of the Savannah*, the leader of the Abazonian Delegation to Bassa tells his fellow Abazonians that the Almighty has divided humans into three: those apportioned the gift to tell their fellows that the time to get up has finally come; those given the eagerness "to rise with racing blood and put on their garbs of war and go to the boundary of their town to engage the invading enemy boldly in battle"; and those others whose part is to recount the story when the struggle is ended. (1998:113). To him, "[t]he sounding of the battle-drum; the fierce waging of war itself; and the telling of the story afterwards" are all important but the story takes the eagle-feather because it continues "beyond the war and the warrior; outlives the sound of war-drums and the exploits of brave fighters; saves our progeny from blundering like blind beggars; owns, escorts and directs us; makes us different from cattle; sets one people apart from their neighbours; [and it is] everlasting" (Achebe 1998:114). I have paraphrased/quoted the Abazonian leader's three categorizations at length because since independence, the persistence of inequalities especially between Francophones and Anglophones produced a cacophony of self-opinionated Achebesque-like or Abazonian timekeepers, warriors and storytellers whose activities, since 2016, have crystalized into an Anglophone crisis that has balkanized the country into four anti-fundamentalist fundamentalism groups: separatists, restorationists, federalists and unitarists.

The Anglophone crisis has been raging and ravaging for more than three years. As I struggle to conclude This chapter, a paraphrased version of the image painted by W. H. Auden in his poem, "September 1, 1939," keeps coming to my mind: Mimbolanders sit on the monument of the Fiftieth Anniversary of Independence and Reunification in Buea, uncertain and afraid as their clever hopes expire, of a low dishonest half a century of independence. Waves of anger and fear circulate over the bright and darkened lands of Cameroon, obsessing their private lives; the unmentionable odour of death offends the atmosphere. All they crave, just like the musicians in *SF*, *ANFM*, *TTOD* and *MBA*, is a voice to sing to undo the folded lie, the romantic lie in the brain of the sensual man-in-the-street and the lie of authority whose buildings grope the sky: there is no such thing as the Mimboland state and no one exists alone; hunger allows no choice to the Mimboland citizen or the police; they must love one another or die. Defenceless under the night their Mimboland world in stupor lies; yet, dotted everywhere, ironic points of light flash out wherever the just exchange their messages (1979: 86, 88).

Perhaps, the lesson we learn from the musicians in *SF*, *ANFM*, *TTOD* and *MBA* is that very few problems can be solved by pretending that they do not exist. In a Cameroonian society plagued by pervasive hegemonic stratification and subordination, marginalization-bound problems require marginalization-based remedies. Yet the idea that Cameroonians can and should be marginalization-blind has emerged as the preferred response to Anglophone crisis in both public policy and private life in Cameroon. Separatists, restorationists, federalists and unitarists are a series – indeed, a tangle of Lipstzian (1994: 6-7) dangerous crossroads. And although the Anglophone Cameroon crisis crossroads like any other crossroads is a tricky, even dangerous place, it has the advantage of being a site from which Cameroonians can look in many directions and walk in many directions at once going beyond the Achebesque timekeeper, warrior and storyteller to give peace a chant and chant peace a gift.

Chapter 7

Longue Longue: History, Identity and Music and the 2016 Anglophone Crisis in Cameroon

Godwin Gham Nyinchiah

Introduction: Origins of Music and history in Cameroon

This study sets out to ascertain whether Longue Longue, the Cameroonian artist, produce his art primarily to inform, educate and entertain his audience or for a revolutionary purpose of changing society. The chapter further analyses how Longue Longue was able to capitalize on orality, and his personal terminological innovation to oppose the Biya Regime for its failure to integrate all Cameroonians into one-fold. He sees the attempt by the minority Anglophones in Cameroon to secede as a failure on the part of the regime that is oppressive and dictatorial. In order to facilitate the task of the research, the following two main analytical approaches are employed: new historicism and pragmatic functionalism. New historicism is appropriate primarily because it cuts across other disciplines like culture, sociology, linguistics, politics, and anthropology. Since music is part and parcel of a people's culture, the approach becomes very relevant here. Pragmatism on the other hand, highlights the commitment of the artist. The study posits that due to the entrenchment of capitalist/materialistic attitudes among the people in Africa in general and Cameroon in particular, revolutionary oral artists will always be needed to create awareness in the people relative to a change of mentality. It also argues that Longue Longue as an artist under reference is committed and determined to 'change his society'. The study further avers that the artist is a true practitioner of realism and will as long as people exist; continue to produce such songs to reflect the changing nature of society.

Perhaps it might be an over statement to state that music in Cameroon is a new creation as most scholars and researchers have been attempted to conclude. Music as used in this chapter is linked to post independence Cameroon and decolonization. The decolonization of Africa saw the rise to power of a political class in some countries that has further alienated the population. This political class is dictatorial in nature-the dictators have simply decided to hang on to power in total disregard of the wishes of the-often, poor and disillusioned-population. As a result, the post-colonial history of Africa is plagued by military coups, human rights abuse, corruption, poverty, tribalism, and identity crisis with some groups within the nation state attempting to secede and create their own nation. However, in many of these countries, the crackdown on most dissident voices has continued with impunity. As a consequence, political activists have had to find other ways of opposing those in power. In Cameroon, one way out has been the return to oral tradition where singers have borrowed lexical items, concepts, and practices to illustrate the excesses of those in power.

The relationship between history, music and society has long been established by Classic as Plato and Aristotle. Aristotle in *The Poetics* (Plato 1955:17) while acclaiming poetry/music above history, distinguished the latter as dealing with the particular and the former as dealing with the universal. This distinction consists in the methods of these art forms. Bearing in the mind that history is party of society, so is music. This chapter foregrounds the relationship between musicians and the reconstruction of identities in post-colonial Cameroon. In order to make a case for understanding the dynamics of agency and identity politics among musicians, Longue Longue picked up the case of the Anglophone Struggle for recognition in the post-Colonial Cameroun State. It argues that musicians have tended to appropriate their creative efforts as part of their drive for the reconstruction of history and identity. It further argues that politicians in Cameroon have tended to appropriate musicians and their creative efforts as part of their drive for power. Some musicians have refused to be at the beck and call of politicians and have tended to criticize and ridicule those in power. Others have seen in such invitations an opportunity for greater recognition and respectability. Some have sought to straddle both worlds, serving politicians while also pursuing their art in the interest of other constituencies. Their different responses notwithstanding, there is evidence that the fortunes and statuses of musicians have been transformed with changing political regimes and notions of identity politics.

The manner in which music is produced and appropriated, by whom and how, is inseparable from power relations: political, cultural, economic, and gendered (Nyamnjoh and Fokwang 2005:252). However, over the past decades, visual as well as non-visual sources have evolved as powerful means of gaining access to alternative histories. Nkwi (2010:39), holds that, it is increasingly, acknowledged that non-visual and visual records, whether art or documentary offer new routes to the past, especially where the life experiences and expression of people in most societies have been marginalized in the conventional dominant written words. This chapter shows how orality/music amongst some Cameroonian musicians (for the purpose of this chapter Longue Longue) can be used as an alternative source of history. The significance of this chapter lies in the fact this source of history has not been adequately handled by Cameroonian scholars, researchers (Nyamnjoh and Fokwang 2005); Nkwi 2010; Jick 2012, 2015; Tala 2013; Vakunta 2014; Kah, 2016) and musicians that have worked in the domain of Anglophone nationalism and history.

Longue Longue focuses his songs not only on ex-raying the evils of colonialism in Africa but as from 2008 maintain that the post-colonial Cameroon regime has maintain and continue to exploit the masses. More so, he opined that the Anglophones in Cameroon have been subjected to marginality and second-class citizens within Cameroon. Hitherto, Lapiro De Mbanga, came up during the reintroduction of multiparty politics in Cameroon, as a prominent musician whose genre of protest music attracted wide popularity. The Biya regime's attempt to co-opt Lapiro, and his consequently ambiguous position, led to deep tensions between him and his supporters, on the one hand, and between him and members of the Biya regime, on the other. However, by becoming a member of the ruling party, Lapiro has made known his political stance, although he remains deeply critical of the regime and of Paul Biya in particular. Some musicians who came up in the era of pluralism in Anglophone Cameroon where; Prince Yerima Afo-Akom, John Minang, Eric Rogers Ngringeh (aka Zuluman),and Loh Benson. In as much as their songs showered praises to the Social Democratic Front opposition Party (SDF), and its leader Ni John Fru Ndi, they however, included the reconstruction of Anglophone identities in Cameroon. They were of the hope that the SDF and the era of the reintroduction of multiparty politics in African and Cameroon was to be a window through which Anglophones contribution to nation building would be recognized and projected (Nyinchiah 2016: 59). Yet to a majority of Anglophone Cameroonians it was an era of their further exclusion, assimilation, the politics of divide-and-rule, and more the enactment of legislations to further co-opt them in the Francophone dominated administration.

In Cameroon, therefore, the role of democracy in societal transformation and nation-building has been compromised by political and social structures created during more than three decades of autocratic rule that still underline the practical and moral workings of the state today. Western democracy remains mired in rigging cleavages that find expression in parochial tendencies ranging from divide and rule to ethnicity and to regionalism being orchestrated by the state's political elites and those loyal to the ruling regime in a neo-patrimonial manner (Nkwi 2013). As a result, the ability to mobilise all and sundry towards a meaningful democratic culture and development is limited. This chapter therefore is a contribution towards the utilization of orality in the historical reconstruction of Anglophone identity in Cameroon. However, much remains to be known about the relationship between music and politics, and on how musicians, politicians and political communities all strive to appropriate each other in different ways and contexts.

The Evolution and features of Political folk-songs and music in Anglophone Cameroon.

The evolution and subsequent development of folk songs in Anglophone Cameroon and elsewhere in the country dates back to the early 19th century when the different Fondoms were founded, the song evolved from the socio- cultural and political realities of the people and they started as forms of entertainment and gradually developed into an expression of rejection of native social, cultural and political issues that surrounded the Grassland people[39] and post-colonial Cameroon. The songs were stored in people's memories and were usually provoked by various events. Such events could either be pleasant or unpleasant.

These songs are short lyric text which is set to music and which

---

[39]Personal discussion with Joko Evaristus, August, 10, 2020.

appeals to a wide range of people. It is an integral part of the peoples culture and heritage and contributes to ceremonial and festival occasions. It is spontaneous and takes the whole of the people's experience as its subject matter. It is performed generally for the artistic gratification of the folk singer and his audience in a restricted context. According to Bole Butake (1994:44):

> The song is the most basic and profuse form of emotive expression in African societies. The African manifests his feelings through an outburst of song when he loves and when he hates, when he works and when he plays, when he is at peace and when he fights, when a child is born and when death takes its toll....

Therefore, the songs are a function of correct and acceptable moral conduct of the society and are intended to have a positive moral influence on the community. In other words, they, they exert a strong moral force and are often used didactically and as social correctives.

Music have developed in Cameroon differently, appropriated and projected differently by the post-colonial Cameroon regimes. It is vital to note that Cameroon graduated from the British and French colonial cultures, with different values. One section of the Country-French Cameroun gained independence on the 1 January, 1960, while the British zone gained independence through a United Nation Organized (UNO) Plebiscite on the 11 February 1961 and by 1 October achieved independence by reunifying the majority French zone.

From the Cameroun first Republic under President Ahmadou Babatoure Ahidjo (1960-1982), to the second Republic Under President Batholomewe Bi Mvodo Paul Biya (1982-2020) it is observe that two principal genres of music have dominated the urban landscape, namely, makossa, which emanated from the Douala area, and bikutsi, principally from the Beti ethnic group, whose prominence is linked to the emergence of the Biya regime. This historical narrative is intertwined with the history of prominent artists, such as Manu Dibango, whose genre of makossa brought world fame to Cameroon's popular music, but whose attempts to win recognition for music as art and musicians as artists met with repeated frustrations by politicians(Nyamnjoh and Fokwang 2005). If makossa started as the music of Douala and assumed a nationwide appeal, nowhere did it face stiffer internal competition than in Yaoundé, especially after the coming to power in 1982 of President Paul Biya. Bikutsi, the music of the Beti, has risen to rival makossa nationally and internationally (Ibid). This has set the stage of the crux of the matter (Nyamnjoh and Fokwang 2005). Hardly has it been a policy in a country with cultural diversity, over 250 ethnic groups with different cultures has only one being dominant and imposed on the people. The Anglophones in Cameroon have hardly have an hour to savour the test of music from their own communities.[40] This sometimes is done when there are traces of resistance and attempt to secede that the national Television Cameroon Radio and Television (CRTV) will within seconds and for a few days have the some of the music screened.

Not only have Biya's governments been dominated by ministers

---

[40]This fact holds true because from independence, the post-colonial Cameroon state leadership has been in the hands of two powerful Francopnones leaders, who from every indication have been projecting the culture of their different ethnic groups. For the Anglophones it is sign of the fact that they do not possess real political power to force their culture be screen frequently on the national television. The local and regional levels the Anglophones do enjoy and savor the test of their own genre of music.

from his Beti ethnic group,(Takougang and Krieger;1998)they have consistently paid special attention to the promotion of Bikutsi and other cultural products from his home area, notwithstanding official rhetoric on balanced regional development and national integration (Nyamnjoh and Fokwang 2005). The advent of national television in 1985, with a Beti as the general manager, brought Bikutsi to the living rooms of viewers even in regions originally dominated by makossa and other music forms. The fact that the management of the national television corporation CRTV has remained firmly in Beti hands since the advent of television has meant more than 35 years of privileged attention for Bikutsi (Nyamnjoh and Fokwang 2005).

Meanwhile, the Bamenda Grasslands are arguably the region where there has been the least achievement in producing local pop stars. The reasons are obvious; it is part of the minority region of Anglophone Cameroon, secondly, the people and the region have been labelled as rebellious, opposing any decision coming from Yaoundé and the Francophone regime and thirdly, it is the birth place of the first opposition party in the era of the reintroduction of multiparty politics in Cameroon in the 1990s as well as the strong hold of the called for the returned of the Federal system and state arrangements of 1961 and of extreme secession and independence for the former British Southern Cameroons.[41] The grassland song are deeply rooted in traditional folk-songs that were popularized in the 1990s. Lob Benson and John Minang submits that:

> We animated in the political rallies in Bamenda organized by the opposition parties who came in to campaign…. The rallies to the buildup of the October 1992 Presidential elections made our local music and some of the artist in this region to be popular ….From the piano, I

---

[41] My fieldwork notes for my, Phd field, 2020.

added other genres of music, typical of the Bamenda Grassland like the popular Jang music, John Minang and others appropriated Bottle Dance and Mbakugalum ... The identity of the North West people….(Nyinchiah 2016:101).

From all intent, the artists from the Anglophone regions of Cameroon use the political platform of the 1990s to showcase their talents in music and orality. Nyamnjoh and Fokwang (2005) argues that orality and music in Cameroon varied and change with the advent of the Biya Regime, which laid emphasis on Bikutsi,- the local music of the Betis/Ewondos, the Presidents ethnic group, in favour of the popular Sawa makossa of the Duala. It was therefore, hoped that if an Anglophone becomes president, he would popularized their own brand of music and orality. John Minang a popular *Mbakugalum* and *Bottle Dance* artist opined that:

> ... 'All of us who played music during this period, paid homage to the new political party that was born in our town'…. Loh Benson animated with the piano. When he got tired, the *Mbakugalum* took over, and then the bottle dance and njang…Most of the artists in Bamenda fine-tuned their current songs from this period… It was an opportunity for us to portray are culture, the kind of music, songs, and dance of the people typical of this region (Nyinchiah 2016:102).

Jang, bottle dance and Mbakuglum were appropriated within the period of multi-party politics in Cameroon. As the region of the strongest political opposition party in Cameroon and the Anglophone 'strong man' John Fru Ndi , the songs were played to signify his entrance and exit in a political rally. It became a symbol for the Anglophone musical identity in Cameroon. It is clear that Grasslanders love their indigenous music heritage. Gatherings and occasions at home in Cameroon or in the diaspora are always an excuse for singing, drumming, and dancing to Grassland rhythms. Amateur audio and video recordings are easy to come by, and are reproduced infinitely and circulated among Grass landers at home and abroad. Dedicated performers of various dances are not difficult to find in cities where Grassland elites may want to show off or entertain their guests with a bit of 'our culture'. Not wanting to be totally eclipsed, some elites have attempted to sponsor the production of local Grasslands talents, some of whom (Francis Ndom, Prince Afo-a-kom, and 'Bottle Dance' musicians like Richard Nguti, John Minang, Ni Ken and Depipson) have made it to the national scene with music from their home area. These and other budding talents in the region and elsewhere shop around for sponsors ranging from businesses to NGOs and publicity-seeking elites, through other artists and the national orchestra.

Given the agitations and forceful recognition of the Anglophones in the political space in Cameroon, a majority of the Francophone musicians have appropriated within their music genre to include pidgin English in their songs. Lapira the De Mbanga who had been a township taxi driver in Bamenda gained that popularity among the English-speaking population and more within the scholarship world among the Anglophone writers. Most of the literature on Lapiro point to him as a great critic of the Biya regime, which is welcome by Anglophone scholarship. Its hardly, a surprised that other francophone singers like Petite Pay, Sergeo Polo and Longue Longue are among the popular Francophone musicians in Anglophone Cameroon. This would set the stage for our ex-tray of Longue Longue and his songs.

Why Longue Longue-the Choice of Artist

In spite of the long list, this study limits itself to Longue Longue . This choice has been influenced first, by the bilingual nature of Cameroon. Longue Longue has blind his Francophone background with some pidgin English for the understanding of his English-Speaking audience. Secondly, I submit that Longue Longue is not only a highly "acerbic critic and articulate commentator but also one of the most eloquent, singers as from the year 2000, when he was highly celebrated in Africa and Cameroon, when he release the album, 'Ayo Africa', future in the film with one of Guinness and South African star Michael Power. The fact that he has not caught the attention of most Anglophone scholars like Lapiro and, he now represent one of popular musicians in contemporary Cameroon" intense of the political space and critic of the regime also influenced this researcher's choice. Third, the artist has address theme of Anglophone nationalism and refer to himself as liberator of the people, thereby sympathizing with the Anglophone unlike other Francophone and Anglophone musicians who have remained mute since the event of the 'Anglophone spring' in 2016. Fourth, the artists is aware that the popular song is folklore and not just a political song, so he graft on the body of the social and political ideas, artistic feathers that are sometimes, surprising in his brilliance. Fifth, Longue Longue as an artist do not only criticize the evils of the society, but also propose revolutionary trends that will hopefully restore the permanent values of society, namely, justice, freedom, and human dignity. This essay is convinced by the foregoing views that the choice of Longue Longue of is not mistaken but quite representative of pop music in contemporary Cameroon.

Longkana Agno Simon, aka Longuè Longuè, is a Cameroonian music artist born in Douala in 1973. Longuè Longuè, son of Agno

Simon, belongs to a family of five children. His father sent him to Yabassi in 1980 when his mother died.

Unhappily accepted by his uncle who did not want to consider him as a son, Longuè Longuè quickly finds himself in the street of Bessengue neighbourhood in Douala. He was perceived by his peers and other family members as a good for nothing. Like most African children, Longue Longue had a difficult childhood. Without the possibility of going to school and receiving formal education, he grew up in the streets of Douala and in formerly learned formerly. He did not allowed himself to be swallowed by the negative values of street life like banditry, pick-pocketing and scamming. He engaged in petty trading(selling of water along the streets and car wash). His passion for music leads him into the local fabrication of musical instruments from recycled materials produce his guitar and a drum kit. With these instruments he started singing in popular bars and in cabarets in Douala and Yaoundé. He participated in music competitions organized by Le Brasseries du Cameroun (A Cameroun Brewery company, that does not only involves in the production and sale of drinks, but also involved in detecting and promoting talents in music and in football in Cameroun). It was during this period that he caught the attention of musicians like Sergeo Polo and Belka Tobis. He sang with them before the *La Brasseries* produced his first musical album.

It was only 2001 that he gained fame with the release of the album title *Ayo Africa* produced by Prince Dedy Eyango.[42] The flagship song of the album hits a phenomenal success in Cameroon and Africa at large. One quickly finds him a nickname, that of the "liberator". His stage name, Longuè means in Douala dialect "life". It was not surprising that in 2003, Longue Longue and his song future

---

[42] http://www.musiques-afriques.com/frames/art-eyango.html

in the film, whose main actor was South Africa's' Michael Power.(An African star advertising for Guinness Africa.

Longue Longue Le*Libérateur*

The singer thus earned himself the nickname of *Le Libérateur*. Two years later, the follow-up album *'Privatisation'* has the difficult task of living up to the expectations of the public. The album, with a cover version of *'Criseéconomique'*, originally from Gabon's *HilarionNguema*, had a slow start in Cameroon, but in the end one song *'Demander à Dieu'* gained popularity on Cameroon's dance floors. The singer has close to 29 songs in different albums, which have earned him credit in the national and international scene. In the following part of this work, some of the themes and historical undercurrents of the songs under reference in this study will be discussed. This section argues that by highlighting the good and evil aspects of the society in order to teach the people to learn from their shortcomings and mistakes, the singer is being revolutionary. Some of the themes to be discussed include: poverty, discrimination, corrupting power of money and position, excesses of government, economic crisis/exploitation, national integration, national unity, materialism, lack of political vision, migration among others.

In 2003, Longue Longue hit the air waves with a stinker on the ways the government of Cameroon had perceived and carries on with the privatization of state on corporations. Central to the song title *Privatisation'* under reference is a strong sense colonial exploitation of Africa and Cameroon in particular. Privatization has become a cornerstone of the good governance structural adjustment linkage formulated by western donors and creditors. In Cameroon, however, shows that the privatization scheme have often failed to promote any transparency and accountability in public-sector or to encourage greater participation of civil society in the decision-making process. (Konings 2003: 5-7).

On 21 November 2016, the Anglophone lawyers and teachers called for an indefinite strike asking the government of Cameroon to maintain the bijural nature of the legal system as well as the British-inspired subsystem of education which was being assimilated and sub-colonized by the French system of education and culture. By 'sub-colonize', we mean that France had colonized French Cameroun and French Cameroun is attempting to establish a further subordinate colony in Anglophone Cameroon. The strike paralyzed the education sector, and Common Law lawyers were brutalized by the military for attempting a peaceful match to express their grievances after memos to the government fell on deaf ears. This strike in 2016 was the result of longstanding and ongoing marginalization and the attempted assimilation and sub-colonization of the Anglophones and their identity in Cameroon(Nkwi 2018:117) The strike caused the artist to call on the Francophone led government to relinquished power to the Anglophones. The causes of the conflict goes as far back as 1961, when the Cameroun Republic and the British Southern Cameroons gave up their identities and became known simply as East and West Cameroon states in the new Federal Republic of Cameroon. His song was popularized following the 2016 ruling Cameroon People's Democratic Movements (CPDM) party's rally in Bamenda. The failed rally saw the death of eight civilians in Bamenda following open confrontation between the Gendemarie, the police and the angry population. In sending out his message, Longue longue inter play between French and pidgin English. His use of French and pidgin English in his song is to highlight the bicultural nature[43] of the reunified Cameroon in 1961. This factor influences the drive for the 1961 state arrangement, whose aim was to accommodate the different colonial heritage. Thus, for the post-colonial Cameroon state to uphold the sovereignty of the state, it is vital to keep and respect this biculturalism, in which every Cameroonian has the right and freedom to express him or herself in public without fear of been tacked 'that Francophone or that Anglophone'. Longue Longue's song which was aimed at achieving this, the singer titled his song *Gouvernement des vieux* . The song goes thus:

Francophones deux fois présidents, Passez le pouvoir à un Anglophone

Si l'on était bien au pays, est-ce qu'on allait prendre la route de l'aventure ?Ahh Monsieur le Présidents ohh…

Un pauvre qui vote pour celui l'a rendu, pauvre si l'on était bien au pays est-ce qu'on allait predre la route de l'etranger?

A l'assemblée il y'a un vieux vraiment!

Au Senat il y'a un vieux, wonderful!

A la Presidence il ya un vieillard

---

[43]See Articles 1 and 2 of the Cameroon Federal Constitution, cited in Anthony Ndi, ,(2013) *Southern West Cameroon Revisited 1950-1972*(Bamenda: Paul's Press), 355-356..

Dans tout le gouvernement, il n'y'a que des vieux, des vieux, des vieux.

Des jeunnes prennent le chemin de la Libye pour devenir des esclaves ohh eeh

Des jeunes prennent la route du desert pour entre en Europe oh oh

A l'assemblée il y'a un vieux vraiment!

Au Senat il y'a un vieux, wonderful!

A la Presidence il ya un vieillard

Dans tout le gouvernement, il n'y'a que des vieux, des vieux, des vieux

Docteur! Doux Joseph! Proviseur à Los Angeles comment pouvez-vous nomme un individu à un poste pendant 25ans? 20ans directeur de tant tant tant, 30ans vous vous partagez le pouvoir dans vos familles.

Since the attainment of political independence by Cameroon in 1960 and effective reunification of the French and the British sectors of the Cameroon in 1961, the leadership of the Country has been in the hands of the majority francophones; from the executive which is highly centralized and authoritarian, to state ministers, heads of services and heads of parastatals. This situation over the years has done on the minority Anglophones that there cannot and will never handle sensitive positions in the country whose foundation was based on the status of 'equality' (see Article 1 of the federal constitution). This meant that in the process of the political evolution of the country, the Francophones have disrespected the union accord of 1961. The minority have seen themselves at the margins of the Cameroon society. This has resulted to what became known as the 'Anglophone Problem'. This problem led to an increasing spirit of Anglophone nationalism and mutual suspicion between Anglophone and Francophone dichotomy in the political, economic, and socio-cultural domains. The singer in this first stanza opined that since independence francophones have had two presidents, it's time to hand over power to the Anglophones. According to him the francophone dominated administration is made up of very old people. More so, with individuals holding some positions as long as 30 years and more.

The Republic of Cameroon gained independence on the January 1, 1960 with Ahmado Ahidjo as its first president (*Le Republique du Cameroun*). By 1961 owing to the United Nations organized plebiscite the British Southern Cameroons voted to be reunited with *La Republique du Cameroun* to form the federal Republic of Cameroon. From 1961 Ahidjo (a Francophone) became the president of the federation, with John Ngu Foncha (an Anglophone) as the Vice President of the federation. The Cameroon federation ceased by 1972 owing the financial, political and economic differences between the state of West Cameroon and East Cameroon, Ahidjo that had been a *de facto* Head of State, created the united republic of Cameroon through a referendum that was organized in May 1972. From this date the name of the country was changed. The state of West Cameroon became just a one of the provinces within the United Republic of Cameroon. The statist identity of the state of West Cameroon was annihilated. The President argued that for the sake of national unity, integration and harmomisation there is the need to create the united Republic. In as much as a handful of Anglophone elites and political class participated and were co-opted into the hegemony alliance, a vast majority since 1972 were not comfortable with the change. This was because it reduced the former West Cameroon state just as any other region within the republic of Cameroon and its statist identity rub out. Ahidjo silence his critics by creating a police state, the politics of divide-and-rule and a heavily centralized system was put in place (Mukong 1990). A reserved, modest and astute politician, he ruled with a stern hand until his resignation as president of the United Republic of Cameroon on 6 November 1982.

From 1982 the second republic was created with Paul Biya as the President (1982-2021). Biya followed in the foot steps of Ahidjo, he continued and maintained a police state,. Beyond the smokescreen of reform, however, Biya did not dismantle the repressive structures and institutions bequeathed him by his predecessor(kofele-Kale,1987:136), and that he had used effectively to enable him to remain in power for over two decades. Both *Service de Documentation* (SEDOC)- despite the name change to *centre National des Etudeset des Recherches* (CENER)- with its complex network of spies, and the *Brigades Mixtes Mobiles* (BMM), were retained as institutions of surveillance and intimidation. In fact, the decision by President Biya, after the failed military coup in 1984 to reappoint Jean Fochive, whose ability and effectiveness as head of SEDOC for over fifteen years under the former President Ahidjo in ferreting out 'enemies of the state', to lead the same agency was a clear indication that Biya was not yet ready to renounce the use of force and intimidation as vehicles for maintaining the political status quo that he had inherited. In 1985, for instance, Gorji-Dinka , a prominent Anglophone Lawyer was arrested and detained for several months for questioning the President's authority and the constitutionality of changing the name of the Country from the United Republic to the Republic of Cameroon. The Anglophones considered it as assimilation and a move to further deny the Anglophones of their statist identity.

> Vous vous partagez le pays avec vos amis ehh
> Vous vous partagez le pays avec vos familles
> Vous vous partagez le pays avec vos amis ehh
> Et après quand ils ont volé vous appelez l'épervier les attraper
> Et après quand ils ont volé, vous appelez les l'épervier les attraper

Qui les avaient nommé d'abord à ce poste la?

C'est toi qui les a nommé Papa, tu as oublié? Il a seulement oublié

C'est toi qui les a nommés ohh, tu as oublié ehh.

Nguélé Rafael du Kenya c'est les mêmes qui sont toujours Ministres ils vont au quartier pour quelque temps et ils reviennent après ils font le tour des Ministères. Aujourd'hui, Ministre de la communication demain ministre des sports.

A neoptrimonial state structure was put in place as the president has decided to reward his family and friends by recycling them from one ministry to the other, while at the National Assembly (the lower House of Parliament) and the Sanate (The Upper House of Parliament) he has appointed the very old people like Cavaye Yeguie Djibril (80years old) and Marcel Niat Njifenji (85 years old) respectively. The implications hers are twofold; first,the systematic appointment of francophones in high places and decision making bodies-the legislative and judicary arms of the government occupied by francophone, the system is legitimising the francophone hegemony over the Anglophone that has conditioned the rise for the demand for the creation of the West Cameroon state following the 2016 trike throughout the Anglophone communities. Secondly,this has given the the president the prerogative to be changing the constitution at will. These are signpost to keep the Anglophones far from the corridors of the executive power and certain positions which seems to be the right and priviledge of the presidents family friends and people of his ethnic Beti origin. This is elucidated by the singer as he opined that power has been distributed to family members and friends.

Longue Longue in the second stanza argues that the francophone led regime has gone as far as converting the government into a family and friends affair. When Ahidjo has consolidated power after independence and reunification, he acted in the belief that national unity and integration could be forged by all Cameroonians. His successor Paul Biya echoed that the Country does not belong to one ethnic group and that all Cameroonians were equal (Biya 1985: 74). A reading of this was that most Anglophones considered that these were just sloganeering, and political propagandist meant for public consumption and to satisfy the international community. For the notion of national unity, national integration has been the means and apparatus used by the majority led regime to for alienate, sideline and assimilated the Anglophone in the francophone hegemonic alliance. From Ahidjo to Biya to an average Anglophone it was simply a change and continuity but for the external pressure that conditioned Biya to accept multiparty politics in the 1990s. But the events following the launch of the Social Democratic Front (SDF) Party in Bamenda, the militarization of the town and the killing of Anglophone six youths in Bamenda, an Anglophone town(Nyinchiah 2016) convinced them that just like Ahidjo, Biya's intent was to silence the voice of the Anglophone within Cameroon and thus their identity. The singer has used his song to remind the *'ancien'* regime that if national unity, integration is anything worth it then power should be transfer power to the Anglophones.

> A l'Assemblée il y una vieux vraiment!
> Au Senat il y'a un vieux, wonderful!
> A la Presidence il ya un vieillard
> Dans tout le gouvernement, il y'a que des vieux, des vieux, des vieux
> Ils ont volé des milliards.
> Et vous, vous avez amené mon pays à la dérive
> Sa majesté Theodore Swan, empereur du Haut-peller, Guy Simo, SKG E l'enfant de Nkongsamba Vous vous partagez le pays avec vos familles (2x)

Et après quand ils ont volé vous appelez l'épervier.
Qui les avait nommés d'abord dans ces postes l' à ehhh ?

The singer has used his song to report to the authorities and calling their attention of the excessive of the dominant Francophone leadership. Here, Longue Longue has used his songs to indirectly or informally communicate to the leaders. A leadership in which it is made up of the old; from the president, the members of the National Assembly and the Senate, more so, there is the recycling of one and the same persons within the system. Using his song, the singer he alludes the government to a family affair. A system in which an individual can occupy a post for even 25 years or more without any interruption. The youths who are supposed to be the leaders of tomorrow are not given the chance. It is for this reason that the youths have embarked on the dangerous path to Europe through Libya and the high seas. The long run effect of such movements has been the politicisation of identity. The recent upsurge of the Anglophone crisis has been fueled by the mass migration of the Anglophones and other Cameroonians abroad. This diaspora had come in contact with much more liberal ideas and free societies. This has motivated them to stimulate political activism back at home. This has raised the issue of the politics of identity and belonging which the government of Cameroon is finding it difficult to contain with.

The aim is usually to influence policy while avoiding the consequence of speaking to men openly (Finnegan 1970:275). Longue Longue use his song to argues that there is the lack of will by the hegemonic Francophone government to hand power to the Anglophone who are in union with the Francophone. When music is used to informed, it is intended to put things straight and unite factions for greater action and productivity in different aspects for the good of society. This is vividly handled by Longue Longue in his song Francophone two Presidents hand over power to an Anglophone. It is important to note that following the United Nations Organisations Plebiscite of 11 February 1961, the Anglophones voted in union with the Republic of Cameroon on the bases of equality. Ahmadou Ahidjo became the first President of the Federal Republic of Cameroon, John Ngu Foncha an Anglophone was the vice President. From 1982 Mr. Paul Biya another Francophone inherited the presidency. It was the hope of the Anglophones that in 1990 an Anglophone will ascent the presidency following the collapse of communism and the called for democratization in Africa. The euphoria that accompanied this event in Cameroon died down after the first presidential elections in the multiparty era. The Anglophone candidate lost. From this date the Anglophones have continue to see themselves as 'outsiders'. This is been promoted and it almost a policy by the government that continuously appoints only Francophones to key ministries. While regional administrators more than three quarters are Francophones. Longue Longue profiles that the poor people who keeps on voting the same government, the government that perpetually keeps them poor. This has conditioned the youths who have no hopes in the government to take dangerous paths to Europe to look for a better life. Finnegan (1970:272-3) contend that songs serve the purpose of reporting or commenting on current affairs. Others like Kah (2016:178) holds that songs are also used for political pressure, propaganda to reflect and mould public opinion.

In his next song titled 'Song for Southern Cameroon Struggle', the singer focused on identity and migration, he submits that owing to the marginalization of the Anglophones in general and the Bamenda people in particular; they want to migrate to where they came from. Like his other songs, the singer makes use of pidgin and French in this song in presenting his message. The lyric of the song goes thus:

> L'histoire est la connaissance du passe base sur les écrits
> Depuis l'existence de l'écriture jusqu' à nos jours
> Je l'ai apprise à l'école
> L'école est bien
> Longué libérateur, the liberator
> L'écrivain publique
> L'histoire dit que les Duala viennent du Congo
> Un Congolais qui est venu pêcher au Cameroun
> L'histoire dit que les Bamiléké viennent du Soudan
> Avec le commerce sur la tête avec les cracks à la main
> L'histoire dit que les Bassas viennent de l' Egypt. Ils avaient fuit l'ésclavage et la dictature des Pharaohs.
> Dans une querelle familiale, Bassi quitta son frère Bassa et alla créer sa famille a Yabassi.
> Voilà d'où sont venus les Yabassi. Ces congoiais faisauent de la merde et jetaient partout dans la foret, ils étaient trop sales.
> Les Bassas les abandonnèrent au coeur de la villa à cause de la saleté.
> Certains Douala avaient pris la direction de département de l'océan et ont crié leur village, Batanga, Kumba et Mabéa là -bas à Kribi.
> D'autre ont pris la direction du sud ouest et ont cree leur village appelé Bakweri.
> A Buea aussi les Bakweri
> D'autre ont continué à Kumba, se sont fait appelés Bafour, Bakoundou, Bakossi.
> Voilà donc l'histoire sur les écrits
> D'où viennent donc les Bamenda oohhh
> D'où viennent donc les Mbororo
> D'où viennent les Magida
> D'où viennent les Bandem, les Mbongo

In postcolonial Cameroon orature and politics have become interwoven to the extent that the orature and the artist has become more visible on the political scene and they are part of the writing of history and their sings are being used by those who appropriate power as well as those who are the recipients of the exercise power. This is typical with the singer under review. He has captured the history of migration of the different ethnic groups in Cameroon. He opined that the ethnic difference in Cameroon is supposed to be an asset for the political development of the country. But he further noted that owing to the fact that one ethnic group the Betis have held on to power to the detriment of the rest. It is for this reason that he paints a picture of the migratory routes of the peoples of Cameroon. In this connection, he identifies that the Anglophones are a different people that came into the union after the partition of 1916 and reunited in 1961. In this stanza the singer argues that what the Anglophones wants is a system similar to the state structure that operates in Canada that is the federal system. It is for this reason that he traces the root of the migratory history of Cameroon.

Like the majority of modern African states, the migratory history of Cameroon can be trace to the Bantu speaking people from the Congo. Whose linguistic line could be trace to the central Benue Valley along the present-day Cameroon-Nigeria border. From Lake Chad the Bantu speaking people moved westwards to the Niger region where they fused with the already existing speakers of non-Bantu languages within this border line within the savannah.

They are been referred to as the peoples of central Cameroon or the Tikar (Nkwi 1987:15; Nkwi 2017:135). Chilver and Kaberry (1967:11) holds that is neither a linguistic nor an ethnic term. It originates from the Germans and applied to the people who descended from the migrant royals of Tikar villages of Kimi, Ndobo and Rifum in the northeast of Bamum stretching from the north of Nigeria. The second wave of the Bantus to Cameroon were the coastal and southwestern Bantus who moved inland along the wouri and Mungo rivers and extending through the greater part of Cameroon This are the present day Bassa-Bakoko Ewondo, Bakweri, Bakundu, Batanga. The Duala provided leadership in this migratory trend from the Congo through to Mungo via floating logs.(Fanso 1989:10-53) However, linguistic evidence is not exclusive in determining the pre-existing Bantu speaker and those who pick it up along the way. Future archeological and linguistic research will clarify this doubt. For the purpose of this work the singer attempts to show that in as much as colonial tendencies have provided new routes in to migration history, it is evident that all Cameroonians owed their roots from the Congo and are all from the Bantu background. However, the new dispensation calls for the respect of the different identities inherited. In a typical Lingala rhythm-original from the Congo, Langue Langue puts it that the Anglophones are tired of the domination of the Francophones and as such they want to live and have their own 'country'.

> Bamenda était un état indépendant avec comme Premier Ministre John Ngu Foncha
> De l'autre cote le Cameroun
> Independent aussi avec Ahmadou Ahidjo les blancs les ont flattés oohh.
> Maintenant les Bamenda demandent un état Fédéral.
> Ills savent qu'ils sont Camerounais
> Ambazonia together
> Bamenda them say dey wangt na Federal State like a Canada
> You must know where you commot, you must know where di go ohh

Bamenda want for know where dem commotm, where them di go ohh(2x)

Bamenda together we can

Bamenda nova deny for be for Cameroon, The only thing them di ask na equality.

The art of storytelling by artist has come to an end in Cameroon. Like other artist, the artist Longue Longue has focused his song by giving a reinterpretation of the post-colonial history of Cameroon. The Anglophone problem that has metamorphosed into the desire for secession and the quest for independence for the former British Southern Cameroons independence. This was intensified during the 2016 lawyers and teachers strike. The Lawyers and the teachers had requested for the protection of the Anglophone legal and educational system. This was a means that they wanted to protect the Anglophone identity. To protect this from being annihilated, they demanded for the return of the 1961 state arrangement- recreating the state of West Cameroon. The peaceful strike was turn violent owing to the involvement of the military, the police, and the gendarme. It was for this reason that Langue Longue captures the events following the 2016 strikes. In his song he noted that the Anglophones are tired of the francophone marginalization and thus want to break and form the state of Ambazonia. In this stanza the singer called on the regime to return to the federal system or engaged into total decentralization failing this the Anglophones will form the state of Ambazonia.

In this song the singer paid homage to John Ngu Foncha the architect of Cameroons reunification. From 1959 Foncha when Foncha became the second Premier of the British Southern Cameroons, he rigorously with his Kamerun National Democratic Party (KNDP) pursue the desire for the British Southern Cameroons to gain independence by reunifying with republic of Cameroon. In the 1961 UN organized plebiscite this was achieved. He led his British Southern Cameroon to the Foumban Conference of July 1961 to negotiate the terms of the reunified Cameroons on 'equal' status and on a loose federal system because of linguistic, economic, political, judicial and educational backgrounds (Ngoh 2019); more so, to protect the statists identity of the British Southern Cameroons within the majority Republic of Cameroon. The British Southern Cameroons had enjoyed autonomy within Nigeria with a Prime Minister, a government and a vibrant judiciary and a strong democratic culture (Ndi 2016). He had hoped to maintain this within the republic of Cameroon (Nyinchiah, PhD filed work). The singer has alluded and praise the commitment of Foncha and the entire Anglophones who come into the union to be treated as equals but that seemed to have been dashed to the wind. Foncha became the Prime Minister of West Cameroon (1961-1970), the Vice President of the Federal republic within the same period. When Biya became the second president of Cameroon, he changes the name of ruling party the Cameroon National Union (CNU) to the Cameroon People's Democratic Party (CPDM), he was made the Vice National President of the party. He resigned in 1990 following the killing of Anglophones in Bamenda during the Launching of the SDF. He embarked on the restoration of the statehood of the British Southern Cameroons when he attended the All Anglophones Conferences of the 1993 and 1994 in Buea and Bamenda respectively. In 1995 Foncha and Solomon .T Muna-former Prime Minister of west Cameroon, Vice President of the Federal Republic of Cameroon, Speaker of the National Assembly of Cameroon, took to the UN to demand of the restoration of the statehood of the British Southern Cameroons (Cameroon Times 1995). It was as result of their frustration and the frustration of the Anglophones within the union that the architects of the reunified Cameroon felt it was necessary for the union to be abrogated. Longue Longue in his song opined that the francophone regime has not kept its own share of the bargain.

More so, the singer praises the town of Bamenda that has always stood up against any centralized policy by the Yaoundé Government. The Fathers of the reunified Cameroon are from this Anglophone regime. The first opposition party that has agitated and demanded for greater political space in Cameroon was born in Bamenda. Longue Longue holds that his song can truly liberate Cameroon if Bamenda defends and protect him from a regime he knows governs with the hammer and it can fall on him. If that happens, he knows Bamenda will stand for him. Longue Longue further maintains that the Anglophones have named their new territory Ambazonia. The name of the territory 'Ambazonia' was derived from *Ambass Bahia*. The Portuguese are said to have arrived the territory which later became Victoria on December 7, 1492, Feast Day of St. Ambrose. They named the Bay, *Ambass Bahia* which referred to an Island in the Bay which was named Victoria or Nicoll Island near Bimbia. The people of the area were called Ambous. They were said to be tall, well-built and cannibal (Ardener 1996). The British missionaries and traders later referred to the area as Ambass Bay. The name Ambazonia was used in 1984 by Fon Gorji-Dinka (leader of the Ambazonia advocacy group). This name has been popularize following the 2016 Anglophone uprsing in Cameroon.

Joshua and Edith Kah Wahla na wuna don go big big school. I beg wuna liberate we. Longué Longué don talkam all. Bamenda wina no leave me oh, if wuna leave me them go killi me.

Décentralisez le pouvoir!

On va ou là?!

Woside we di go with this francophone them?

Decentralization e dey for Cameroon, then Bamenda, Kumba, Limbe, Buea for be fine.

Avant la réunification du Cameroun,

Le drapeau Camerounais était frappé de deux étoiles sur la couleur verte ce qui représentait le Cameroun oriental et le Cameroun occidental.

Après la réunification fût retenu une seule étoile frappée sur la couleur rouge du drapeau Camerounais.

Symbole de l'unité

Bravo Longué Longué Bravo Bravo super.

Issues pertaining to migration form part of the most salient topics in Africa today (IOM 2004). Although most of the literature tends to examine migration through the lenses of South-North movements, there have been considerable migrations within the continent of Africa itself (Bakewell & De Haas 2007). Its ramifications are seen in social, cultural, and political domains. The long run effect of such movements was the politicisation of identity (Nkwi 2017:131). The recent upsurge of *ivoirité* denoting the "true Ivoirians" as opposed to the "other" in 1995, and the *makwerekwere* in South Africa, coined to describe settler immigrants tickles us to the perennial issue of migration and politicization of identity which has been given birth by the colonial and post-colonial regimes (Whitman 2000). In the Central/West Africans state of Cameroon the concepts of *allogenes* and *autochthones* was evoked to include and exclude some of the citizens (*Nouvelle Expression* 1996; Awasum 1998; Nyamnjoh and Geschiere 1998).

In this song the singer attempts the migratory path that has been followed by the different peoples that made up contemporary Cameroon. In effect the cultural, social, and political specificities of the different group should have been respected and included in the nation building project. This according to Longue Longue has given rise to the Bamenda people and the entire Anglophone community attempt to secede from the rest. Given that as minority their cultural trait has been neglected in Cameroon. However, he noted that the Anglophones are not asking and or demanding secession because they really want it so because they are not being treated as equals with the francophones *'Bamenda nova deny for be for Cameroon, The only thing them di ask na equality'*. The article of quality enshrined in the federal constitution has been overlooked by the post-colonial Cameroon leadership. More so, the quality principle was to be best protected within the federal system[44] owing to the reunification of the British and French zones of Cameroon in 1961. Longue Longue holds that federalism would be the best form of government to keep the Anglophones within Cameroon. It is for this reason that the singer opines that *'Maintenant les Bamenda demandent un état Federal.* The much-acclaimed decentralization in Cameroon has not been implemented and as such the Anglophones feel cheated in every spheres of life in Cameroon the singer noted. His use of pidgin English in his song is to show the bicultural nature of the country. He maintains that Bamenda should protect him from the heavy hammer of the state of Cameroon that has always responded to criticism with imprisonment, *'Longué Longué don talkam all. Bamenda wina no leave me oh, if wuna leave me them go killi me'.* Longue Longue has shown a mastery of the predicaments of the Anglophones in Cameroon which was transformed into a crisis in 2016.

In 2016, the Anglophones in Cameroon, demanded the return to the 1961 state arrangement and or an outright independence for the Anglophones out of the Republic of Cameroon. This has been

---

[44] Cameroon operated a federal system of government from October 1961 to May 1972.

conditioned by the haste with which the Anglo-French partitioned the territory in 1916. The partition was unequal, France took 4/5 and Britain 1/5. Then in 1961 with the supervision of the UN, the reunification of the British and French sectors of the country was negotiated. From all intent the haste in the events which was not accompanied by adequate preparations and total readiness by the two sectors of Cameroon has conditioned the majority and minority question in Cameroon.

It was with this historical trajectory, failed decolonization in Cameroon that the singer profiles the mobility of the different groups that made up Cameroon. This song profile the December 8, 2016 CDPM rally in Bamenda Town, that saw the shooting and killing of unarmed civilians by the military. Longue Longue takes a historical perspective when he traces the migratory routes of the different communities that made up Cameroon. He uses music to show why there is resistance against the dominant role of the Yaoundé administration by these different groups. This was not peculiar to Cameroon and the Anglophone resilience to French Cameroun administrative and political domination. In South Africa, Anne Schuhmann in *'The Beat that Beat Apartheid'* takes a historical perspective when she traces the role of music in the resistance against apartheid in South Africa (Englert 2018:12).

Music has been used to assert identity as well nationhood. Henry Kah (2016:179) opines that throughout the colonial era, political songs were composed and sung throughout the length and breadth of Africa to marshal a common feeling of belonging and heritage. This was against the backdrop of European colonial administration that needed to be flushed out. During the post-colonial ere, music became vital tool to arouse nationhood among the Biafrans of Eastern Nigeria between 1967 and 1970. This was when they wanted to break away from the Federation of Nigeria to create the state of

Biafra. In Cameroon the 2016 Anglophone revolt has taken the same path. It is for this reason that the singer Longue Longue composed is song to allude about the intending break away by the Anglophones from the Republic of Cameroon. Boni (2000:176) has observed that in the present dispensation, singers are composing songs to address contemporary issue like instability and the search for unity. In the case of the Anglophones they are in search of an identity.

This song by Longue Longue was banned and it was not popularized within the Cameroon music industry. Its popularity was limited to Anglophone population who could only access the song on *Youtube* and other social media network. This was an indication that censorship was extended to songs and music. One way of keeping the state void of any criticism from the citizens was the introduction of strict policy of censorship, This policy works well in a full or semi police state. The advent of the Anglophone crisis in Cameroon proof that the government has reintroduced a police state; instances of the police harassing citizens to check their phones on the kind of literature they read and the kind of music they listen to was a feature of the Anglophone crisis. It explains why Longue Longue's songs on the Anglophone crisis have been limited to social private Anglophone media space. The liberal space provided by the brief tenets of democracy has faded with the passage of time. Yet it is a truism that post-colonial African states are mired in a pool of social, economic, and political challenges. The 1990s ushered in a brief period of democracy whose concrete roles in solving it copious problems remain a forlorn cry of disillusionment and political frustrations in most of the African countries. The case of Cameroon is even truer.

How did we Get Here

On 8th December 2016, a planned political rally of the ruling party, CPDM, which was scheduled to hold in Bamenda, the administrative capital of the assumed marginalized Northwest Region of Cameroon turned out to be bloody as a confrontation with the armed forces led to the death of eight people. The event in Bamenda quickly spread to other towns and villages in the Anglophone regions. The incidence showed resilience of the Anglophones within the political repression of the ruling government of Paul Biya. The events around the last months of 2016 and the first two quarters of 2017 in light of a durable situation of political repression in Cameroon that fed the spirit of dissent, resilience and Anglophone Cameroon at large called to question the modalities of decolonisation in Africa as a whole and the process of the hasty conclusion of the reunification question in Cameroon, that has of late created an identity crisis within the country. The events also internationalized the once internal 'Anglophone problem' into the 'Anglophone crisis'. The singer in the above song captures the events and holds that *Maintenant les Bamenda demandent un etat Federal.*

More particularly, the Anglophone crisis had rocked the state of Cameroon for the past five decades and the two communiques were just revealing the dill-dallying nature of the government in handling. It brought to the forefront, issues that are so central to this study- how suppression, resistance and protest have influenced and continue to influence political choices in the present-day Cameroon and entire Anglophone Cameroon. How music the use of orality and pop music and people did became connected during this period both in Cameroon and the diaspora. This is because langue Longue who is a Francophone singer transcended politically barrier to unite the two cultural and politically different people in Cameroon through music. His music on the woes of the Biya regime was widely listened to and danced by Anglophone Cameroonians in the diaspora. Can music and the musician be a panacea to the current impasse in the Cameroon nation building project?, Can musicians of both sides of the political divide in Cameroon replace the guns, bullets with songs. Or the declaration of war on the Anglophones by the president of the republic of Cameroon in late 2017 be the solution to the crisis?

The declaration of war by the president transformed the already volatile and fragile crisis into a real warfare with the Cameroon regular forces and the Anglophone youths who have pick up dun guns, under the code name the Ambazonia Restoration Forces, to defend themselves, create and defend their own 'state'- The Federal Republic of Ambazonia, against the brutality of the Cameroon military. This event is, however, not new, in French Cameroon pre to the demand for independence in French Cameroon by the *Union des Populations du Cameroun* (UPC). From the French colonial administration to the post-colonial administration under Ahidjo, the declaration of war was used as a means to force those Cameroonians clamouring for freedom from colonial rule into submission (Richard Joseph, 1978). It was the successes recorded during this period that motivated the Biya government to decide on war as a solution to the grievances of the Anglophones. His use of force to silence the Anglophones has met with stiff resistance from the minority Ambazonia Restoration Forces (Aka Amba Boys)who are greatly motivated from home and abroad.[45] The Amba Boys have been

---

[45]The Amba Boys have been receiving financial and other logistic support from the Anglophone community at home and abroad. Their camps are interspersed in the villagers of the Anglophone regions of Cameroon. Food and other locally made guns have been supplied to them by the people of the different communities to

making use of hit and run tactics to outsmart the Cameroon Republican forces in their drive to keep the sovereignty of the state intact, and holding on to a 'one and indivisible Cameroon'. The intensity and gravity of the events that happened in Anglophone Cameroon in general from mid-November stretching into 2017 is deeply rooted in the Anglophone problem. Much has been devoted to this problem and our focus here will not be to repeat what has already been done (Konings 1996; Konings and Nyamnjoh 1997; Mbaku 2002). Yet it suffice to mention that the problem transformed into a crisis exposed and internationalized the crisis.

Conclusion

The main objective of This chapter was to analyse how Longue Longue uses his music to oppose the Yaoundé-regime. The first section provided background information on the political situation in Cameroon with particular attention to human rights abuse, corruption, and embezzlement. The second section focused on Longue Longue his biography and his songs. He stayed at the forefront of civil society politics in Cameroon despite the banning of his music on CRTV-the official radio and television channel. He pleaded the case of handful Anglophones who have been sideline in the body politics of Cameroon and limited only to certain positions while other like the president is the exclusive prerogative of the Francophones. He sees the strike actions by the Anglophones as an

---

which they belong and hub there. This local collaboration and support from the locals have made the total defeat of the Amba Boys and bring the Anglophone Community into total submission to the state very difficult for the Cameroon Republican Forces. For details of the support of the Amba Boys see Nyinchiah PhD field work, October 2020.

attempt to gain recognition in Cameroon. This work contends that in as much as the songs of the artist under reference are meant for pleasure, its revolutionary explanations goes beyond pleasure. There is every indication holds that, in the new millennium, protest music will play a more influential role in the political landscape in Cameroon. They had taken Lapiro's genre of music that has inspired a younger generation of musicians, as more protest music seems to emerge from both bikutsi and makossa artists. Some of these artists have become actively involved in local and national politics, the most popular of them being Lapiro himself, and Longue Longue has follow suit. It is also important to observe today that many studies have also been carried out to highlight the power of music in societal transformation.

Chapter 8

Epilogue: Which way Forward?

Walter Gam Nkwi

The Unfinished Business

This chapter is not intended to recapitulate what the contributors have already done. It is meant to tickle the reader(s) to chart new paths for further research since any research endeavour is a work in progress and research itself stands on ruling stairs. Even though the foregoing chapters have provided profound reflections on music in Cameroon, there is no gainsaying that they still allow some gaps for the future researchers to take over. For instance, there is no chapter on female Cameroonian musicians. This is not to suggest that the contributors were oblivious of the existence of the female musicians in Cameroon. Rather, the point is that their interests were focused on male musicians. For further research, gender perspectives would be of paramount relevance. For example, musicians like Anne Marie Ndze, Charlotte Mbango, and Grace Decca just to name a few could be the focus of future research.

If we define and explain music as a collection of coordinated sound or sounds and that making music is the process of putting sounds and tones in an order, often combining them to create a unified composition; if we accept that people who make music creatively organize sounds for a desired result, like the well venerated Beethoven symphony or one of Duke Ellington's jazz songs; if music is made of sounds, vibrations, and silent moments, and it doesn't always have to be pleasant or pretty; if music can be used to convey a whole range of experiences, environments, history and emotions (Titon 1984); then almost every human culture, be it African, European, American, or Asian has a tradition of making music. Archaeologists and ethno-musicologists have done some in-depth work about music and musical instruments. For example, early instruments like flutes and drums have been found dating back thousands of years. Furthermore, ancient Egyptians are said to have used music in religious ceremonies. Many other African cultures have traditions related to drumming for important rituals. Today, rock and pop musicians tour and perform around the world, singing songs that make them famous.

According to the Encyclopaedia of African Music, African music is as vast and varied as the continent's many regions, nations, and ethnic groups. The African continent comprises approximately 20 percent of the world's land mass and has a population of roughly 934 million (Tracey 1961). African music is as diverse as its cultures and peoples and has flowered in many indigenous forms and has been shaped by several foreign influences. Although there are many different varieties of music in Africa, there are a number of common elements to the music, especially within regions. The concept of music in Africa, especially in sub-Saharan Africa is different from that in other regions and cultures. The roles of music and dance are tightly woven together in sub-Saharan Africa, and music intersects with every aspect of life by expressing life through the medium of sound. By helping in marking the important moments in life, music helps to underscore the divine and eternal value of human life (Schmidt-Jones 2008; Tenaille 2002).

As the African society keeps changing in response to the forces of colonization, independence, neocolonization, and globalization, the role of music keeps changing as well, adapting to the new situations in which the people of Africa keep finding themselves. Though there have been changes in some of the forms of the music, including the infusion of instruments, musical styles, and genres from outside the African continent, music remains very important in Africa today. Also, because Africans travelled from Africa to other parts of the world, both as a result of African slave trade and later migrations, the music and dance forms of the African diaspora have influenced a number of international musical styles and genres, including many Caribbean and Latin American music genres like Rumba and Salsa, as well as providing the foundation of the musical tradition behind African American music.

Granted these mixtures and influences, one of the germane research areas could be folklore music (Peek 2002; Lomax 1998). When one talks about folklore music, Francis Ndom and Prince Martin Tubou alias *Afo-a-kom* from the Northwest of Cameroon immediately come to mind as representative artists of that musical genre. Also, researchers could as well examine Talla Andre Marie and a whole lot of his kind from the Eastern Grassfields because the commentary in their music blends traditional and national politics. Further research could be taken up to dig deeper into the instruments which they are using and the messages which they blend with modern politics as well as love, economy, environment, illness, and church. The chapters largely have focused on what Nyamnjoh and Fokwang (2005: 272) call "protest music". This is in reaction to their call that, focus is thus one of the possible numerous reactions to Nyamnjoh and Fokwang's assertion that "There is every indication that, in the new millennium, protest music will play a more influential role in the political landscape in Cameroon" (p.273). Further research on music and politics could focus on comparing the role of music in Cameroon's two republics – the First Republic from 1960 to 1982 and the Second Republic from 1982 to the present.

How does one meaningfully conceptualize music in Cameroon with its mosaic of indigenous groups and languages? And how does one research music beyond the conventional methodological tools that have been used hitherto? Musicians who have the latitude to produce music need the attention of researchers. Consequently, one of the questions that beg for further answers is who are these musicians? What are their backgrounds and from where did they take their inspirations? What is the relationship between music and identity? At the beginning of the 21 Century there was already serious research on music and identity more generally. Annemette Kirkegaard while at the Nordic Institute brought together some refined scholars whose researches were brought together by African and Nordic scholars on the theme of Music and identity in Africa. The anthology maintains that (2002) the musics of Africa play a particularly important role in expressing and forming identities. The authors came from musicology and other disciplines to analyse various aspects of the complex issues of playing with volatile identities in music in Africa today. Taken together these papers shed new light on the assumed or real dichotomies between the countryside and city, collective and individual, tradition and modernity, the authentic and alien (Kirkegaard 2002). These particular methods and themes could fit further into our Cameroon case study in multiple and varied ways.

When scholars of music are discussing African music, the term "traditional music" is often used to refer to the characteristics of African music prior to the colonization of the continent by European countries especially during the late nineteenth century. Traditional African music leans much more on utilising local instruments, voice forms and dancing styles that one can situate and trace their origin within a defined geographical location. Though there have been many changes ever since colonisation and the various migrations, one can still locate some of this music in areas where empires rose and fell. The pre-colonial period was full of social changes and dynamism. Great African empires and kingdoms rose and fell, but many of their traditions and cultures are still prevalent to this day throughout African villages. Can we start to carry out effective research on our different societies that existed long before the advent of colonialism and reconstructing what has been lost? What have been the technological changes in terms of the instruments? What type of history can we decode from music in these societies long before the advent of the colonial period? How did colonialism conceive and perceive traditional music and musicians? What type of literally genres were employed in this music? What methodologies or methodological tools would best suit research on music? Do we need to be passionate and compassionate when studying music and musicians in Cameroon? How do the researchers position themselves in the society in which they are researching on music or we could also add the role of the church which defined African traditions as paganistic or heathen? There are also questions of positionality and reflexivity. Investigations into the above inquisitions and many others not cited here could open fleshpots for future research in Cameroon music.

References

Achebe, C. 1958 *Things Fall Apart*. Heinemann.
Achebe, C. 1987, *Anthills of the Savannah*. London: Heinemann.
Achebe, C. 1998. *Anthills of the Savannah*. New York: Anchor Press.
Achebe, C.1989. *Hopes and Impediments: Selected Essays*. New York: Doubleday.
Aderinto, S. A. 2010. "Sexualized Nationalism: Lagos and the Politics of Illicit Sexuality in Colonial Nigeria, 1918-1958" PhD Diss. University of Texas.
Aderinto, S.A. 2007. "The Girls in Moral Danger: Child Prostitution and Sexuality in Colonial Lagos, Nigeria, 1930s to 1950" *Journal of Humanities and Social Sciences*, 1, 2: 1-22.
Adorno, F. 1988. *Introduction to the Sociology of Music*. Translated by E. B. Ashton. New York: Continuum.
Agostino. G.; J.P. Dunne and L. Pieroni. 2016. "Corruption and Growth in Africa." *European Journal of Political Economy* 43: 71-88.
Alleyne, M. (2000) "White Reggae: Cultural Dilution in the Record Industry, *Popular Music and Society* 24:1:10.1080/03007760008591758
Amutabi, M. 2002. "The Role of Traditional Music in the Writing of Cultural History: The Case of the Abaluyia of Western Kenya" In *Africanising Knowledge: African Studies across the Disciplines*, Edited by Toyin Falola and Christian Jennings. New Brusnwick, N.J.: Transaction Publishers,.
Andersen, K. 2012. "You Say You Want a Devolution?". *Vanity Fair*. Retrieved 22-11-2020.
Ardener, E. 1967. "The Nature of the Reunification of Cameroon" *African Integration and Disintegration: Case Studies in Economic and Political Union.pp.285-337* Edited by A. Hazlewood (ed) London: Oxford University Press.

Ardener, E; Ardener and W.A. Warmington (1960). *Plantation and Village in the Cameroons: Some Economic and Social Studies.* Oxford: Oxford Press.

Ariba, C.2012. "Bobi giving back to the hands that lifted him up" *New Vision.* Retrieved 21 January 2021

Arlt, V, ed 2004'Der Tanzder Christen: Zu den Anfängen derpopulären Musik an der Goldküste, ca. 1860–1930', *Jahrbuch für Europäische Überseegeschichte,* 4,3: 151–90.

Arlt,V.2002. 'The scholars' dance: popular culture and the appropriation of Christianity on the southeastern Gold Coast, c.1890–1918', Paper presented to the conference on 'Performing Culture: The politics and aesthetics of cultural expression in contemporary Ghana', Amsterdam.

Arnault. Karel. 2018. "Mediating Matonge: Relocations of Belgian Postcoloniality in Four Films." *Afrika Focus* 31, 2: 149-163.

Assiter, A.1996. *Enlightened Women: Modernist Feminism in a Postmodern Age.* London: Routledge.

Auden, W. H. 1979. *Selected Poems.* New York: Vintage.

Awasom, N. F., 2003-2004. "Anglo-Saxonism and Gallicism in Nation Building in Africa: The Case of Bilingual Cameroon and the Senegambia Confederation in Historical and Contemporary Perspective." *Afrika Zamani,* 11&12: 86-116.

Barchiesi, F. 2012. Precarity as capture: A conceptual reconstruction and critique of the worker-slave analogy. Retrieve from http://www.uninomade.org/precarity-as-capture/ (accessed 09.07.2020).

Barchiesi, F. 2012. Precarity as capture: A conceptual reconstruction and critique of the worker-slave analogy. Retrieve from http://www.uninomade.org/precarity-as-capture/ (accessed 09.07.2020).

Barnes, T. 2002. "Virgin Territory: Travel and Migration by African

Women in Twentieth-Century Southern Africa". In Jean A. Susan, G. and Nakanyke, M. (eds) *Women in African Colonial Histories*. Indiana: Indian University Press.

Bayart, J. 1993. *The State in Africa: the Politics of the Belly*. London: Longman

Baye, M., & Amongwa, F. 2002. "Decomposition of Inequality in the Distribution of Living Standard in Cameroon" *African Journal of Economic Policy,* 9, 2: 51-75.

Bennett, A. 2007. "The Forgotten Decade: Rethinking the Popular Music of the 1970s," *Popular Music History,*2:1. DOI :10.1558/pomh.v2i1.5. Retrieved 23 November 2020

Birgit, E, ed 2008 'Popular Music and Politics in Africa-Some Introductory Reflections'. In Wiener Zeitschrift für kritische Afrikastudien, vol 4,2: 72-92.

Blacking, J. 1976. *How Musical Is Man?* London: Faber & Faber

Bloom, B.S. 1956. *Taxonomy of Educational Objectives*. New York: David McKay Co.Inc.

Bordowitz, H. 2004. *Noise of the World: Non-Western Musicians In Their Own Words*. Canada: Soft Skull Press.

Boserup, E. 1970. *Women's role in Economic Development*. London: Allen and Unwin.

Brown, S. 1999. "The 'musilanguage' model of music evolution," in *The Origins of Music*, eds N. L. Wallin, B. Merker, and S. Brown Cambridge: The MIT Press), 271–301. doi: 10.7551/mitpress/5190.003.0022

Brunner, A. 2013. The singer Anne-Marie Nzié and the song" liberté": on popular music and the postcolonial state in Cameroon. *African Music: Journal of the International Library of African Music, 9*(3), 40-58.

Brunner, A. 2013.The singer Anne-Marie Nzié and the song" liberté": on popular music and the postcolonial state in

Cameroon. *African Music: Journal of the International Library of African Music*, 9(3):40-58.

Brunner, A. 2017. Popular Music and the Young Postcolonial State of Cameroon, 1960–1980. *Popular Music and Society*, 40(1):37-48.

Brunner, A.2016.. "The Singer Anne-Marie Nzié and the Song "Liberté": On Popular Music and the Postcolonial State in Cameroon." *Journal of International Library of African Music*

Cameroonian Saxophonist Manu Dibango Dies of Coronavirus, https://www.theafricareport.com/25017/cameroonian-saxophonist-manu-dibango-dies-of-coronavirus/, retrieved on April 30, 2020.

Camus, A.1971. *The Rebel*. Harmondsworth: Penguin.

Chem Langhee, B. 1995. "The Anglophone-Francophone Divide and Political Disintegration in Cameroon: A Psycho Historical Perspective" *Regional Balance and National Integration in Cameroon: Lessons Learned and the Uncertain Future*. Leiden: African Studies Centre.

Chiabi, E. 1989. "British Administration and Nationalism in Southern Cameroons, 1954-1964" in M.Z. Njeuma, (ed) *Introduction to the History of Cameroon Nineteenth and Twentieth Centuries*. London: Macmillan.

Cockburn, C. & Lynette H. 1999 "Transversal Politics and Translating Practices." *Soundings* (Special issue: *Transversal Politics*), 12: 89–93.

Cohen, A.D. & Dornyei, Z. 2020. *Focus on the Language Learner: Motivation, Styles and Strategies*. Ed. Smith. *An Introduction to Applied Linguistics*. London: Arnold.

Cohen, A.D. & Susan, W. 1966. *Styles-and Strategies- Based Instruction: A Teacher's Guide*. Minneapolis: University of Minneapolis. CARLA.

Coplan, D.D. ,2000 'Eloquent knowledge: Lesotho migrants' songs and the anthropology of experience'. In Barber, *Readings in African Popular Culture*, London: Oxford University Press.

Cross, I. 2016. "The nature of music and its evolution," in *Oxford Handbook of Music Psychology*, eds S. Hallam, I. Cross, and M. Thaut (New York, NY: Oxford University Press), 3–18. doi: 10.1093/oxfordhb/9780198722946.013.5.

Dave, N. 2014. The Politics of Silence: Music, Violence and Protest in Guinea. *Ethnomusicology*, 58(1):1-29.

De Mbanga, L. & Brown, D. 2010. Voice to the Voiceless. *Index on Censorship,* 39/3:. 123-130.

DeLancey, Mark W. 1966. "The Ghana-Guinea-Mali Union: A Bibliographic Essay." *African Studies Bulletin* 9, 2: 35-51.

Denselow, R. 2015. "Nigeria's new president Muhammadu Buhari – the man who jailed Fela Kuti". *The Guardian*. Retrieved 4 October 2020.

Dissanayake, E. 2012. The earliest narratives were musical. *Res. Stud. Music Educ.* 34, 3–14. doi: 10.1177/1321103X1244814.

Douglas, M.1966 *Purity and Danger*. London: Routledge.

Ebune, J. B. 1992. *The Growth of Political Parties in Southern Cameroons, 1916-1960*. Yaounde-CEPER. Editions Tribord.

Editor.2021. " Bobi Wine Biography, Early Life, Age, Family, Education, Career and Net Worth. *Information Guide Africa*. Retrieved 20 January 2021.

Elango, L. Z. 1987. *The Anglo-French Condominium in Cameroon 1914-1916: History of a misunderstanding*. Limbe, Cameroon: Presbook.

Emielu, Austin Maro. 2008. "Towards a Global 21st Century African Popular Music: Assata Band as a Case Study." *Legon Journal of the Humanities* 19: 135-149.

Englert, B. 2008. Ambiguous relationships: youth, popular music and politics in contemporary Tanzania. *Stichproben. Wiener Zeitschrift für kritische Afrikastudien, 14*(8): 71-96.

Erlmann, V.1997. 'Africa civilized, Africa uncivilized: local culture, world system and South African music'. Pages are missing In K. Barber (ed.), *Readings in African Popular Culture,* Oxford: James Currey.

Fanon, F. 1966. *The Wretched of the Earth.* Trans. Constance Farrington. New York: Grove Press.

Fanon, F. 1967. *Black Skin, White Masks.* New York: Grove Press.

Fanso, V.G. (1985). "African Traditional and European Colonial Boundaries: Concepts and Functions in Inter-Group Relations with Special Reference to South Western Cameroon" *Journal of Historical Society of Nigeria,* Xii, 3 &4: 23-43.

Fanso, V.G. 1989. *Cameroon History for Secondary Schools and Colleges Vol. II: Colonial and Post-Colonial Times.* London: Macmillan.

Fanso, V.G. 1999. "Anglophone and Francophone Nationalisms in Cameroon" *Round table* 350, April.

Feld, S. 2000. "A sweet Lullaby for World Music" *Public Culture,* Vol. 12, No.1: 145-148

Ferreira, Carolin Overhoff. 2011. "Ambivalent Transnationality: Luso-African Co-Productions after Independence (1988-2010)." *Journal of African Cinemas* 3, 4: 231-255.

Fest, J. (1963)*The Face of the Third Reich: Portraits of the Nazi Leadership.* Translated by Michael Bullock, London: Bloomsbury.

Finnegan, R. 1970. *Oral Literature in Africa.* Oxford: Oxford University Press.

Fuh, D. 2011. "Quand la femme se fache': Popular Music and Constructions of Male Identity in Cameroon." Institute of Social Anthropology/Centre for African Studies, University of Basel.

Fuh, D. 2020. Precarity, Fixers, and New Imaginative Subjectivities of Youth in Urban Cameroon." In *The Oxford Handbook of Global South Youth Studies.* Edited by Sharlene Swartz, Adam Cooper,

Clarence M. Batan, and Laura Kropff Causa. DOI: 10.1093/oxfordhb/9780190930028.013.38

Fuh. D. 2020. 'Quand La Femme Se Faché: Popular Music and Construction of Male Identity. pp. 1-13.

Garfinkel, David A. 2013. "Cosmopolitanism and Patriotism in Ghanaian Hiplife Lyrics." MA Thesis, University of California San Diego.

Geschiere, P. (1986). "Paysans, régime national et recherché hégémonique" *Politique Africaine*, Vol. 22: 88-103.

Gilliland, John 1969. "Play A Simple Melody: American pop music in the early fifties". *Pop Chronicles*. University of North Texas Libraries.

Glanville, J. 2010. Music and Silence. *Index on Censorship*, 39 (3):3-5.

Gordon, L. 2010. Theory in black: Teleological suspensions in philosophy of culture. *Qui Parle: Critical Humanities and Social Sciences*, 18, (2), 193-214

Gordon, L. 2010. Theory in black: Teleological suspensions in philosophy of culture. *Qui Parle: Critical Humanities and Social Sciences*, *18*(2), 193-214.

Grosh, B . & Makans dala, R. S. (eds) 1994 *State-Owned Enterprises in Africa*. Boulder/London: Lynne Rienner Publishers.

Halliday, M.A.K. 1977. *Language as a Social Semiotic: The Interpretation of Language and Meaning*. Baltimore: University Park Press.

Hersch, R. 2007. "Music of Oppression, Music of Resistance." Retrieved January 7, 2007 from http://canadiandimension.com/articles/1805

Higham, T., Basell, L., Jacobi, R., Wood, R., Ramsey, C. B., and Conard, N.J. 2012. Testing models for the beginnings of the Aurignacian and the advent of figurative art and music: the radiocarbon chronology of GeißenklÃsterle. *J. Hum. Evol.* 62, 664-676. doi: 10.1016/j.jhevol.2012.03.003.

Igbi, O. 2015. "Nigerian Highlife Music: A Survey of the Socio-Political Events from 1950-2005." *EJOTMAS: Ekpoma Journal of Theatre and Media Arts*, 170-179.

Jacques, W. 1989. Benoit's Comment faire l'amour avec un negré sans se fatigue. In Cinema Canada Film Reviews April-May 1989, 18-19.

Jayawardane, M. M. 2018. Mixtapes, Sonic Landscapes and the Poverty Archive: The Politics and Poetics of the Im/mobilised "Semi-politan African Nobilities, German Federal Cultural Foundation.

Jenks, C. 2003. *Transgression*. London and New York: Routledge.

Jervis, J.1999. *Transgressing the Modern: Explorations in the Western Experience of Otherness*, Oxford: Blackwell.

Jick, H. & Ngeh, A.T.2008. 'Popular Song as a Vehicle for Social and Political Commentary in Post-Colonial Cameroon'. *Epasa Moto* 3, 2,: 51-82.

Jick, H. and Ngeh, A.T2006. "Poetry in the Service of Nationalism in an Unjust Setting: The Anglophone Cameroon Experience"pp.106-109. In Chia, E.N, Tala Kashim and Tanda Vincent (eds.) *Perspectives on Language Study and Literature in Cameroon*. Limbe: Anucam.

Jick, H. K. 2005. 'Oral Literature: The Lacuna in Contemporary Cameroonian Education'. Pages are missing In Chia,pp.89-90.In E.N., Tala K.I. and Jick H.K. (eds.) *Globalisation and the African Experience: Implications for Language, Literature and Education*. Limbe: Anucam.

Jick, H. K.2009. 'Contemporary Historical Reality as Source and Beneficiary of the Popular Song in Post-Independent Cameroon',pp.102-105. In Danail Abwa, E.S.D. Fomin, Albert Pascal and Willibroad Dze-Ngwa (eds) *Boundaries and History in Africa: Issues of Conventional Boundaries and Ideological*

Frontiers(Festschrift in Honour of Verkijika G Fanso, Yaoundé: University of Yaoundé.

Jick, H. K.2015. 'The Cameroonian Urban Oral Artist As Revolutionary Thinker'. *International Journal of Liberal Arts and Social Science*, 3, 2: 27-29.

Johnson, W. R. 1970. *The Cameroon Federation: Political Integration in a Fragmentary Society*. Princeton: Prince University Press.

Joseph, R. (ed) 1978. *Gaullist Africa: Cameroon Under Ahmadu Ahidjo*. Enugu, Nigeria: Fourth Dimension Publisher.

Joseph, R.1978 *Radical Nationalism in Cameroun: Social Origins of the U.P.C. Rebellion*, England: Cambridge University Press.

Jua, N. 1989. "The petty bourgeoisie and the politics of social justice in Cameroon", In *Proceedings of the Conference on the Political Economy of Cameroon*, Leiden: African Studies Centre Monograph Series.

Jua, N. 1991. "Cameroon: Jump-starting an economic crisis" *Africa Insight*, Vol.21, No.3:162-170.

Kah, H. K. 2015. "Understanding Conflicts in Cameroon History through "Awilo's" Song "contri don Spoil". *East-West Journal of Business and Social Studies*, Vol.4, 1: 80-104

Kah, H.K. 2016. 'Music, Gender and History Among the Laimbwe Urchin Group of Bu, Cameroon, In *Trames*, 20(70/65),2:36- 40.

Kale, P.M. 1967. *Political Evolution in the Cameroons*. Buea, Cameroon: Government Printers.

Kashim, I. T.(2013) *Power and Marginality in Contemporary Cameroonian Orature*. Kansas: MAP Mircalaire Publishing.

Kigambo, G. 2017. "Bobi Wine calls win a renewal of leadership" *The East African*. Retrieved 20 January 2021.

Kirkegaard, A. & Mai, P. 2002. *Playing with Identities in Contemporary Music in Africa*. Uppsala: Nordic African Institute.

Kirkegaard, A.(2007)'Tourism industry and local music culture in contemporary Zanzibar'. In Baaz and Palmberg, *Same and Other*. 59-76.

Kofele-Kale, N. (1980). *An Experiment in Nation Building: The Bilingual Cameroon Republic since Reunification*. Boulder, Colorado: Westview Press.

Konings, P. 2003. 'Privatisation and Ethno-Regional Protest in Cameroon'. *Africa Spectrum*, 38, 1:5-26.

Leach, M. (ed) 1986. *Standard Dictionary of Folklore, Methodology and Legend*. New York: Frank and Wagnall.

Lipsitz, G.1994. *Dangerous Crossroads: Popular Music, Postmodernism and the Politics of Place*. New York: Verso.

Lomax, A. & Edwin E. E. 1968.*Folk Song Style and Culture*. New Brunswick: Transaction Books.

Lukács, G.1970. *Writer and Critic*. London: Merlin Press.

Mahama, John Dramani. 2014. "Telling and Retelling of Each Story: From the Maghreb to Madagascar." *The Journal of Pan-African Studies* 7, 3: 115-120.

Mamdani, Mahmoud. 2008. "Higher Education, the State and the Marketplace." *Journal of Higher Education in Africa* 6, 1: 1-10.

Mandela, N. 1994. *Long Walk to Freedom*. Boston: Back Bay Books.

Mano, W. 2007. Popular music as journalism in Zimbabwe. *Journalism Studies*, *8*(1): 61-78.

Mano, W. 2007. Popular music as journalism in Zimbabwe. *Journalism Studies*, *8*(1), 61-78.

"Manu Dibango Obituary," https://www.theguardian.com/music/2020/mar/24/manu-dibango-obituary, retrieved on April 30, 2020.

"Manu Dibango." https://en.wikipedia.org/wiki/Manu Dibango, retrieved on October 22, 2020.

"Manu Dibango: African Saxophone Legend Dies of COVID-19," https://www.bbc.com/news/world-europe-52017834, retrieved on April 30, 2020.

Masquelier, C. 2019. Bourdieu, Foucault and the politics of precarity. *Distinktion: Journal of Social Theory, 20*(2): 135-155.

Mbembe, A. 2001. *On the Postcolony*. California: University of California Press.

Mbembe, A. J. 1986. "Pouvoirs des morts et langage des vivants" *Politiques Africaine*, 22 :37-72

Mbile, N.N. 2000. *Cameroon Political Story: Memories of an Authentic Eye Witness*. Limbe, Cameroon: Presbook.

Mbuagbaw, T.E., R. Brian and R.Palmer. 1987. *A History of the Cameroon* New Edition. Essex: Longman.

Mc Quillar, T. & Johnson, F. 2010. *Tupac Shakur: The Life and Times of an American Icon*. Cambridge: Dacapo Press.

McLuhan, M. 1964. *Understanding Media: The Extensions of Man*. New York, McGraw Hill.

McLuhan, M. 1964. *Understanding Media: The Extensions of Man*. New York, McGraw Hill.

Mignolo, W.2000 *Local Histories/Global Designs: Essays on the Coloniality of Power, Subaltern Knowledges and Border Thinking*. Princeton, New Jersey: Princeton UP.

Millar, K. 2017. Toward a critical politics of precarity. *Sociology Compass, 11*(6):24-83.

Milne, M. 1999. *No telephone to Heaven: From Apex to Nadir-Colonial Service in Nigeria, Aden, the Cameroons and the Gold Coast*. Hants: Meon Hill Press.

Mithen, S., (ed.). 2005. *Creativity in Human Evolution and Prehistory*. London: Routledge. doi: 10.4324/9780203978627.

Mohanmedbhai, G. 2015. "The Challenge of Graduate Unemployment in Africa." *International Higher Education* 80: 12.

Mokake, F.M. 2013. "Youth and Currency Counterfeiting at Crossroad with a Special Reference to Mutengene (Cham),

Cameroon" *Childhood in Africa: An Interdisciplinary Journal*, 3, 1: 1-16.

Monnakgotla, K. 1997. "From Confrontation to Cooperation: New Security Challenges Facing Post-Apartheid Southern Africa." M.A Thesis, Rhodes University.

Moore, C. 2009. *Fela, Fela! This Bitch of a Life*. With Introduction by Margaret Busby and Foreword by Gilberto Gil. Allison & Busby. UK: New edition Chicago Review Press.

Moorsom, T. L. 2011. *Africa: The Frontlines and the Margins of a Global Anti-Poverty Movement*, Carleton: University Canada Press.

Mundundu, A, M. 2005. "The Recontextualisation of African Music in the United States: A Case Study of Umoja African Arts Company." PhD Thesis, University of Pittsburgh.

Mukong, A. 2009. *Prisoner Without a Crime: Disciplining Dissent in Ahidjo's Cameroon*, Mankon, Bamenda: Langaa Research Publishing and Common Initiative Group.

Murisa, H. 2013. "Up Close And Personal With The Ghetto President Bobi Wine". *Chono8 Magazine*. Retrieved 20 January 2021.

Muzee, H., & Enaifoghe, A. O. 2020 "Social Media and Elections in Uganda: The Case of Bobi Wine and the Arua Primary Elections." In *Social Media and Elections in Africa*, Volume 1:195-213. Palgrave Macmillan, Cham.

Muzee, H., & Enaifoghe, A. O. 2020. Social Media and Elections in Uganda: The Case of Bobi Wine and the Arua Primary Elections. In *Social Media and Elections in Africa, Volume 1* (pp. 195-213). Palgrave Macmillan, Cham.

Naanen, B. 1999. "Itinerant Gold Mines: Prostitution in the Cross River Basin of Nigeria, 1930-1950" *African Studies Review*, 34, 2: 57-79.

Ndjio, B. 2005. "*Carrefour de la joie:* popular deconstruction of the

African postcolonial public sphere." *Africa*, 265-294.

Ndjio, B. 2008. *Cameroonian feymen and Nigerian "419" scammers: Two examples of Africa's "reinvention" of the global capitalism* (African Studies Centre Working Paper 81/2008). Leiden.

Ngo N, N. L.2016. "Voix féminines de la chanson au Cameroun: émergence et reconnaissance artistique." pp. 177-196.

Ngoh, V. J. 1999. "The Origin of the Marginalisation of Former Southern Cameroonians (Anglophones), 1961-1966: An Historical Analysis." *Journal of Third World Studies*, Xcl: 165-183.

Ngoh, V.J. 2001. *Southern Cameroons, 1922-1961: A Constitutional History*. Aldershot: Ashgate,.

Ngoh, V. J. 1996. *History of Cameroon since 1800*. Limbe, Cameroon: Presbook,

Ngongkum, Eunice. 2017. "Urban Orature and Resistance: The Case of Donny Elwood." *TYDSKRIF VIR LETTERKUNDE* 54, 2: 61-73.

Ngu, J. N. (1989). "The global economic crisis and sub-Saharan Africa" *Afrique Unie*, 1: 52-75

Njeuma, M.Z. (ed) 1989. *Introduction to the History of Cameroon Nineteenth and Twentieth Centuries*. London: Macmillan.

Nkwi, G.W. 2010.*Voicing the Voiceless, Contributions to Closing the Gaps in Cameroon History, 1958-2009*. Mankon, Bamenda: Langaa Research &Publishing CIG.

Nkwi, G.W. 2017.'Migration and Identity in Southwest Region of Cameroon: The Graffie *Factor, C.1930s-1996'.Brazilian Journal of African Studies*, 2, 3:40-50.

Nkwi, W.G. 2006 b. "Folk Songs and History amongst the Kom of Northwest Cameroon: The Pre-Colonial and Post-Colonial Periods" *Humanities Review Journal*, 6,: 62-76.

Nkwi, W.G. 2006. "Elites, Ethno-Regional Competition In Cameroon, and the Southwest Elites Association (SWELA),

1991–1997" *African Study Monographs,* 27(3): 123-143.

Nkwi, W.G. 2015. " Cell Phone Repairers in Cameroon, 2000-2-13" *Journal for the Advancement of Developing Economies,* 4, 1:6-18.

Nkwi, W.G. 2016 c. "Prostitution in colonial Lagos and Accra: Evidence from the National Archives Buea, Cameroon, c.1930s-1950s" *Vestiges Journal,* 1, 2: 89-109.

Nkwi, W.G. 2016d. "*Salt Wata* Modernity: The Port City of Victoria (Cameroon) ca. 1920's-1980" *CORIOLIS: Multi-Disciplinary Journal of Maritime Studies,* 6, 2,: 34-52

Nkwi,G.W,2018.'Words Cannot be Found : Terrorism and Extreme Violence in Anglophone Cameroon,2016-2018, In *African Journal for the Prevention and Combating of Terrorism,* 17,1:214-127.

Nkwi, W. G. 2017., "Rivers and Ports in Transport History of Cameroon" *OGIRISI: A New Journal of African Studies,* 13: 200-235

Nkwi, W.G, & Nyingchiah, G.G. 2017 ' Bamenda Again, Memory, Strikes, Social Media in Anglophone Cameroon,2016-2017', In Mirjam de Bruijn and Jonna Both, eds, *Conference on connecting in Times of Duress, in Understanding Communication and Conflict in Middle Africa's Mobile Margins. N'Djamena.*(Forthcoming)

North, A. C., and Hargreaves, D. J. 2008. *The Social and Applied Psychology of Music.* New York, NY: Oxford University Press. doi: 10.1093/acprof:oso/9780198567424.001.0001.

Novotney, A. 2013. "Music as Medicine". *Science Watch.* Vol.44. No.10: 46-62

Nyairo, J., & Ogude, J. 2005. Popular music, popular politics: Unbwogable and the idioms of freedom in Kenyan popular music. *African Affairs,* 104(415): 225-249.

Nyamnjoh F. 2019. "ICTs as *Juju*: African Inspiration for Understanding the Compositeness of Being Human through Digital Technologies." Keynote Address at the 2019 Digital

Humanities Conference on the theme of 'Complexities', Utrecht University, The Netherlands, 9th – 12th July 2019.

Nyamnjoh F.2008 *Souls Forgotten*. Mankon, Bamenda: Langaa RPCIG.

Nyamnjoh, F 2009. *Married but Available*. Mankon, Bamenda: Langaa RPCIG.

Nyamnjoh, F. 2013. *The Travail of Dieudonné*. Mankon, Bamenda: Langaa RPCIG

Nyamnjoh, F. and Jude F.2005. "Entertaining Repression: Music and Politics in Postcolonial Cameroon," *African Affairs*, 104(415): 251–274.

Nyamnjoh, F. B. 2005a. "Fishing in troubled waters: disquettes and thiofs in Dakar". *Africa*, 295-324.

Nyamnjoh, F. B. 2005b. *Africa's media: Democracy and the politics of belonging*. Zed Books.

Nyamnjoh, F.2007a *Mind Searching*. Mankon, Bamenda: Langaa RPCIG.

Nyamnjoh, F.2007b. *The Disillusioned African*. Mankon, Bamenda: Langaa RPCIG.

Nyamnjoh, F.2015. "Incompleteness: Frontier Africa and the Currency of Conviviality," *Journal of Asian and African Studies*, 52(3): 1-18.

Nyamnjoh, F.B. & Fokwang, J. (2005). "Entertaining repression: Music and politics in postcolonial Cameroon." *African affairs*, *104*(415), 251-274.

Nyamnjoh, F.B. 2006. *A Nose for Money*. Nairobi, Kenya: East African Educational Publishers.

Nyamnjoh, F.B. 2015. "Incompleteness: Cross, I. (2016). "The nature of music and its evolution," in *Oxford Handbook of Music Psychology*, eds S. Hallam, I. Cross, and M. Thaut (New York, NY: Oxford University Press), 3–18. doi:

10.1093/oxfordhb/9780198722946.013.5.Frontier Africa and the Currency of Conviviality"

Nyamnjoh, F. B. and Page, B. 2002. "*Whiteman Kontri* and the enduring allure of modernity among Cameroonian Youths" *African Affairs,* 101:607-634.

Nyinchiah, G.G.2016 'Multiparty Upheavals in Cameroon: A History of Coping Strategies in Bamenda, 1990-2011'. Unpublished M.A Thesis, University of Buea , Cameroon

Ogbonnaya, Joseph. 2012. "Religion and Sustainable Development in Africa: The Case of Nigeria." *International Journal of African Catholicism* 3, 2: 1-22.

Ogunnaike, L. 2003. "Celebrating the Life and Impact of the Nigerian Music Legend Fela". *The New York Times.* Retrieved 18 November 2010.

Olaniyan, T. 2004. *Arrest the Music! Fela and his Rebel Art and Politics.* Indiana: Indiana University Press.

Olatunji, M. 2007. "Yabis: A Phenomenon in the Contemporary Nigerian Music" *The Journal of Pan African Studies.* 1: 26–46

Olorunyomi, S. 2002. *Afrobeat: Fela and the Imagined Continent Africa* USA: World Press.

Ong, W. 1981. *The Presence of the Word.* Minneapolis: University of Minneapolis Press.

Ong, W. 1982. *Orality and Literacy. The Technologizing of the Word.* New York:

Onyeji, C.2004. "Music and the Search for Beauty" *Nsukka Journal of the Humanities,* No.14: 151-165.

Oxford, R. L. 1990 *Language Learning Styles: What Every Teacher Should Know.* Boston: Heinle & Heinle.

Oxford, R.L. 1990 *Language Learning Strategies.* New York: Newburg House/ Harper and Row.

Palmsberg, M. and A. Kirkegaard (eds) 2002. *Playing with Identities in*

Contemporary Music in Africa. Uppsala: Nordiska Afrikainstitute.

Peek, Philip M., & Kwesi Y.2004 *African Folklore: An Encyclopedia.* New York: Routledge.

Pettman, J.1992 *Living in the Margins, Racism, Sexism and Feminism in Australia.* Sydney: Allen & Unwin.

Pongweni, Alex. J. C. 1982. *Songs that Won the Liberation War.* Harare: The College Press

Pufleau, Luis-Velasco. 2014. "Reflections on Music and Propaganda." *Contemporary Aesthetics* 12: 1-12.

Rahmato, Dessalegn. 1988. The Crisis of Livelihood in Ethiopia. Working Papers on Ethiopian Development, Ethiopian Research Programme College of Arts and Science, University of Trondheim.

Rathnaw, D. M. 2010. "The eroticization of bikutsi: reclaiming female space through popular music and media." *African Music: Journal of the International Library of African Music*, 8(4), 48-68.

Reuster-Jahn, U. 2014. English versus Swahili: Language choice in Bongo Flava as expression of cultural and economic changes in Tanzania. *SWAHILI FORUM,* 21, 1-25.

Reuster-Jahn, U. 2014. English versus Swahili: Language choice in Bongo Flava as expression of cultural and economic changes in Tanzania. *SWAHILI FORUM,* 21, 1-25.

Reviews: 1994. *Three Kilos of Coffee: An Autobiography by Manu Dibango* in Collaboration with Danielle Rouard, translated by Berth G. Raps, Chicago and London: University of Chicago Press, 1994. 146pp.

Rubin, N. 1971. *Cameroon: An African Federation.* London: Pall Mall.

Said, E. 1991 *Musical Elaborations.* New York: Columbia University Press.

Scheub, H. 1971. Translation of African Oral Narrative Performance to the Written Word. *Yearbook of Comparative and*

General Literature, 28-36.

Schellenberg, A. and Weiss, M.W. 2013. "Music and Cognitive Abilities". *American Psychological Society*. Vol.14, No.6:201-220.

Scheub, H. 1985. A Review of African Oral Traditions and Literature. *African Studies Review,* (28) 2-3: 1-72.

Scheub, H. 2002. *The Poem in the Story: Music, Poetry, and Narrative*. Madison: University of California Press

Schleiermacher, F. and Bowie, A. (1998). *Hermeneutics and Criticism: And Other Writings*. Cambridge: Cambridge University Press.

Schmidt-Jones, C. 2008. "Talking Drums." *Connexions*. January 14, 2008. Retrieved November 11, 2020.

Schoonmaker, T. (ed) 2003. *Black President: The Art & Legacy of Fela Anikulapo Kuti*. New Museum of Contemporary Art, New York:

Schoonmaker, T. (ed) 2003. *Fela: From West Africa to West Broadway*. London: Palgrave Macmillan.

Shepler, S. 2010. Youth music and politics in post-war Sierra Leone. *The Journal of Modern African Studies*, 627-642.

Shepler, S. 2010. Youth music and politics in post-war Sierra Leone. *The Journal of Modern African Studies*, 627-642.

Sikod, F.2006. "The Completion point of the HIPC initiative; what it means for the Cameroon Economy" A presentation in Hilton, Sponsored by the British Council.

Sithole, T. 2012. "Fela Kuti and the Oppositional Lyrical Power", *Journal of Music Research in Africa*, 3, 4: 34-53.

Sone, E. 2009. Lapiro de Mbanga and Political Vision in Contemporary Cameroon. *The International Journal of Language, Society and Culture*, (27):18-26.

Sone, E. M. & Mesumbe, N.N. 2014. "Female identity in Cameroon in the 1990s: female prostitution and the song, "*Muziki*, 11,2: 103-115.

Stallybrass, P. and Allon W. 1986. *The Politics and Poetics of*

Transgression, London: Methuen.

Stamatescu, Ioana. 2017. "Le Freak, C'est Chic! Disco Culture and Whit Stillman's The Last Days of Disco." *Synergy* 13, 1: 60-74.

Standing, G. 2011. *The Precariat: The new Dangerous Class.* London: Bloomsbury Academic.

Steedman, C. 1988. "Rural development planning and budgeting in Cameroon" Washington, DC: Development Alternatives Incorporated , April.

Stewart, A. 2013. "Make It Funky: Fela Kuti, James Brown And The Invention Of Afrobeat." *American Studies* 4,: 99-115

Street, J. 2003. 'Fight the power': The politics of music and the music of politics. *Government and Opposition, 38*(1): 113-130.

Street, J. 2003.'Fight the power': The politics of music and the music of politics. *Government and Opposition, 38*(1), 113-130.

Takougang, J. & Krieger, M. 1998. State and Society in Africa: Cameroon at the Crossroads. Westview: Boulder.

Takougang, J. and Krieger, M. (1998)*African State and Society in the 1990s: Cameroon's political crossroads,* Boulder: *Westview Press.*

Tala, K.I. 1987/1988. Aesthetics from an African Perspective: A Case of the *mbag'alum* of the Mezam People" *Science and Technology Review*, Vol. V: 101-106.

Tambi, M. D. 2015. "Economic Growth, Crisis and Recovery in Cameroon: A Literature" *International Journal of Industrial Distribution and Business,* Vol, 6, No 1: 5-15.

Tangem, D. F. 2016. Oral history, collective memory and socio-political criticism: A study of popular culture in Cameroon. *Tydskrif vir letterkunde, 53*(1):160-178.

Tangri, R. 1999.*The Politics of Patronage in Africa: Parastatals, Privatisation and Private Enterprise.* Oxford: James Currey.

Tazanu, P. M. 2012. *Being Available and Reachable: new media and Cameroonian transnational sociality.* Mankon, Bamenda: Langaa

Research and Publishing CIG.

Tazanu, P. M. 2016. Practices and narratives of breakthrough: Pentecostal representations, the Quest for Success, and Liberation from bondage. *Journal of Religion in Africa*, 46(1), 32-66.

Tazanu, P. M. 2018. Of polluted spirits and compromised identity: Pentecostal depictions of causality and the repositioning of human agency in Cameroon. *Journal of Asian and African Studies*, 53(6), 970-983.

Tehranian, M. 2002. "Taming Capital, Holding Peace." In *Democratizing Global Governance*, edited by Esref Aksu and Joseph A. Camilleri, New York: Palgrave Macmillan, pp. 28-54.

Tenaille, F. 2002. *Music is the Weapon of the Future: Fifty Years of African Popular Music*. Chicago: Lawrence Hill Books, 2002.

Terdman, Moshe. 2008. Somalia at War – Between Radical Islam and Tribal Politics. Research Paper No. 2. The S. Daniel Abraham Centre for International and Religious Studies, Tel Aviv University.

The World Bank, 1984. "Toward Sustained development in Sub-Saharan Africa: A joint program of action". Washington, DC: The World Bank.

The World Bank. 1981. Accelerated development in Sub-Saharan Africa. An Agenda for action. Washington, DC: The World Bank.

Thorsen, Stig-Magnus. 2004. "Sounds of Change – Social and Political Features of Music in Africa." *Sida Studies* No. 12.

Titon, J.T. 1984. *Worlds of Music: An Introduction to the Music of the World's Peoples*. New York: Schirmer Books.

Tlostanova, M. 2013. "Transcultural Tricksters beyond Times and Spaces: Decolonial Chronotopes and Border Selves." *Language Philology Culture*, vol. 2-3: 9–31.

Tracey, H. 1961. *The Evolution of African Music and its Function in the Present Day.* Johannesburg: Institute for the Study of Man in Africa, 1961.

Tsing, A. 2015. *The mushroom at the end of the world: On the possibility of life in capitalist ruins.* Princeton: Princeton University Press.

Underhill, E. B. 1958. *Alfred Saker: Missionary to Africa: A Biography.* London: The Carey Kingsgate Press.

Vail, L & White, L. 1983. Forms of Resistance: Songs and Perceptions of Power in Colonial Mozambique" *The American Historical Review*, 88, 4: 883- 919.

Vakunta, P. 2014. *The Life and Times of a Cameroonian Icon: Tribute to Lapiro De Mbanga Ngata Man: Tribute to Lapiro De Mbanga Ngata Man.* Mankon, Bamenda: Langaa RPCIG.

Vakunta, P. 2004. *The Life and Times of a Cameroonian Icon: Tribute to Lapiro De Mbanga Ngata Man*, Mankon, Bamenda: Langaa RPCIG.

Van der Walle, N. 1989. "The politics of non-reform in Cameroon", Paper presented at the 1989 meeting of the African Studies Association, November 2-5, Atlanta, Georgia.

Vande W. N. 1993.'The Politics of Nonreform in Cameroon' In Callaghy T.M. and J. Ravenhill (eds): *Hemmed In: Responses to Africa's Economic Decline*. New York: Columbian University Press

Veal, M. E. 1997. *Fela: The Life of an African Musical Icon.* Philadelphia: Temple University Press.

Verschave, F. X. 2004. *De la Françafrique à la Mafiafrique.* Bruxelles:

Waterman, C. A 1982 "'I'm a Leader, Not a Boss': Popular Music and Social Identity in Ibadan, Nigeria." *Ethnomusicology* 26/1:59-72.

Welch Jr. Claude E. 1967. *Dream of Unity: Pan-Africanism and Political Unification in West Africa.* Ithaca: Cornell University Press.

Welch, G.F., and McPherson, G. E., (eds.). 2018. "Commentary:

Music education and the role of music in people's lives," In *Music and Music Education in People's Lives: An Oxford Handbook of Music Education* New York, NY: Oxford University Press), 3–18. doi: 10.1093/oxfordhb/9780199730810.013.0002 *West African Europhone Novel*. Amsterdam: Rodopi.

Williame, J.-C. 1986. "The practices of a liberal political economy: Import and Export substitution in Cameroon" *The Political Economy of Cameroon*. Eds . Michael Schatzberg and I.Michael Zartman. New York: Praeger.

Wolkerseder, Daniel Stefan. 2015. "It's a Decent thing to Bring Cool Sounds into the World – Musical Mediators and Cultural Production." M.A. Thesis, Wien Vienna.

Wright, D. 1991. "Oligarchy and Orature in the Novels of Nuruddin Farah," *Studies in 20th Century Literature*, (15)1:86-99.

Yuval-Davis, N. 2006. "Intersectionality and Feminist Politics." *European Journal of Women's Studies*, 13(3):193–209.

Yuval-Davis, N.1999. "What is 'Transversal Politics?" *Soundings* (Special issue: *Transversal Politics*), 12:94-98.

Yuval-Davis, N.2019. Georgie Wemyss and Kathryn Cassidy. *Bordering*. Cambridge: Polity.

Zabua, C. 1991 *The African Palimpsest: Indigenization of Language in the West African Novel*. Amsterdam, Atlanta, Rodoph.

Zeleza, P.T. 2010. "Dancing to the Beat of the Diaspora: Musical Exchanges between Africa and its Diasporas." *Africa and Black Diaspora: An International Journal* 3, 2: 211-236.

Discography

Bona, Richard Bona – Allô Fokou (Official Audio) Buy and stream "Allô Fokou" now: https://richardbona.lnk.to/AlloFokou.

Lapiro, de M. (2012) *Démissionnez!* Retrieved August 10, 2012 from http://www.youtube.com/watch?v=v5xy2xg9774

Lapiro, de M. (2009) *Lef am so*. Retrieved August 15, 2009 from http://www.youtube.com/watch?v=LVYEAs-OtXM

Lapiro, de M. (2010) *Constitution constipée*. Retrieved June 19, 2010 from
http://www.youtube.com/watch?v=LVYEAs-OtXM

Lapiro, de M.(2008) *Na You*. Retrieved August 15, 2008 from http://www.youtube.com/watch?v=Thqb_aTByAE)

Lapiro, de M. (2010) *Kop nie*. Retrieved September 21, 2010 from http://www.youtube.com/watch?v=Thqb_aTByAE)

Lapiro, de Mbanga (2010). *Mimba wi*. Retrieved September 16, 2010.
http://www.youtube.com/watch?v=Thqb_aTByAE

Lapiro, de M. (2010) *Pas argent pas amour*. Retrieved July 18, 2010 from http://www.youtube.com/watch?v=Thqb_aTB

Lapiro, de M (2010). *Qui n'est rien n'a rien*. Retrieved September 21, 2010 from http://www.youtube.com/watch?v=Thqb_aTB

Lapiro, de M.(2010) *Jolie fille*, Retrieved July 18, 2010 from http://www.youtube.com/watch?v=Thqb_aTB

Lapiro, de M.(2010) *Mi nding mi be, foua*. Retrieved July 18, 2010 from http://www.youtube.com/watch?v=Thqb_aTB

Lapiro, de M. (2010) *Overdone*. Retrieved November 12, 2012 from http://www.youtube.com/watch?v=pzBbHqhLQi0

Lapiro, de M. (2010). *Nak Pasi*. Retrieved March 17, 2014 from http://www.youtube.com/watch?v=hasn-1BPFfk

Lapiro, de M. (2014). *Na wou go pay?* Retrieved April 2, 2014 from http://www.youtube.com/watch?v=_aB_luGtXG8

Lapiro, de M. (2013). *No woman no cry*. Retrieved March 12, 2013 from
http://www.youtube.com/watch?v=Zkicp8KsWLM

Lapiro, de M. (2014). *Fogwa ma wo*. Retrieved April 3, 2014 from http://www.youtube.com/watch?v=fz7xISSewvQ

Lapiro, de M. (2014). *No make erreur.* Retrieved April 1, 2014 from http://www.youtube.com/watch?v=Qkb4LihLfY8

Lapiro, de M. (2012). *Dem se.* Retrieved January 23, 2012 from http://www.youtube.com/watch?v=hcrAo0mz_AA

Lapiro, de M. (2014). *Qui n'a rien n'a rien.* Retrieved April 4, 2014 from
http://www.youtube.com/watch?v=ru-1gcyxeSI

Lapiro, de M. (2013). *Bayam Sellam.* Retrieved October 12, 2013 from
http://www.youtube.com/watch?v=FsJ54dMJPKM

Lapiro, de M. (2013). *Foua Foua.* Retrieved December 30 2013 from http://www.youtube.com/watch?v=ibg6rl3MNEQ

Lapiro, de M. (2000). *Souviens-toi chéri.* Retrieved March 12, 2000 from
http://www.youtube.com/watch?v=OjCJNyY2-gw

Valsero a.k.a Le Général. *Lettre au président.* Retrieved May 11, 2009 from
http://www.youtube.com/watch?v=a28WhRWrrx4

Valsero a.k.a Le Général. *Ce pays tue les jeunes.* Retrieved January 26, 2009
from http://www.youtube.com/watch?v=Z4XJDegyuYE

Valsero a.k.a Le Général.. *Réponse du président à Valsero.* Retrieved March 30,
2012 from http://www.youtube.com/watch?v=ys-xf3cLPX0

Valsero a.k.a Le Général.. *Valsero répond.* Retrieved December 27, 2009 from
http://www.youtube.com/watch?v=cBuPpx1KmQo

Valsero a.k.a Le Général.. *Valsero, ne me parle pas du Cameroun.* Retrieved March 22,
2009 from http://www.youtube.com/watch?v=siGRwpgvliY

Valsero a.k.a Le Général.. *Holdup*. Retrieved July 7, 2010 from http://www.youtube.com/watch?v=14UEWJ_TGhI

Valsero a.k.a Le Général.. *Va voter*. Retrieved February 7, 2010 from http://www.youtube.com/watch?v=BwRYZkD3JYU

Valsero a.k.a Le Général.. *3e lettre au président*. Retrieved September 28, 2011 from http://www.youtube.com/watch?v=A_qo8l9oCcA

Valsero a.k.a Le Général.. *Femme seule*. Retrieved November 8, 2012 from http://www.youtube.com/watch?v=7-aB5b89Tek

Valsero a.k.a Le Général. *Quitte les choses*. October 5, 2012 from http://www.youtube.com/watch?v=77pMLUquBfk

Valsero a.k.a Le Général.. *Je porte plainte*. Retrieved June 2, 2013 from http://www.youtube.com/watch?v=14H2onzcFEI

Valsero a.k.a Le Général.. *Le langage des armes*. Retrieved December 6, 2012 from http://www.youtube.com/watch?v=dlaBXHDyN5g